chaord [kay'-ord], *n., fr.* E. chaos [GR. and L. *chaos, n.* formless, primordial matter; utter confusion; utterly without order or arrangement] and fr. E. order [ME. *ordre,* fr. OF. *ordre,* fr. L. *ordo, ordinis, n.* line, row, regular arrangement in accordance with rules]
1. any self-organizing, self-governing, adaptive, nonlinear, complex organism, organization, community or system, whether physical, biological or social, the behavior of which harmoniously blends characteristics of both chaos and order. 2. an entity whose behavior exhibits observable patterns and probabilities not governed or explained by the rules that govern or explain its constituent parts.

chaordic [kay'-ordic], *adj.,* fr. E. <u>cha</u>os and <u>ord</u>er.
1. the behavior of any self-governing organism, organization or system which harmoniously blends characteristics of order and chaos.
2. patterned in a way dominated by neither chaos or order. 3. characteristic of the fundamental organizing principles of evolution and nature.

Birth
of the
Chaordic
Age

Birth
of the
Chaordic
Age

DEE HOCK

Founder, and CEO Emeritus
VISA

Berrett-Koehler Publishers, Inc.
San Francisco

Berrett-Koehler Publishers, Inc.
450 Sansome Street, Suite 1200
San Francisco, CA 94111-3320
Tel: (415) 288-0260 Fax: (415)362-2512 www.bkconnection.com

ORDERING INFORMATION

Quantity sales. Special discounts are available on quantity purchases by corporations, associations, and others. For details, contact the "Special Sales Department" at the Berrett-Koehler address above.

Individual sales. Berrett-Koehler publications are available through most bookstores. They can also be ordered direct from Berrett-Koehler: Tel: (800) 929-2929; Fax: (802) 864-7626; www.bkconnection.com

Orders for college textbook/course adoption use. Please contact Berrett-Koehler: Tel: (800) 929-2929; Fax: (802) 864-7626.

Orders by U.S. trade bookstores and wholesalers. Please contact Publishers Group West, 1700 Fourth Street, Berkeley, CA 94710. Tel: (510) 528-1444; Fax (510) 528-3444.

Printed in the United States of America

 Printed on acid-free and recycled paper that is composed of 50% recovered fiber, including 10% postconsumer waste.

Library of Congress Cataloging-in-Publication Data

Hock, Dee, 1929–
   Birth of the chaordic age / Dee Hock.—1st ed.
      p. cm.
   Includes index.
   ISBN 1-576-75074-4 (alk. paper)
      1. Hock, Dee, 1929– 2. Businessmen—United States—Biography. 3. VISA International—History. 4. Bank credit cards—History. I. VISA International. II. Title.

HG1643.H63 A3 1999
332.1'78—dc21
[B]   99-044779
                                                                      CIP

First Edition

   05   04   03   02   01   00   99   10 9 8 7 6 5 4 3 2 1

CHAORD® and CHAORDIC® are registered trademarks of The Chaordic Alliance

This book is dedicated to all grandchildren, their children, and the children's children. Would that I could know and name them all.

Seven I shall:

Brian
Martin
Karan
Heather
Sarah
Andy
Katie

Contents

Author's Note to the Reader

This is a chaordic book. There are many ways to read it.

If you wish to sample a few highlights, you can scan the pages for the *MiniMaxims* and read a few pages surrounding each.

If you would prefer the inside story of a lifetime exploring new concepts of organization that led to the formation of a unique organization that, in two decades, became one of the largest enterprises on earth, you may wish to begin with Chapter One and read only that portion of the book set in the type style you are now reading.

If you would like to dive into the depths of the thinking and beliefs underlying its formation and explore new concepts of organization that could provide a path to a more liveable future, you may wish to also read those portions set in the type style of this paragraph. The first is the Prologue, "On the Nature and Creation of Chaordic Organizations." It is not essential to understanding or enjoying the story, but it will provide important perspective. By all means, return to it later if you wish, for the story also provides important perspective on the Prologue.

If you seek the deepest understanding, you may wish to compare your daily life with the contents and return to the pages from time to time, to argue, reformulate, or replace the contents with your own belief and understanding.

✍❦

I am not a lover of lists. It would take more time and space than this book allows to list all the people whose behavior, integrity, character, judgment, and intellect have shaped my becoming. I do not wish to select among them. The few who appear at some length in this book are not there to set them above others, but as symbols of the decency, generosity, and integrity inherent in all people, should they choose to use them, and of the many I have encountered along the way who have.

Nor am I fond of pages of footnotes and bibliography. From childhood, I have been an incessant, eclectic reader, and when good fortune allowed, buyer of books. For thirty years past, I have lived and worked in the midst of thousands. The adventure and wisdom they contain is so integral to my becoming, that I could not select among them if I wished or properly know their influence. Let the selections that found a place herein stand for the countless number that are deserving, but did not.

How you choose to explore this book, or whether you choose to explore it at all, is not for me to say, for choice is the very heart and soul of chaordic organizations. What happens to it is yours alone to determine.

Is anyone afraid of change? Why, what can take place without change? What then is more pleasing to the universal nature? And canst thou take a bath unless the wood undergoes a change? And canst thou be nourished unless the food undergoes a change? And can anything else that is useful be accomplished without change? Dost thou not see then that for thyself also to undergo change is just the same, and equally necessary for the universal nature?

—Marcus Aurelius Antonius

In Search of a More Liveable World

Four-nineteen in the morning. Wind wanders around the house drumming fingers of rain on the window, muttering discontent at being locked out. Owls in the alcove of the chimney share a liquid word with one another about the splendor of the night. My aching body, dripping nose, and congested lungs do not impress the computer. It stares at me with its dead, milky-white eye and nags with an incessant hum.

Old Monkey, my rational mind, who has pestered me since I can remember, escapes into the infinity of imagination and the kind of questions that led us here. Did the silence of a billion nights shape the owl's gentle voice? What happens within owl when it hears owl? How can we know so much *about* owl, and nothing of what it is *to be* owl? Do our intentions toward owl shape owl becoming? Do owl intentions shape our becoming? How did evolution *organ*-ize owl, man, earth, and all therein as a vast harmonic—infinite cohesion of infinite complexity—infinite coherence of infinite diversity? How and why did man wander off on another path and organize society into mechanistic, linear, combative institutions so in discord with the human spirit and the natural world? I grab Old Monkey by the tail and drag him, complaining, back to the demands of an eager editor.

Harriet Rubin left at five-thirty yesterday with my twenty-year tangle of notes under her arm, fixing me with dark brown eyes, and disguising a sliver of steel with a smile as she insisted for the twentieth time, "You must write *Birth of the Chaordic*

Age. You've been dreaming it, believing it, and living it since you were a child. Now you must share it. I know you're convinced you don't have time. I understand your feeling that the last thing the world needs is another book, but you *must* do it! *Please*, sit down in the morning and write an introduction. The book will follow."

There it is again, my old nemesis, *must*, however charmingly packaged by an editor I met only yesterday. The hair on the back of my neck rises as I reply, "Harriet, you don't understand. Chaordic organization is about releasing what people desire in the depth of their being—the passion they have for it—the integrity they bring to the attempt. If you want me to write the book, make me love the idea." And so she did.

So, what *is* this book about?

It's about an introverted, small-town child, passionate to read, dream, and wander the woods, the youngest of six, born to parents with only an eighth-grade education. It's about crushing confinement and interminable boredom in school and church, along with sharp, rising awareness of the chasm between how institutions profess to function and how they actually do—what they claim to do for people and what they too often do to them. It's about sixteen years in the bowels of three institutional beasts; years filled with pleasure and pain, success and failure, dwindling hope and growing despair.

It's about three compelling questions, which arose from that awareness—questions that came to dominate my life:

Why are institutions, everywhere, whether political, commercial, or social, increasingly unable to manage their affairs?

Why are individuals, everywhere, increasingly in conflict with and alienated from the institutions of which they are part?

Why are society and the biosphere increasingly in disarray?

It's a story of an odyssey in search of answers to those questions, and how it led to the formation of VISA International, perhaps the largest enterprise on earth.

It's a story of harboring the Four Beasts that inevitably devour their keeper, Ego, Envy, Avarice, and Ambition, and of a great bargain, trading Ego for humility, Envy for equanimity, Avarice for time, and Ambition for liberty; a story of ten years of isolation, anonymity, study, and manual labor, while restoring two hundred acres of ravaged land to health and beauty.

It's a story of events impossible to foresee that have set a man of seventy on another odyssey more improbable than VISA and infinitely more important, along the knife's edge between massive institutional failure and societal transformation. It is the story of a word, "Chaord" (*kay*-ord), and how it arose from realization that all things, even life itself, are a seamless blending of chaos and order.

It is not a story of the past, although the past is in it. It is not my story, although I am in it. It is not the story of VISA, although VISA is in it. It is not the story of credit cards, although credit cards are in it. And it is not your story, although you are in it.

Beyond all else, it is a story of the future, of something trying to happen, of a four-hundred-year-old age rattling in its deathbed as another struggles to be born—a transformation of consciousness, culture, society, and institutions such as the world has never experienced.

It is written with deep conviction that it is far too late and things are far too bad for pessimism. In times such as these, it is no failure to fall short of realizing all that we might dream—the failure is to fall short of dreaming all that we might realize.

We must try.

On the Nature and Creation of Chaordic Organizations

To follow, not to force, the public inclination, to give a direction, a form, a technical dress and a specific sanction to the general sense of the community, is the true end of legislation.
— EDMUND BURKE

I agree to this constitution with all its faults, if they are such; because I think a general government necessary for us, and there is no form of government but what may be a blessing to the people if well administered. . . . [It] can only end in despotism, as other forms have done before it, when people shall become so corrupted as to need despotic government, being incapable of any other.
— BENJAMIN FRANKLIN

We are living on the knife's edge of one of those rare and momentous turning points in human history. Liveable lives for our grandchildren, their children, and the children's children hang in the balance.

The Industrial Age, hierarchical, command-and-control institutions that, over the past four hundred years, have grown to dominate our commercial, political, and social lives are increasingly irrelevant in the face of the exploding diversity and complexity of society worldwide. They are failing, not only in the sense of collapse, but in the more common and pernicious form—organizations increasingly unable to achieve the purpose for which they were created, yet continuing to expand as they devour resources, decimate the earth, and demean humanity. The very nature of these organizations alienates and disheartens the people caught up in them. Behind their endless promises of a peaceful, constructive societal order, which they never deliver, they are increasingly unable to manage even their own affairs, while society, commerce, and the biosphere slide increasingly into disarray. We are experiencing a global epidemic of institutional failure that knows no bounds. We must seriously question the concepts underlying the current structures of organization and whether they are suitable to the management of accelerating societal and environmental problems—and, even beyond that, we must seriously consider whether they are the primary cause of those problems.

Poised as we are on the knife's edge between socioenvironmental disaster and a liveable future, one question cuts to the core of our future: Will the result be chaos and the even more repressive and dictatorial regimes so often arising from chaotic conditions? Or will we emerge from the eggshell of our Industrial Age institutions into a new world of profound, constructive organizational change?

The answer lies in the very *concept* of organization and in the *beliefs* and *values* of individuals.

Our current forms of organization are almost universally based on compelled behavior—on tyranny, for that is what compelled behavior is, no matter how benign it may appear or how carefully disguised and exercised. The organization of the future will be the embodiment of *community* based on *shared purpose* calling to the *higher aspirations of people*.

Formation of a chaordic organization is a difficult, often painful process, but one also filled with joy and humor. Entirely different dynamics of judgment, behavior, capacity, and ingenuity can evolve. Small shifts in deeply held beliefs and values can massively alter societal behavior and results—in fact, may be the only things that ever have. That is my hope for our future.

I know it can happen. I've been there—or at least gone part of the way—during the formation of VISA and other chaordic organizations revealed later in this book. It's very difficult to put in words, for in truly chaordic organization there is no destination. There is no ultimate being. There is only becoming.

Forming a chaordic organization begins with an intensive search for *Purpose,* then proceeds to *Principles, People,* and *Concept,* and *only then* to *Structure* and *Practice.* It can't be done well as a linear process. Each of the six elements can be thought of as a perspective, a sort of "lens" through which participants examine the circumstances giving rise to the need for a new concept of organization and what it might become. The most difficult part is to understand and get beyond the origin and nature of our current concepts of organizations; to set them aside in order to make space for new and different thoughts. Every mind is a room filled with archaic furniture. It must be moved about or cleared away before anything new can enter. This means ruthless confrontation of the many things we know that are no longer so.

The process can easily begin with a deceptively simple question: "If anything imaginable is possible, if there are no constraints whatever, what would be the nature of an ideal organization to . . . ?" Finishing that question is all-important. It is essential to determine with absolute clarity, shared understanding, and deep conviction the *Purpose* of the community. From that, all else must flow. It is what will bind the group together as worthy of pursuit. The first attempt nearly always results in platitudes; impressive words full of smoke and mirrors with which everyone can quickly agree without discomfort and easily implement with a bit of institutional cosmetology. To get beyond platitudes, it becomes necessary to agree on what a "purpose" really is.

To me, purpose is a clear, simple statement of intent that identifies and binds the community together as worthy of pursuit. It is more than what we want to accomplish. It is an unambiguous expression of that which people jointly wish to become. It should speak to them so powerfully that all can say with conviction, "If *we* could achieve that, *my* life would have meaning." Making a profit is not a purpose. It may be an objective; it may be a necessity; it may be a gratification; but it is not a purpose!

It is not necessary to perfect the purpose, or any other part of the process, before proceeding to the next. It is only necessary to obtain agreement that the present expression of purpose is good enough to permit exploration of principles, and that each expression of a principle is good enough to go on to the next. Every principle will call into question and refine the purpose. Every principle will call into question and refine every other principle. In looking through each "lens," that is, each perspective of the process, both that which precedes it and that which lies ahead, will be illuminated and improved.

Conceiving the *Principles* is an extremely complex part of the process. The same difficulty returns. Platitudes inevitably emerge. It is necessary to reach agreement on what a principle is. By principle I mean a behavioral aspiration of the community, a clear, unambiguous statement of a fundamental belief about how the whole and all the parts intend to conduct themselves in pursuit of the purpose. A principle is a precept against which all structures, decisions, actions, and results will be judged. A principle *always* has high ethical and moral content. It never *prescribes* structure or behavior; it only *describes* them. Principles often fall quite naturally into two categories: principles of structure and principles of practice.

Purpose and principle that can lead to a chaordic organization cannot be devised by leaders and imposed on a community as a condition of participation. They must be evoked from the minds and hearts of members of the community. They are not frozen mandates to be obeyed under penalty of banishment from the community. They are a living set of beliefs capable of evolving with the participation and consent of the community. Properly done, they will never be capable of full realization. "Honor thy father and mother" is a true principle, for we all understand what it means, yet it gives us no instruction as to method. There are infinite ways to honor a father and mother.

The whole of the purpose and principles should constitute a coherent, cohesive body of belief, although it is inevitable that one principle may be in conflict with another. Where conflict exists, decisions should be balanced so that no principle is sacrificed to another. Paradox and conflict are inherent characteristics of chaordic organization.

It is not uncommon for even the most perceptive group to meet bimonthly for three days of intense discussion, for more than a year, before arriving at clarity and agreement on such a body of belief. Long before they are through, they will discover that it is not a somber process, but full of laughter and joy. There will be growing respect and trust. There will be growing commitment. There will be realization that what they are doing is as much about personal transformation as it is about organizational reconception. If there is not, the effort will never achieve its full potential.

When a sound body of belief is reasonably complete and agreed upon, the group can then begin to explore the *People* and *Organizations* that would need to be participants in the enterprise in order to realize the purpose in accordance with the principles. It sounds simple, but rarely is. When people set aside all consideration of existing conditions, free themselves to think in accordance with their deepest beliefs, and do not bind their thinking with structure and practices before considering meaning and values, they usually discover that the number and variety of people and entities to participate in governance, ownership, rewards, rights, and obligations are much greater than anticipated. They usually find their deepest beliefs require transcendence of existing institutional boundaries and practices. Determining the people and institutions required to realize the purpose in accordance with the principles brings realization of just how narrow and restrictive existing institutions are in relation to the exploding diversity and complexity of society and the systemic nature of seemingly intractable social and environmental problems.

Awareness arises in all members of the working group that they cannot represent only their own views and beliefs, for a good many members of the community they hope to form are not at the table. They must, to the best of their ability, act on behalf of the larger potential community and not bind its hands by trying to perfect the work they have begun. They are really trustees attempting to bring into being a chaordic organization capable of attracting a diversity of others and enabling them to continue its evolution. It is at this point that most groups more fully realize the magnitude of the task in which they are engaged. It is well that they do, for the point of frequent failure lies just ahead.

With *Purpose, Principles,* and *People* well established comes realization that it is unlikely that any existing form of organization can enable those people to achieve the purpose in accordance with their principles. Something new must be imagined; a new concept of organizing relationship. Again, definition helps. By *Concept* I mean a visualization of the relationships between all of the people that would best enable them to pursue the purpose in accordance with their principles. An organizational concept is perception of a structure that all may trust to be equitable, just, and effective. It is a pictorial representation of eligibility, rights, and obligations of all prospective participants in the community. The feedback part of the process never ends. Developing a new concept calls into question purpose, principles, and people. Every part of the process illuminates all subsequent and preceding parts, allowing each to be constantly revised and improved.

The conceptual part is where the old internal model returns time and again to derail the process. It is impossible to describe how difficult it is to imagine all the permutations and possibilities of human relationships that arise when one truly accepts that organizations exist only in the mind; that they are no more than conceptual embodiments of the ancient idea of community. At this point in the process it is so easy, so comfortable, so reassuring to avoid the difficulty by allowing old concepts to emerge camouflaged in new terminology. Breaking through the old eggshell to stand wet and shivering in a new world of possibilities is a frightful thing. Especially when crawling back in is clearly an option. Extraordinary insights emerge when there is realization that any concept of relationships that can be imagined can be codified and legally brought into being.

Once a group makes its way through *Purpose, Principle, People,* and *Concept* and can see the harmony that can be achieved between them, a transformation takes place. By this time, they have filled the practice part of the process with a rich variety of objectives and activities that might be realized if the organization they visualize can be brought into being. The questions shift from "Are we going to do this?" to "How quickly can we achieve it?" Success is by no means assured. The group may fail to communicate it properly to others. They may fail to obtain the resources. They may fail to achieve enough understanding and support from others to bring it into being. If they are an existing organization, they may fail to develop a successful process of transformation. But nothing will keep them from the attempt.

The most frustrating part then begins. They must shift from conceptual thinking, to which they have become accustomed and grown to love, to the pragmatic, meticulous, grinding work of *Structure.* By structure I mean the embodiment of purpose, principles, people, and concept in a written document capable of creating legal reality in an appropriate jurisdiction, usually in the form of a charter and constitution or a certificate of incorporation and bylaws. It is the written, structural details of the conceptual relationships—details of eligibility, ownership, voting, bodies, and methods of governance. It is the contract of rights and obligations between all participants in the community.

Many difficult questions arise in the structural process, primarily because it is rare when the deepest beliefs of people fit old concepts of organization. Every such effort raises new structural questions different from all others. How to embed purpose and principles in the constitutional documents? How to create equal legal responsibility of directors and management to guide the organization in accordance with the purpose and principles as well as in accordance with sound financial management? How to create new concepts of ownership not dominated by monetary markets? How to involve all affected parties in deliberations and decisions free of domination by any? How to preserve purpose and principle from capricious change, yet provide adequate means for their evolution? How to embody in the constitution an immune system to the recentralization of power and wealth? How to ensure and protect rights of self-organization? How to equitably balance competition and cooperation? The answers are emerging and are improving with every attempt.

Long before the structural work is finished, everyone realizes that they need not worry about the practices of the community. By *Practice* I mean the deliberations, decisions, and acts of all participants in the community functioning within the structure in pursuit of purpose in accordance with principles. They realize they should not bind participants in the new community to any practice, no matter how desirable it may appear in advance. Their responsibility is to bring into being an organization in which all participants can have an active, creative, equitable role in deciding what practices will best achieve the purpose in accordance with the principles, and effectively undertake them. The organizers have long since realized that they are engaged in the process not to command and control, but to act as trustees to bring into being an organization more in harmony with the human spirit and the natural world—an enabling organization aligned with the higher aspirations of humanity. They will be faced by the thousand and one difficulties required to bring it into being and nurture it to maturity, but that will no more dissuade them than the difficulties of birthing and raising a child will dissuade an aspiring parent.

When the structure is complete, the entirety of the work results in a charter package, which is temporarily frozen. It is usually in the form of a massive civil contract between an unlimited number of people and institutions which meet eligibility requirements for participation. The contract of participation is often no more than a single page acknowledging receipt of the structural documents and agreeing to abide by them as they then exist or are thereafter modified, which is relatively risk-free. Modifications are determined by the participants, of which they are one. No participant has inferior or superior rights and obligations. The contract creates irrevocable rights, but allows withdrawal at any time should the participant judge benefit no longer outweighs obligation. If sufficient participants accept the new concept and structure, it comes into being, its governance structures are formed, its momentary state of arrested development ends, and it resumes evolutionary self-organization. The process of actualization may be considerably different with respect to an existing hierarchical organization, particularly one constrained by institutionalized monetization. However, the fundamentals of reconception will be much the same.

When such an organization is brought into being, it will inevitably attract the people required for its success, since they will be drawn to the clarity of shared purpose, principles, concept, and structure. With clarity of shared purpose and principles, the right people, an effective concept, and proper structure, practice will be highly focused and effective since human spirit, commitment, and ingenuity will be released. Purpose will then be realized far beyond original expectation. People will come to see that the process is not a closed circle. Achieving purpose beyond expectation enlarges confidence and calls into question the original purpose and principles. And an enlarged and enriched purpose will enlarge and enrich in concept an ever widening and ascending spiral of complexity, diversity, creativity, and harmony—well, let's call it what it is—evolution. And what about profit? Well, from my experience, profit becomes a barking dog begging to be let in.

So let the story begin.

CHAPTER ONE

Old Monkey Mind

No single thing abides, but all things flow.
Fragment to fragment clings; all things thus grow
Until we know and name them. By degrees
They melt and are no more the things we know.
Globed from the atoms, falling slow or swift
I see the suns, I see the systems lift
Their forms; and even the systems and their suns
Shall go back slowly to the eternal drift.
　　　　—LUCRETIUS

Nine hours we have happily worked the hillside together, a sixty-five-year-old man and Thee Ancient One, a diesel crawler-tractor of indeterminate age and lineage. Thee roars and clanks across the ground, a squat old creature with massive winch and rippers behind, dozer and brush rake ahead, huge hydraulic cylinders port and starboard, and roll cage overhead. It is more than Thee was designed to bear, but she labors on patiently beneath her appendages.

It was quiet and cold when we began at dawn on land savaged by a century of overcropping, abandoned decades ago to the ravages of wind and rain. Where soil remains, masses of poison oak and coyote brush have scabbed the land to begin the healing. We are here to repay a debt to nature we did not incur. Fair enough, for we have incurred many a debt elsewhere that others must now repay.

It is 1993, nine years since I abruptly severed all connection with the business world for life on the land. It is still hard to believe. After sixteen years of intense conflict with Industrial Age, command-and-control corporations; after thirty-five years dreaming of new concepts of organization and experimenting with them; after two impossible years bringing one of those dreams into being; after fourteen grueling years leading it to maturity; after all that, turning my back on VISA and walking away at the pinnacle of success was the hardest thing I have ever done.

The reason is still difficult to explain, but it is not complicated. That inner voice that will not be denied, once we learn to listen to it, had whispered since the beginning, "Business is not what your life is about. Founding VISA and being its chief executive officer is something you must do, but it's only preparatory."

Each time I replied, "You're crazy! Preparatory for what—and where—and why?" There was no answer, only silence. In time the voice became incessant and demanding.

"You don't understand, VISA's not an end. It's only an archetype. Give it up, and the business world as well—completely—irrevocably—now! Then you may understand!" It was frightening. It was maddening. I felt a damned fool to even think about it. A rational, conservative, pragmatic, hard-nosed, fifty-five-year-old businessman who'd never smoked a joint or dropped a drug, listening to "inner voices?" Absurd! Throw away a lifetime of work—success, money, power, prestige—as though it had no value in the vague hope that life had more meaning? Madness!

But the voice would not be silent. This was not my friend and companion Old Monkey Rational Mind, the certified expert of logic, talking. This was another voice entirely. And I knew it was right. In 1984, I abruptly left VISA and pulled down an iron curtain, offering the only possible explanation: "I feel compelled to open my life to new possibilities." No one believed it. Why should they? I could scarcely believe it myself. I hadn't a clue what those possibilities might be. But I was certainly going to be open to them.

Seven years later, in 1991, in a brief acceptance speech at induction into the Business Hall of Fame, I struggled to put it in perspective.

> This moment brings to mind an old parable. Picture a wagon drawn by four lathered horses racing down an unpaved country road. A fly, perched on the tailgate looking backward, swells with pride as it exclaims, "Wow! Look at all the dust I raised."
>
> In the audience are a few individuals representing all the splendid people at VISA, who built a far better wagon and pulled it farther, faster than the world thought possible, proving once again that from no more than dreams, determination, and liberty to try, quite ordinary people consistently do extraordinary things. To all you wonderful people at VISA, my undying gratitude for an incredible ride, and for letting me be your symbol.
>
> As for those kind, generous people who made this moment possible, at the risk of appearing ungracious, I have a bone to pick. A half-century ago, while reading Thoreau, my mind tripped over his admonition, "Beware of any enterprise requiring new clothes." It made sense, leading to ambition to get through life without wearing a tux. For sixty-two years I have never—not once—participated in anything requiring formal dress.
>
> Through those years, I greatly feared and sought to keep at bay the Four Beasts that inevitably devour their keeper: Ego, Envy, Avarice, and Ambition. In 1984, I severed all connections with business for a life of isolation,

anonymity, and study, convinced I was making a great bargain, trading Ego for humility, Envy for contentment, Avarice for time, and Ambition for liberty, hoping that the Beasts were securely caged.

With the call notifying me of this event, old Ego came roaring from his cage and "black tie" echoed in my ears. Instinct said, "Decline," but as the days passed pondering how that might graciously be done the truth emerged. My character is too weak; the honor too great. So here I am, for the first time in my life adorned in tux, beneath which old Ego is feasting on my vitals. Therein lies the bone I wish to pick, for it *feels just grand!*

So, from a Utah country kid to you all, for recognition beyond my wildest dreams and a memory beyond measure, my deepest gratitude and heartfelt thanks. And for temptation beyond power to endure and destruction of a lifelong ambition, you have my forgiveness as well.

The nine years since Old Monkey Mind and I left VISA and opened our life to new possibilities have been good years, filled with things we deeply love—family, grandchildren, nature, books, isolation, privacy, the infinities of imagination—more than enough to make a fine life. From time to time during the first few years after we left VISA, we heard that familiar inner voice with its old refrain, "This is not what your life is about; this is merely preparatory." But we dismissed it as an echo and came to believe that life on the land was the possibilities we were meant to realize. As this day dawned, how could we possibly have known that before it ends other threads of life will emerge and begin to weave a new pattern of possibilities beyond imagining?

It has been one of those spirit-lifting, mind-soaring, diamond days. Hands and feet fly between track brakes, clutches, hydraulic levers, gearshift, and throttle; nine levers simultaneously manipulated. We are a symphony of motion, Thee and me. No sissy automatic controls for us. Thee has been a good teacher. After nine years working together, motions require no conscious thought. We are not separate things. Thee manipulates my hands and feet as surely as I manipulate her pedals and levers. We function as a single system, recognizing one another's strengths, excusing one another's foibles, communicating in ways neither of us understands, expecting no more than the other can give. We are bound to the same earth by the same gravity. We breath the same air. We both live by processes of combustion, and our excess heat dissipates into the same space. We are a microcosm of the infinite interconnectedness of all things: at once particulate and whole, self and not-self, at one with the universe.

Old Monkey Mind pulls me into one of those thickets of thought we have been trying to penetrate these many years. Is man machine? Is machine man? Are both inseparably connected and related in ways we can't comprehend? Why and how did we begin to think of making machines like men and men like machines? When and why did we begin to think of the earth as separate from mankind; a warehouse of free material to make gadgets for consumption in a mechanistic money economy; a free dump for our poisons and waste? How and why did we begin to break everything apart in the rational mind? Is there any way to break things apart in the mind without breaking them apart physically? Does the one breaking inevitably result in the other? Just who or what determines this breaking apart, locking our thoughts and lives into ever more confining boxes of specialization and particularity? What if the very concept of separability (mind or body, cause or effect, mankind or nature, competition or cooperation, public or private, man or woman, you or me) is a grand delusion of Western civilization, epitomized by the Industrial Age, useful in certain scientific ways of knowing but fundamentally flawed with respect to understanding and wisdom? What if our notions of separability, particularity, and measurement are just a momentary aberration in the great evolution of consciousness?

Old Monkey and I have long chuckled at the absurd notion that mind, body, and spirit are separate things, like cogs, cams, and springs of a clock. We're certain that machines, people, and nature are not as separate as Francis Bacon, Isaac Newton, Descartes, and the science they spawned would have us believe. Science has insisted for two hundred years that the few pounds of gray matter in the bone box on my shoulders is nothing but electrical and chemical impulses flickering about between separate particles of matter in obedience to rigid, universal laws of cause and effect.

> **MiniMaxims**
>
> *Particularity and separability are infirmities of the mind, not characteristics of the universe.*

Old Monkey and I don't think so. For all the wonders of modern science and its obsession with measurement and particularity, we don't believe Life will ever surrender its secrets to a yardstick. Old Monkey and I are not confused. Where he is, so am I, and where I am, so is he. Body, mind, and spirit are inseparably one and they are one with all else in the universe. We are not put off by notions to the contrary.

Thee Ancient One and I have carefully worked our way around the half-dozen stunted Douglas fir that have found enough sustenance to begin forming a new forest. I have no design for the land. It will design itself, yet visions of how it might look when reseeded with native grasses and flowers interspersed with groves of native trees flow through my mind. We have been laboring on these two hundred acres of pasture, hill, and forest for nine years. Early visions are already young reality. The first fields restored are deep in grass, surrounded by groves of Douglas fir, madrone, oak, and redwoods carefully transplanted as seedlings from the surrounding forests.

Within three years, air and sunlight will transform into clay the subsurface mudstone we are shattering with Thee Ancient One's rippers. The clay will suck nitrogen from the roots of the grasses and mix with dying stems. Each year, the grass will be taller, thicker. Trees will explode with growth. Animals and birds will return to make their contribution. In time, the more porous soil will absorb and distribute water from the heaviest storms, and the lateral ditches that now control runoff can be filled. Soil is building as thousands of gophers, mice, and moles work assiduously carrying grass underground and dirt to the surface.

Beneath us, billions of worms, ants, beetles, and other creatures till the soil around the clock. Trillions of microscopic creatures live, eat, excrete, and die beneath my feet, fulfilling their destiny and mine as well, just as surely as I fulfill theirs. Could this abundance of interdependent diversity be the deeper meaning of the biblical injunction, "Multiply and replenish the earth?" Could it mean we are here to enable the multiplication and replenishment of all life on earth, not just our own? Is it possible that the "nature" we were told to subdue is our own?

We work submerged in the roar of the engine and clank of tracks. Nose-tingling clouds of dust rise, spiced with the pungency of weed and brush crushed beneath the tracks. Four red-tailed hawks scream greetings as they float high above, scribing invisible parabolas in the sky before sliding swiftly down the slope of the wind, then rising again. Five jet-black vultures spiral into view, outspread wings powered by the wind, tip feathers spread like fingers against the sky. Thee is idled as I grab binoculars to join them for a quarter hour. I am no longer on a tractor. A bit of glass before the eye and we are one, bird observed and bird observer.

Every feather moves in intimate, intricate converse with the wind. Language is such clumsy communication compared with that between breeze and bird. Inseparability and wholeness are everywhere about. Bone and feathers, flesh and spirit, space and time—wind, bird, sunlight, earth, man—irrevocably interconnected, defining one another. All simultaneously competing and cooperating, separate yet inseparable, a whole of parts and a part of wholes, none in control but all in order. The simple, fundamental, undeniable truth is obvious. *Everything is its opposite.* All things define one another. It is impossible to conceive of "thing" without the concept of "no thing." There is no bird without man, and no man without bird. Where are the borders except in the mind?

If the universe is truly a meaningless mechanism composed of separable, physical particles acting on one another with precise, linear laws of cause and effect, and people are no more than an assemblage of particles, as science has demanded we believe for two hundred years past, whence came these eternal questions that so fascinate Old Monkey Mind and me? Why, at long, long last, can't science explain such simple things as love, trust, generosity, and honor?

For decades, Old Monkey and I have puzzled over the essential nature of desire for certainty and control, and where it originates. Why do we strive to structure institutions as though they were predictable, controllable machines, and labor to make people behave as though they were predictable cogs and wheels? It led to a fascinating question. What would it be like if one had perfect ability to command and control?

It would be necessary to know every thing and event that ever had happened, for how could one know what total control meant without infinite knowledge of past events and their consequences? It would require omniscience about the future; necessity to know with absolute certainty every thing that could ever be and every event that could ever occur, when and how it would happen, and every nuance of what its effects would be. One could never control that which could not be known until it happened. Mystery and surprise could not be tolerated.

Perfect knowledge of past, present, and future would not be enough to achieve perfect control. It would be necessary to know the thoughts, emotions, and desires of every human being: their hopes, joys, fears, and urges. *And not just those other folks.* It would be necessary to know everything self might ever feel, think, know, or experience, past, present, and future. Even beyond that, it would be necessary to be rid of all emotions, feelings, beliefs, and values, for such things catch us unaware and affect our behavior. Compassion must go, love must go, admiration, envy, desire, hate, nostalgia, hope—along with every aesthetic sensibility. If perfect control existed, couldn't emotions be called up and controlled at will? But how to know which to call up, to what degree, and why? Such encumbrances would be intolerable. Perfect control would require absolute knowledge of everything that came before every before, and everything to come after every after, and so on ad absurdum.

But all that reveals nothing. It is only conditions. It still leaves the question unanswered. *What would it be like to be the possessor of total, infinite, absolute control?* The first thought is that it would be akin to being a god, at least as gods are normally perceived. With more intense thought and a good deal more intuition, it hits like a bolt from the blue. *It would be death. Absolute, perfect prediction and control is in the coffin.* It requires complete denial of life.

> **MiniMaxims**
>
> *Desire to command and control is a death wish. Absolute control is in the coffin.*

Life *is* uncertainty, surprise, hate, wonder, speculation, love, joy, pity, pain, mystery, beauty, and a thousand other things we can't yet imagine. Life is not about controlling. It's not about getting. It's not about having. It's not about knowing. And it's not even about being. Life is eternal, perpetual becoming, or it is nothing. Becoming is not a thing to be known or controlled. It is a magnificent, mysterious odyssey to be experienced.

At bottom, desire to command and control is a deadly, destructive compulsion to rob self and others of the joys of living. Is it any wonder that a society whose worldview, whose internal model of reality, is based on belief of the universe and all therein as machine should turn destructive? Is it any wonder that a society that worships the primacy of measurement, prediction, and control should result in destruction of the environment, maldistribution of wealth and power, mass destruction of species, the Holocaust, the hydrogen bomb, and countless other horrors? How could it be otherwise, when for centuries we have conditioned ourselves with ever more powerful notions of engineered solutions, domination, compelled behavior, and separable self-interest? Tyranny is tyranny no matter how petty, how well rationalized, how unconscious, or how well intended. It is that to which we have persuaded ourselves for centuries, in thousands of subtle ways, day after day, month after month, year after year. It did not need to be so, ever. It need not be so now. It cannot be so forever.

Old Monkey and I are yanked back into the moment by a gust of wind laden with icy drops of rain. While we have wandered, the sky has darkened, the wind has picked up, and daylight has dimmed. No doubt of it, we're in for a heavy storm. Better hurry. Rain will soon saturate the soil and work will be impossible. A flick of the throttle and Thee Ancient One roars to life. We crawl across the land, pushing a huge pile of brush toward the ravine. Unconsciously, instinctively, I slip out of harmony with my surroundings to take control of the situation. One hurried pass, then another and a third. Faster, faster—fifteen minutes more and the job will be done.

Thee Ancient One screams with metal on metal, bucks, and stops, to the hammering of drive-wheel spokes jumping the track sprocket. Damn and double-damn! Idiot! Fool! *I would try to impose control* and demand more than the situation required or Thee could give. I shut down the engine and sit quietly in the rain as anger and frustration slowly drain away. I begin to grin. Plus one for Thee Ancient One. Minus one for you, old man. I sit motionless for ten minutes, gradually returning to harmony with the whole, enjoying the sound of gusting wind, the first drops of cold rain, the ocean restless under darkening clouds, trees and grass in a supple dance with the wind. Everything is in its timeless, seamless rhythm of conflict and cooperation. The earth, each blade of grass, each tree, the man, the tractor, the storm—each a whole of parts and a part of wholes, acting on and acted upon. Everything both infinitely understandable and infinitely mysterious, including an old man sitting on a tractor, smiling and running a hand over stubble on a crooked jaw.

Jogging the half-mile to the equipment barn, I slip into boots, rainpants, slicker, and hood. Into the back of the truck go steel crowbars, hydraulic jack, four-foot crescent wrench, shovel, and smaller tools. Rain is misting the windshield as I drive back to Thee Ancient One, silent on the hillside. Kneeling in the mud, positioning thirty pounds of crescent wrench to turn the huge nut controlling tension on the track is no piece of cake. Arms and shoulders are cramping before tension is released. On and off Thee Ancient One for a half an hour as wind and rain increase, alternately raising the front with the dozer blade and the back with the hydraulic jack until the ton of track hangs slack an inch above the mud.

With six-foot steel bars I leverage the massive track away from the frame and in line with the drive wheel. With a satisfying *clank,* the track settles into the sprockets front and back. Grinning, I struggle for three-quarters of an hour restoring tension to the track, removing blocks and throwing muddy tools into the truck.

Truck and tools safely parked in the barn, I call Ferol, my wife, to assure her I will soon be at the house and extract a promise to turn on the sauna. I climb a half-mile of hill in the dark, sucking a bloodied knuckle, staggered by gusts of wind, water sloshing in my boots. Thee rumbles into life with the first revolution of the starter. Engaging the clutch, I revel in diamond slivers of rain lancing through the headlights as we roar down the hill to the dry barn, cold settling to the bone making thought of the sauna grand.

Mud-caked, bloody-knuckled, and shaking, I return to the house to leave rain-soaked clothes draining in the mudroom. Shivering in a towel, I make a quick stop in a poor boy's dream realized. Four walls of books, several thousand volumes, leather chair, fireplace, and study with picture windows overlooking forest, valley, village, and ocean. In a stack of unread books, my eye is taken with the black jacket of a small volume, in the center of which, bursting with light, is the picture of a small sand dune above a single word: *Complexity.*

Cold seeps from the bone as I lie in the heat of the sauna, book propped on a towel on my chest, scanning the Introduction. I haven't the slightest idea that another of those tiny, jeweled bearings on which the future turns has been placed in my path. Two chapters later, I set the book aside, shower, then settle into bed to read it through with growing fascination.

It is the story of a few prominent scientists and academics from several disciplines who formed a small institute to pursue their shared awareness that a new science might emerge from the study of complex, self-organizing, adaptive systems, which they refer to as "complexity." They seem intrigued by the notion that the two-hundred-year-old scientific attempt to explain the universe and all it contains as mechanisms operating with precise, linear laws of cause and affect may be inadequate. Concern that pursuit of specialization, separability, and particularity may have led to a blind alley in ultimate understanding has brought them to a more holistic approach. Constrained by the specialization within universities, they felt compelled to set up a separate institute to pursue the "new" concepts.

They speculate that there is something about the nature of complex connectivity that allows spontaneous order to arise, and that when it does, characteristics emerge that cannot be explained by knowledge of the parts. Nor does such order seem to obey linear laws of cause and effect. They speculate that all complex, adaptive systems exist on the edge of chaos with just enough self-organization to create the cognitive patterns we refer to as order.

It is not so much the concepts that fascinate me. They seem like old, familiar friends. Many sentences and paragraphs contain language similar to that which I've used for years. They echo beliefs about concepts of societal organizations based on nature's way of organizing that I have developed and argued for several decades. What fascinates me is that they are now emerging in the scientific community in relation to physical and biological systems.

Nearly four decades ago, three questions emerged from my growing beliefs. They were fascinating then. They are compelling today. Time and again they return.

Why are organizations, everywhere, whether political, commercial, or social, increasingly unable to manage their affairs?

Why are individuals, everywhere, increasingly in conflict with and alienated from the organizations of which they are part?

Why are society and the biosphere increasingly in disarray?

Today, it doesn't take much thought to realize we're in an accelerating, global epidemic of institutional failure. Not just failure in the sense of collapse, such as the Soviet Union, the Berlin Wall, or corporate bankruptcy, but the more common and pernicious form: organizations increasingly unable to achieve the purpose for which they were created, yet continuing to expand as they devour scarce resources, demean the human spirit, and destroy the environment.

Schools that can't teach

Universities far from universal

Corporations that can neither cooperate nor compete, only consolidate

Unhealthy health-care systems

Welfare systems in which no one fares well

Farming systems that destroy soil and poison food

Families far from familial

Police that can't enforce the law

Judicial systems without justice

Governments that can't govern

Economies that can't economize

Such universal, ever accelerating institutional failure suggests there is some deep, pervasive question we have not asked, some fundamental flaw in the ordering of societal relationships of which we are unaware. It suggests that intractable problems can only get worse until we ask the right questions and discover the flaw. Is that the great new frontier that awaits? Is that the millennial odyssey which cries out to us all?

In the deep silence of the early morning hours, a chapter or two from the end of the book, I am frustrated by the long strings of adjectives, "autocatalytic, nonlinear, self-organizing, complex, adaptive, holistic," with which the scientists attempt to explain their supposed new science. I rise and descend to the library to grub through various lexicons looking for a more suitable word, and finding none, into roots and meanings. Nothing emerges. Why not invent a word? Since such systems are believed to emerge in the narrow phase between chaos and order, I borrow the first syllable of each, *cha* from *cha*os and *ord* from *ord*er, and the word *chaord* emerges. I begin to write a definition, trying to merge lifelong love of nature, sixteen extraordinary years creating such an organization, thoughts from the book, and conviction about the nature of institutions into the meaning of a single, simple word:

chaord. (Kay'ord) fr. E. **Cha'os** [Gr. and L. *chaos*. n. formless, primordial matter; utter confusion; utterly without order or arrangement: and fr.] **Order** [ME. *ordre*, fr. OF. *ordre*, fr. L. *Ordo, ordinis*, line, row, order, orig. a technical term in weaving akin to L. *Ordiri*, regular arrangement in accordance with rules.]

1. any self-organizing, self-governing, adaptive, nonlinear, complex organism, organization, community, or system, whether physical, biological, or social, the behavior of which harmoniously combines characteristics of both chaos and order 2. an entity whose behavior exhibits observable patterns and probabilities not governed or explained by its constituent parts 3. any chaotically ordered complex 4. an entity characterized by the fundamental organizing principle of evolution and nature

I return to bed to finish the final chapters of the book. My last thought before switching off the light is noted in the margin: "The hubris of science is astonishing. It will come as quite a surprise to countless poets, philosophers, theologians, humanists, and mystics who have thought deeply about such things for thousands of years that complexity, diversity, interconnectedness, and self-organization are either new or a science."

It is past midnight and the storm front has passed when memory takes me by the hand, leading me back to the origin of such thoughts. It was a very long time ago.

CHAPTER TWO

A Lamb and the Lion of Life

*The striking of a match is every bit as wonderful as
the working of a brain; the union of two atoms of
hydrogen and one of oxygen in a molecule of water is
every bit as wonderful as the growth of a child.
Nature does not class her works in order of merit;
everything is just as easy to her as everything else: she
puts her whole mind into all that she does . . . [she]
lives through all life, extends through all extent,
spreads undivided, operates unspent.*
— STEPHEN PAGET

Nineteen thirty-four, and I am five years old, wild with excitement, trotting back and forth peering around overall-clad legs bulging with muscle, as neighbors with crowbars strain alongside my father to roll the frame cottage on old telephone poles a quarter-mile down the cement highway to an acre of land purchased from a neighboring farmer. With the cottage on site and a man on either end of a ten-foot crosscut saw, the poles are soon bucked into short sections. They are buried on end under the jacked-up house, which is slowly lowered, creaking as it comes to rest a foot above the ground on the wooden foundation.

Two hours later, with a four-foot-square wooden porch and steps nailed front and back, we pour into our new house, as beds, chairs, and table are moved from the rented, crumbling brick house across the lane. There, five children were born and two died along with a tubercular aunt. In the dusk of the summer evening, the wood-burning iron stove that will do double duty for cooking and heating is installed against a partial wall dividing the single room into cramped sitting and kitchen space. One by one, the neighbors shoulder their tools and trudge into the night to shouts of "Thanks!" and "Welcome."

We christen our new home with a raucous game of kick-the-can as the vast, velvet night and billions of stars arc over our acre. Two hours later, dinner over, dishwater flung out the back door, six people edge their way into wall-to-wall beds on the screened porch. I tumble into the iron crib, which seems to have shrunk by half over the years, pushing me into a curl of comfortable sleep.

The next morning, I trot happily behind a tall, god-like father a quarter mile through fragrant locust trees to the neighbor's flowing well, breathing the pungency of crushed peppermint snatched from the ditch bank. The five-gallon can is slowly filled and shouldered by my father for the return trip, as he proudly explains that there'll be no stale, piped water in our house. We'll have "walking water" from an artesian well. "Nothing finer."

That winter, screens having been replaced by glass, with icicles hanging from roof to snow-covered ground outside, I weigh an extended bladder and cramping bowel against a fifty-yard dash between three-foot snow banks to the icy outhouse. "Nothing finer," my mother explains. Teaches one to "attend to business and not dawdle." Earlier this evening, with great fanfare, my mother produced her special treat, "rich man's soup." Hot water, bread, salt, pepper, and a dollop of melting butter. "Nothing finer," of course. No food spoiled with fancy sauces for this lucky bunch. It is years before realization dawns that there may have been no other food in the house.

A hint that we are not the most fortunate of people and a hundred homilies lurking in the parental mind leap out to assault our ears. "Riches are not in the number of possessions, but the fewness of wants." "Pretty is as pretty does." "Wish not, want not." "Money's manure, no good unless you spread it." "The road to hell is paved with good intentions."

With puberty came hatred of homilies. They buzzed about like flies. It was apparent my parents not only believed such stuff, but tried to live it. They were stupid! They were losers! What did they know? Blind to it, hating it, struggling against it made no difference; the intuitive wisdom of the centuries was being handed down. An imperceptible foundation was being built that would support me through immense storms of good and bad fortune to come. I raged against it, ran from it, ignored it, but it always returned. Still does. Just ask my kids. They have those homilies in their bones. So will their children.

Three years after we move into our new home, I am curled on my side in my favorite place, the floor in the corner next to the warm woodstove, face propped up on my left hand, right hand turning pages of a book. The radio is talking at the family, and they to one another. I've gone to another place and hear nothing. When and how I learned to read, or where the grand passion for books arose, is lost to memory. This is not a bookish family. My parents consider themselves lucky to have graduated eighth grade before pride and necessity drove them to earn their own living. Where the books came from, I have no idea. Probably from people who know the Hock boy is "a little strange; he'll read anything."

Love me as they will, there is a growing feeling of estrangement from family; a feeling of not belonging. In a recurring dream, I was born in a field of flowering grass beneath a warm sun, propped on my side reading, alone but never lonely, until these people took me in. No one shares the reading or wandering. No one directs them either. I live in secret worlds of the imagination, which the others find strange.

A growing jaw propped for thousands of hours on a left hand in order to turn pages with the right is getting a pronounced set to the right, giving my face a belligerent look. Or perhaps it came from years of pretense that I am an Indian kid, for my father calls me "Ewe Bullheaded Littlepup" more often than Dee. The fire dies down as my mother pulls me from the pages. She opens the oven door and removes a round, fifteen-pound rock, which she wraps in flannel, carries to my bed, and slips between the flannel sheets. "Nothing finer," of course, than an icy room, cold feet on a hot rock in the bottom of a bed, and a kid disappearing into the pages of a book.

It is easy to know where the other grand passion, love of nature, came from. The west face of the Wasatch Range of the hundred-mile-wide Rocky Mountains dropped precipitously to the strip of farmland, orchards, and the tiny village nestled more than a mile below the peaks. West of the cultivated land, vast alkali marshes stretched flat and unbroken for miles until they met the barren shores of the Great Salt Lake. Rivers and streams of fresh, cold water from snow banks deep in the mountains tumbled and fell through boulder-strewn canyons bisecting the sheer, mile-high face of the mountains, a haven for wildlife. They slowed as they met the alkali flats, picking up silt until they became turgid, brown sloughs of water imperceptibly wandering westward to merge with the Great Salt Lake. Vast hours and days in the midst of such magnificence are impossible to describe, nor can words convey the abiding love of nature or the deep, intuitive sense of connection to the earth that they aroused.

There was no way then to know how reading would sustain me through the years, intertwining with experience of nature and the ticktock world of business to shape beliefs about institutions and the people who hold power within them. There was a completeness to life then, an inarticulate sense of the universe and all therein as a living, breathing, fragrant whole. Money was scarce, but value was ample. Getting was hard, but sharing was easy. Possessions were scant, but love was abundant. Is that when the seeds of obsession with relationship and connection were sown? Is that where aversion to rational, mechanistic ways of thinking sprouted and took root?

Nothing in the early years prepared me for the shock of institutions. With school and church came crushing confinement and unrelenting boredom. I had no words for it at the time, but the feeling was powerful, often overwhelming. It was as though everyone began to shed wholeness and humanity at the door, along with coats and overshoes, and, one by one, to cut the threads of connection to the inner spirit, the world of nature, and the humanity of others. Idolized adults suddenly turned in a mob to confront one; "All right kid, you've had the joy of life for six years. That's enough. Grow up. Learn what life is really like." To a child passionately in love with nature, and imaginary worlds, the reality of institutions was misery. It was rationally, logically, methodically, and carefully explained, but it made little sense. Failure to conform brought discipline, accepted without realization it was often a form of abuse. One day in particular is burned in memory.

$\mathcal{L}$

Sunday, 1941, I walk along the road on a bitter-cold winter morning, blown snow swirling like fine white sand as the wind works assiduously to build drifts. I am on the way to church to serve sacrament with other deacons, preteen boys on the first step of the patriarchal ladder of lay church officials. At the cross-roads, diminutive, crotchety Old Joe in his white apron is alone behind the counter and half-dozen stools in the warmth and light of the one-room café. Along with a two-pump gas station and small grocery, it passes for the center of town.

"Hey kid, get in here!" Old Joe is standing in the doorway, scowling in my direction. *"Get in here. I can't keep the damned door open all day!"* Oh my God, he means me! What have I done? This is not a town or a time for disrespect of elders, let alone disobedience. I reluctantly cross the street and enter, engulfed by warmth and the smell of hot food. Joe is busy at the grill, scowling over his shoulder as he snaps, *"Sit down."* Moments later he turns, a smoking plate of eggs, ham, and hotcakes in hand. *"Eat!"* I'm not the smartest kid in my class, but eat is something I understand. Momentary panic—I have no money. Does he expect me to pay? This is no time for indecision. He said eat and I do, with a vengeance.

"On your way to church?"

"Yup."

"Uh-huh. Thought so. Well, if you're gonna spend all morning with hypocrites, you'll need all the strength you can get. Have another hotcake." As the last bite disappears, he throws open the door and barks, *"Get movin', you're gonna be late."* The storm seems more friendly as I climb the hill, looking back to see Joe's dwindling figure scowling through the window.

An hour later, we are lined in the back aisle of the church, the organist pumping out a hymn as an elder blesses the sacrament, bits of bread and small paper cups of water on glass plates suspended from wire handles. We march forward to be handed a plate and fan out down the aisle to pass them through the congregation. Ancient Mr. and Mrs. Jones sit on the bench that is my lot. He is enjoying a wee nap, jaw drooping as spittle leaks from the corner of a slack mouth. She accepts the plate, partakes, elbowing him in the ribs as she turns. His eyes fly open, his hand flies up, and it happens. In the deep silence of the church the plate crashes to the floor. In a flash, the elderly Mrs. Jones snatches the handle from the midst of shattered glass and bits of bread and shoves it into my hand.

Every eye in the church turns to stare. The silence speaks. "Guilty! You have smashed the sacrament! The evidence is in your hand!" In that frozen moment, no one knows what to do. A friend loses his cool and giggles. The church fills with suppressed guffaws. But the unctuous, rotund Superintendent of the Sunday School is not smiling. He is slowly swelling with the wrath of God. Days seem to creep by before the sacrament is finished, the handle is out of my hand, the organist launches a march, and the congregation moves to classrooms in the back of the building.

Practicing invisibility in a corner of my class is no protection. The door bursts open and the rotund Super enters. He fixes me with an icy stare as the tirade begins. "Blasphemy! Flesh of the father trampled—nothing humorous about—on your knees to pick up—lack of respect—should have this, should have that—" His bladder of righteousness is bursting as he spews words of condemnation. It would hurt less if he used a whip. I say nothing and endure, but questions *will* rise. Why wasn't he on his knees picking up after it happened? Why did he not behave as he now commands? Later, walking the mile home in sullen, burning silence, something in the back of my mind begins to boil.

What is this chasm between how institutions profess to function and how they actually do; between what they claim to do for people and what they actually do to them? What makes people behave in the name of institutions in ways they would never behave in their own name? Church, school, government, business—all the same. What is this difference between Joe and the Super? Joe in his tiny café, crotchety and generous. The Super in church, unctuous and abusive. Nothing in nature feels like church or school. There's no "principal" blackbird pecking away at the rest of the flock. There's no Super frog telling the others how to croak. There's no teacher tree lining up all the saplings and telling them how to grow. Something's crazy here! Is it me? I can't begin to think about it in a coherent way, let alone understand the resentment, confusion, and doubt. But the sense that something, somewhere, in me or elsewhere, has gone awry is powerful. I look up at the massive mountain peaks under their mantle of snow, towering a mile into the pale winter sky. They don't seem troubled. The turmoil gradually subsides.

Mind and body returned to the church from time to time, but heart and spirit, never. To Joe's we returned whole and happy many times, until the day of his death, and beyond.

✍❦

At thirteen I rebelled. Not the overt, in-your-face rebellion of the sixties. At that time and in that place, it would have been rewarded with a choice between two years in reform school or four years in the army. My rebellion was a persistent, stubborn, at times stupid refusal to accept orthodox ideas, be persuaded by authoritarian means, or seek acceptance by conformity.

Much as I detested confinement and rebelled against it, it was in a fifth-grade classroom that the greatest of good fortune came. In the way of all young boys craving attention from girls, I slyly slipped my hand onto the desk behind, to tip her books to the floor. Without so much as acknowledging my presence or the slightest change of expression in her magnificent brown eyes, with her fingernails, she put four, bloody, crescent moons in the back of my hand. We have been together every step of the way since. Whether without Ferol I would be writing this book is very much in doubt. One thing is certain, I would not wish to be.

The years passed alternating between the abiding, beautiful mysteries of nature, the imaginative joy of books, the dull reality of institutions, and work, work, work. From time beyond memory, I had chores to contribute to the welfare of family. At ten, I was hand-harvesting fruit and vegetables at a penny the pound. At twelve, stoop labor thinning sugar beets at twenty dollars the acre, followed by a first salaried job at farm labor for twenty cents the hour. The first nickel raise was a proud moment, remembered still.

At fourteen, a forged baptismal certificate claiming sixteen brought a job dumping slop in a canning factory. Summer and after-school jobs came one after the other: mucker at a dairy, hot-tar truck-chain dipper under hundred-degree sun, spray-truck operator, hod carrier, slaughterhouse laborer in the offal department. It was not demeaning. It was life. It was making a living. It was what proud men did—without whining. "Root, hog, or die," was the homily of the day.

Hunting and fishing was also a way of life then, and a major source of food. Deer, elk, pheasant, ducks, geese, and rabbits continually found their way to the table, and I was only too willing to be the gatherer. In the fall of my fifteenth year, two pals and I carefully planned the opening day of duck season. We would drive in the dark to the end of a dirt road in the middle of the marshes bordering the Great Salt Lake, build blinds, and wait for the dawn. As it grew light, flocks of ducks and geese would rise from the lake and head east across the marshes to feed in the farmlands. We would be waiting.

When we gathered in the cold and dark of the morning, we were four, not three. My pals had invited a new boy recently moved to an adjacent farm only a week before, loaning him a doubled-barreled, twelve-gauge shotgun. Full of excitement, anticipation, and laughter, we drove west in a dilapidated farm truck. My pals would work further into the marshes in one direction, Ralph, the new boy, would row the boat down the slough in another, and I would keep pace along the shore.

It was a cold, clear morning as light gathered over the mountains far to the east, gradually revealing the vast, flat miles of salt grass and occasional bull rushes that stretched in every direction. There was splendid, absolute silence except for the occasional creak of oars and crunch of my footsteps. A large flock of ducks rose far to the west and moved swiftly in our direction. I called softly to Ralph, pointing them out, and he rowed hurriedly to the far bank. They were moving steadily toward us as he leaped from the boat, turned quickly, and reached for his gun lying in the boat. The hammer caught on the seat. *WHAMM!* The sound of the shot echoed and reechoed over the deathly silence of the marsh. He dropped the gun and grabbed his left hand with his right, clutching both to his chest. My mind flashed. "My God! He shot off his hand!"

Straightening, he screamed, *"I got it, boy, I got it,"* took four staggering steps up the muddy bank, and pitched onto his face. Blood cascaded down the bank. It wasn't his hand. An ounce and a half of lead shot had shredded his heart.

As I tore frantically at bulky boots and clothing, a figure appeared moving swiftly down the far bank, racing toward Ralph. The stranger brought Ralph across the slough in the small boat in the midst of a universe frozen, paralyzed, by the sound of the gun. He quickly left to report the accident, trotting across the vast, flat expanse until he dwindled away to nothing.

In the silent expanse of the barren marsh, for two hours, under that clear, cold morning sky, time froze. Nothing existed, not a single thing, except a boy standing alive, staring at a boy lying dead.

An eternity later, small figures appeared at the edge of the earth, growing larger as they ran toward us, gathering around the boat, among them a father and mother sobbing inconsolably as they bent over their only son. I knew him for only three hours, one alive and two dead. It was not apparent then, but in those three hours everything changed. The relevance and importance of everything shifted. Never again could I think a thought, ask a question, or hear an answer in quite the same way. Answers became less significant, while questions grew more important. The need to know slowly dissolved into desire to understand. An inward eye began to open.

ℒ♥

Like all young boys of the time, sports filled part of my life, although considerably hampered by lack of aggression and aversion to the braggadocio, butt-slapping bonhomie of the locker room. The good fortune of a leg muscle damaged at football, along with a perceptive high school dean, brought me to forensics with success enough to have some idea of both what it means and what it costs to excel. The state high school debate tournament, arguing alternate sides of a proposition, affirmative and negative, for sixteen consecutive wins and the state championship, brought a strange mixture of disbelief that it could have happened to me and elation that it did. It brought a certificate as well, from tiny Weber Junior College for an annual remission of tuition in the amount of $50. Incredible! I went. There, another dean put me in the way of the classics and some understanding of both the powers and limitations of the human mind. At the same time, increasing conflict with the college and other organizations inflamed a growing preoccupation with the paradoxes inherent in institutions and the people who hold power within them.

No doubt those early years in a small mountain town, the intense love of nature, and the shock of institutions began the slow, lifelong process of trying to unravel some of the paradoxes then tying my life in knots. The seeds of many of the perceptions that shaped my life, some now grown to convictions, were planted then.

One concept that Old Monkey Mind and I have puzzled over is an ancient, fundamental idea, the idea of community. The essence of community, its very heart and soul, is the nonmonetary exchange of value; things we do and share because we care for others, and for the good of the place. Community is composed of that which we don't attempt to measure, for which we keep no record and ask no recompense. Most are things we cannot measure no matter how hard we try. Since they can't be measured, they can't be denominated in dollars, or barrels of oil, or bushels of corn—such things as respect, tolerance, love, trust, beauty— the supply of which is unbounded and unlimited. The nonmonetary exchange of value does not arise solely from altruistic motives. It arises from deep, intuitive, often subconscious understanding that self-interest is inseparably connected with community interest; that individual good is inseparable from the good of the whole; that in some way, often beyond our understanding, all things are, at one and the same time, independent, interdependent, and intradependent—that the singular "one" is simultaneously the plural "one."

In a true community, unity of the singular "one" and the plural "one" extends beyond people and things. It applies as well to beliefs, purpose, and principles. Some we hold in common with all others in the community. Others we may hold in common with only some members of the community. Still others we may hold alone. In a true community, the values others hold that we do not share we nonetheless respect and tolerate, either because we realize that our beliefs will require respect and tolerance in return, or because we know those who hold different beliefs well enough to understand and respect the common humanity that underlies all difference. Without an abundance of nonmaterial values and an equal abundance of nonmonetary exchange of material value, no true community ever existed or ever will. Community is not about profit. It is about benefit. We confuse them at our peril. When we attempt to monetize all value, we methodically disconnect people and destroy community.

The nonmonetary exchange of value is the most effective, constructive system ever devised. Evolution and nature have been perfecting it for thousands of millennia. It requires no currency, contracts, government, laws, courts, police, economists, lawyers, accountants. It does not require anointed or certified experts at all. It requires only ordinary, caring people.

True community requires proximity; continual, direct contact and interaction between the people, place, and things of which it is composed. Throughout history, the fundamental building block, the quintessential community, has always been the family. It is there that the greatest nonmonetary exchange of value takes place. It is there that the most powerful nonmaterial values are created and exchanged. It is from that community, for better or worse, that all others are formed. The nonmonetary exchange of value is the very heart and soul of community, and community is the inescapable, essential element of civil society.

If we were to set out to design an efficient system for the methodical destruction of community, we could do no better than our present efforts to monetize all value and reduce life to the tyranny of measurement. Community is more than a mega-balance sheet with the value summed on a bottom line. Money, markets, and measurement have their place. They are important tools indeed. We should honor and use them. But they are far short of the deification their apostles demand of us, and before which we too readily sink to our knees. Only fools worship their tools.

> **MiniMaxims**
>
> *Only fools worship their tools.*

There can be no society without community. In fact, there can be no life without it. All life, all of nature, all earthly systems, are based on closed cycles of receiving and giving, save only that gift of energy which comes from the sun. There can be no life whatever without balanced cycles of giving and receiving.

Nonmonetary exchange of value implies an essential difference between receiving and getting. We receive a gift. We take possession. It is a mistake to confuse buying and selling with giving and receiving. It is a mistake to confuse money with value. It is a mistake to believe that all value can be measured. And it is a colossal mistake to attempt to monetize all value.

When we make that attempt, we methodically replace the most effective system of exchanging value for the least effective. Because we cannot mathematically measure the nonmonetary, voluntary exchange of value, we cannot prove to our rational mind the efficiency of the whole or the parts. Nor can we engineer or control that which we cannot measure. Nonmonetary exchange of value frustrates our craving for perfect predictability and the control that it always promises but can never deliver.

When we monetize value, we have a means of measurement, however misleading, that allows us to calculate the relative efficiency of each part of the system. It allows us to engineer mechanisms to "solve" problems that our measurements have revealed. In a strange way, we measure our problems into existence, then try to engineer them away. It doesn't occur to us that destroying an extremely effective system whose values we can't calculate in order to calculate the supposed efficiency of an ineffective system is fundamentally flawed. It doesn't occur to us that attempting to engineer a society and institutional structures based on mathematical measurement may be equally flawed. As the popular dictum says, "What gets measured is what gets done." Perhaps that's precisely the problem.

Giving and receiving can't be measured in any meaningful sense. A gift with expectation is no gift at all. It is a bargain. In a nonmonetary exchange of value, giving and receiving is not a transaction. It is an offering and an acceptance. In nature, when a closed cycle of receiving and giving is out of balance, death and destruction soon arise. It is the same in society.

When money's rant is on, we come to believe that life is a right that comes bearing a right, which is the right of getting and having. Life is not a right. Life is a gift, bearing a gift, which is the

> **MiniMaxims**
>
> *Life is a gift, bearing a gift, which is the art of giving.*

art of giving. And community is the place where we can give our gifts and receive the gifts of others. When our individual and collective consciousness becomes receptive to new concepts of organization which that way of thinking implies, society and its institutions may yet come into harmony with the richness and abundance of the human spirit, and the earth of which it is an inseparable part. That is the voice that sings to us now, and the song is beginning to be heard throughout the land.

Events of those high school and college days remain much more vivid and clear than the embryonic thoughts then in gestation. The sharpest of all is college graduation. It is 1949. Officials of the tiny, two-year, Weber Junior College are ambitious for increased stature as a four-year school and a new campus. They are obsessed with impressing the legislature about the ability of the institution and acumen of its products. The graduation ceremony is planned with meticulous care to impress a plethora of state officials who are to attend.

At commencement, my parents, numerous relatives, and Ferol, the love of my life, are in the packed auditorium to watch the first member of the family to attend college receive an AA degree. Graduates line up in the corridor outside, waiting their turn to cross the stage. Far to the rear someone yells, "Hey, Hock!" Thinking there is ample time, I bolt from the line for a reunion with friends who graduated the previous year. We are rudely interrupted by officials racing down the hall hurling accusations of egregious error and malignant intent for failure to appear as my name was called over—and over—and over again to an empty stage and ghastly silence. They insist I make an appearance at the end of the line. Nooo way! One thing I have learned is to let bad enough alone. I slip away into the night, later to face the utter devastation of my parents and listen sullenly as my father snaps out the inevitable homily, "Well, there's no point in being stupid unless you can show it."

Thus, at twenty, newly married, unemployed, schooling ignominiously ended, eager to learn but averse to being taught, emerged an absurdly idealistic, naive young man—an innocent lamb stalking the Lion of life. The hungry Lion was swift to pounce.

CHAPTER THREE

The Bloodied Sheep

Begin the morning by saying to thyself, I shall meet with the busybody, the ungrateful, arrogant, deceitful, envious, unsocial. All these things happen to them by reason of their ignorance of what is good and evil.

— MARCUS AURELIUS ANTONIUS

A society of sheep must in time beget a government of wolves.

— BERTRAND DE JOUVENAL

In the summer of 1951, the lamb fell into a job at a small, floundering branch office of a consumer finance company involved in making small loans to individuals and financing the purchase of furniture and automobiles. Within months, the manager departed and his lot fell to the lamb. Protected by remoteness, anonymity, and insignificance, four lambs, whose average age was twenty, trashed the company manual, ignored commandments, and did things as common sense, conditions, and ingenuity combined to suggest. Within two years, business tripled and the office was leading the company in growth, profit, and quality of business. Anonymity was gone and the inexorable fists of hierarchal power and orthodoxy were pounding for conformity. How much better the lambs could do if they would conform to central mandates! Even if they could be trusted with liberty, others could not. Exceptions could not be made without risking anarchy.

It was too much for a lamb already dreaming of greener pastures. He slipped away to open a new office in a smaller, more remote Oregon town, hoping that the pressure to conform was an aberration of regional management and not the true nature of the company. There, the pattern repeated itself. Using the same iconoclastic concepts and ideas, the new office was in the black by the third month, with business and profit increasing rapidly. It inevitably attracted the iron fist of corporate orthodoxy and the itchy fingers of bureaucracy. Confrontation with superiors grew frequent and intense.

In a year and a half, the problems came to a head during a trying visit and review by the regional supervisor. Salary was the final subject. The lamb had been arguing for months that the company policy of annual reviews was absurd, maintaining that performance, time, and pay were related and should not be separated. If performance could be achieved in a quarter the normal time, review and raises should be quarterly as well. He had been politely, completely ignored. The year had crept by, the review of performance was excellent but the promised raise was not forthcoming.

"You'll just have to be patient," Cliff, the supervisor, insists. "I've recommended a raise but the personnel department has mislaid your file. When it's located, it will be taken care of."

"How much did you recommend?"

"It's against company policy to say until it's been approved."

"Cliff, let me make certain I understand. The reason my pay hasn't been raised is that my personnel file is lost. There's no other reason?"

"That's right."

"When the file's located will the raise be retroactive?"

"Dee, you know that's against company policy."

"Is it against company policy to lose my personnel file?" He glares at me, exasperated, refusing to reply.

"Cliff, why don't you step out for a cup of coffee while I make a couple of calls. When you return, I'll have someone on the line with the file in their hand and we can put the matter to rest."

His voice rises in anger. *"You can't do that!"*

"Do you mean I can't because of lack of ability, because you forbid it, or because it may not be lost at all?"

"You can't, and that's the end of it!"

The man is lying. He knows it. I know it. And he expects me to play the silly game. Well, I'm not about to play by his rules.

"Look, Cliff, I want to be helpful, I'm confident I can find the file and happy to make the effort. Ten minutes should be enough. If you like, you can listen."

"This is ridiculous! There's a right and a wrong way to handle these things, and that's all there is to it!"

How can the man use words like right and wrong when he means permitted and forbidden? But that's all there is to it— well, almost. He leaves, and ten minutes later I determine the file is right where it should be, but there is no raise. Instead, within the week there is an "invitation" to visit the head office, where a transfer, skillfully veiled as a promotion, is arranged, ostensibly to handle branch development companywide.

Three months later, on the twelfth floor of a gray, granite headquarters in a maelstrom of smog, traffic, and noise in the heart of Los Angeles, I was taken in tow by a charming man, Dick Simons, an experienced employee in the marketing department, who was to familiarize me with the work. He was extremely literate. Exceptional intelligence and perception lay behind the literacy, and more than a little cynicism. He detested his job. He knew a lamb when he saw one. We swiftly became friends.

Several weeks into the work, a summons came to step into the office of Brown, head of the division, a diminutive, rotund fellow, pleasant enough, though bombastic with subordinates and obsequious with superiors. Visitors, he told me solemnly, were occasionally confused about location of the senior executives' offices. I was to attend to the matter and keep him informed.

Back in the office shared with Simons, I ask for the name of sign companies with whom we customarily dealt.

"How do you intend to handle it?" he asks.

"Call and see what's available in brass, either freestanding or wall-hung, and have it installed," I reply.

His hands go up in mock horror as he comes down hard on every other word. "That will *never* do. You've been assigned a *project*. It will already be in the department *project-control log*, flagged as *important* because it involves *senior executives*. Important projects *always take time*. This assignment will require *months*."

"Yeah, sure, Dick, funny, funny," I reply, reaching for the telephone.

His hand closes over mine. "Am I not responsible for your indoctrination? Trust me. This will be fun, and you'll learn something as well."

For the next half hour he lectures me on the disposition, habits, prejudices, emotions, and capabilities of each executive. It is a dazzling display of analysis and erudition. I am easily taken in hand and, truth be told, quite willing to be taken, for the world of words and ideas is infinitely more intriguing than the mechanics of business. At lunch he explains. "What you don't understand is that in organizations like this, procedure is more important than purpose, and method more important than results." He carefully examines a list of officers, deciding which among them would be most likely to have an opinion on signs and how to make an innocuous approach.

During the weeks to follow I received a fascinating education about both human nature and the nature of organizations. One of the most intelligent, capable people I had ever met skillfully extracted opinions about "the sign problem" from various officers, each opinion different and duly admired. I listened as he casually revealed to Brown the divided opinions in the executive office about "the sign problem" and his concern that no one "upstairs" be offended by what we did. He obtained diverse sketches, samples, and prices from suppliers, exposing them to officers in idle moments to elicit conflicting opinion and avoid decision. Brown's inquiries were skillfully turned aside with allusions to things "going well, or about wrapped up," then digression to other subjects. Not once was a lie told or a person misled. Simons had more integrity and skill than that. He simply left muddy minds unclarified, idle minds free to fuss, and ignorant minds uninformed. Perceptive minds he avoided.

Caught up in a bureaucratic command-and-control organization that would not allow opportunity to use his creativity and ability constructively on substantive matters for important ends, he skillfully honed them on trivial matters to no end at all, always in conformity with the policies and habits of the organization in which he was enmeshed. The difference between Simons and millions of others trapped in mechanistic, Industrial Age organizations is that he chose to be undeceived, either by self or others. He refused to demean his talent by not using it to the maximum, even for wasteful, unproductive ends. He enjoyed every minute of it. And so did I. He was, by far, the person most highly regarded by management.

Fascinated, I watched for months as he manipulated situation after situation. He suggested a story for the company magazine about executive secretaries, causing a muddle of childish

> ### MiniMaxims
> *The doing of the doing is why nothing gets done.*

maneuvers by middle managers while Brown went bonkers trying to adjudicate who would be labeled "executive" by inclusion of their secretary and who insulted by exclusion. Simons organized a move to new quarters and induced months of bickering over allocation of space, layouts, furnishings, and windows. Week after week he took me into his confidence as he meticulously explained what he intended, then brought it about. Why he did so is a mystery, but his confidence was never violated. It was the beginning of another MiniMaxim: *The doing of the doing is why nothing gets done.*

He soon left the company and the world of business, respected, liked, and praised by everyone, quietly determined there must be a place where he could use his ability constructively among kindred spirits. I hope he found it, for he was the right sort.

I have never forgotten Simons. Countless times over the years I have asked diverse groups of people to reflect very carefully on their work within organizations and to make a simple balance sheet. How much time, energy, and ingenuity did they spend obeying senseless rules and procedures that had little to do with the results they were expected to achieve; how much did they devote to circumventing those rules and procedures in order to do something productive with the remainder; how much was wasted interpreting such rules and enforcing them on others; how much did they simply withhold due to frustration and futility? It's is a rare person who arrives at a sum less than 50 percent. Eighty is not uncommon.

A few years ago, I was asked to spend three days in no-holds-barred discussion of chaordic concepts in a major U.S. Army command. The first day included a meeting of the Audie Murphy Club, the best and brightest young noncommissioned officers on the lowest rungs of the hierarchy. The second day included meetings with senior commissioned officers of the command, and the third, a meeting with sergeant majors; grizzled veterans on the top rung of the noncommissioned ladder charged with the day-to-day operation of the command.

The young non-coms are apprehensive when asked to make the assessment of wasted time, energy, and ingenuity. It takes considerable reassurance before they accept that they can safely speak of such things. After much discussion and thought, the estimates emerge. They range from 45 to 85 percent.

The senior commissioned officers are more solemn and deliberate but gradually get into the spirit of it. Their estimates are lower—ranging from 20 to 50 percent. Not surprising, for it is rare when people who write and enforce rules spend much time following them. The third day is the surprise.

The sergeant majors don't take long to make the assessment. I am surprised. Some are as low as 5 percent, none above 20. I point out the discrepancy between the three groups and ask for an explanation. The toughest-looking cookie in the crowd looks through me as though I am the dumbest recruit to crawl from under a rock and roars, "Hell, that's easy. We been gittin' around dumb rules all our lives, and we damned well ought to know how to do it without wastin' time. If a new rule comes down, it don't take ten minutes to figure out how to look good and still do things our way. The young pups haven't learnt how yet, and the brass is too busy tryin' to figure out how we do it." Raucous laughter.

"Well, how *do* you do it? I'd like to know. Can I get a copy of the sergeant majors' manual that explains it?" More laughter.

"There ain't no manual. Any sergeant major calls me and needs something, he gets it, no questions asked or answered. I need something and call another sergeant major, I get it. Same deal."

"OK, but you can't con a country boy. There's more to it than that. You know exactly where what you give comes from, and you have a pretty good idea where what you get comes from as well. How can I learn what really happens?" Laughter again.

"No problem. Go to the Sergeant Majors' War College. Don't worry too much about classes. Take plenty of beer money and don't expect much sleep. If the bunch gets to like you, and you're not too dumb, you can learn plenty."

"Sounds like there are two armies. The official army and the real one. The explicit and the implicit organization. What might happen if the two ever came together?"

"Hell, I don't know about that explicit, implicit crap but I do know the army. It's been this way since war was a pup. You and I ain't gonna live long enough to see that change."

One long look around the room is enough to convince me that knowing more about the real army will have to wait. No way could I hold my own on a beer bust with these boys.

Unfortunately, what the sergeant majors knew and Simons tried to teach, the lamb was not yet ready to learn. At twenty-five, for all his quiet, rebellious, unorthodox ways, he was too naive, too well indoctrinated, and much too enamored of his desire to rise in the company to see clearly the realities. He was conditioned to see a bitter, brilliant man damaging a decent company, rather than inept leaders in a corrupt company degrading and exploiting good people.

The lamb stepped eagerly into the jaws of the beast. He wanted to believe in the company. He wanted it to be different.

He wanted to make it better. It's an old, old story. The lamb was determined to change the company; the company was determined to corral the lamb. It was no contest. Within the year, a badly mauled lamb was out the door, much wiser in the ways of hierarchal, command-and-control organizations and the people who hold power within them.

Old Monkey Mind and I have long puzzled where mechanistic organizational concepts so wasteful of the human spirit and destructive of the biosphere originated, and why we are so blind to their reality. Their genesis has a long history, reaching back to Aristotle, Plato, and even beyond. However, it was primarily Newtonian science and Cartesian philosophy that fathered the modern version of those concepts, giving rise to the machine metaphor. That metaphor has since dominated the whole of our thinking, the nature of our organizations, and the structure of the Western industrial society to a degree few fully realize. And it has rapidly infected the rest of the world. It declared that the universe and everything in it, whether physical, biological, or social, could only be understood as a clock-like mechanism composed of separable parts acting on one another with precise, measurable, linear laws of cause and effect. If we could dissect and understand all the parts and the laws governing them, we could reconstruct the world and all therein as measurable, predictable, orderly machines, presumably much more to our liking than the world we experienced.

For nearly three centuries, we have worked with exceptional diligence to structure society in accordance with that perspective, believing that with *ever more* reductionist scientific knowledge, *ever more* specialization, *ever more* technology, *ever more* efficiency, *ever more* linear education, *ever more* rules and regulations, *ever more* hierarchal command and control, we could learn to engineer organizations in which we could pull a lever at one place and get a precise result at another and know with certainty which lever to pull for which result. Never mind that human beings must be made to behave like cogs and wheels in the process.

For more than two centuries, we have been engineering those institutions and pulling the levers. Rarely, very rarely, have we gotten the expected results. What we have gotten is all too obvious: obscene maldistribution of wealth and power, a crumbling ecosphere, and collapsing societies.

Just as the machine metaphor that arose from Newtonian science and Cartesian philosophy was the father of today's organizational concepts, the Industrial Age was the mother. Together, they dominated the evolution of all institutions. The unique processes of the age of handcrafting were abandoned in favor of mechanistic, dominator organizations, which, in order to produce huge quantities of uniform goods, services, knowledge, *and people,* amassed resources, centralized authority, routinized practices, and enforced conformity. This created a class of managers and specialists expert at reducing variability and diversity to uniform, repetitive, assembly-line processes endlessly repeated with ever increasing efficiency. Thus, the Industrial Age became the age of managers.

It also became the age of the physical scientist, whose primary function was to reduce diverse ways of understanding to mechanistic knowledge through uniform, repetitive laboratory processes endlessly repeated with ever increasing precision. In time, universities obtained an oligopoly on accreditation and the production of both classes. It has led to one of those immense paradoxes of which the universe is so infinitely capable. A paradox that is having profound societal effect. The highest levels of all organizations, whether commercial, political, social, or educational, are now primarily formed of an interchangeable cognitive elite interwoven into a mutually supportive complex with immense self-interest in preservation of existing hierarchal forms of organization, and the ever increasing concentration of power and wealth that they inevitably bring.

At the same time, that complex is spawning an incredible array of scientific and technological innovation; immense engines of change creating enormous diversity and complexity in the way people live, work, and play, which in turn demands radically different concepts of organization; concepts by which power and wealth are more equitably distributed and commonly shared. Concepts by which human ingenuity is unshackled and harmony with the human spirit and the ecosphere restored. As a society, to borrow from Shakespeare, we are "hoist with our own petard."

The essential thing to remember is not that we became a world of expert managers and specialists, but that the *nature* of our expertise became *the creation and management of constants, uniformity, and efficiency,* while the *need* has become *the understanding and coordination of variability, complexity, and effectiveness,* the very process of change itself. It is not complicated. The nature of our organizations, management, and scientific expertise is not only increasingly irrelevant to pressing societal and environmental needs, it is a primary cause of them.

> ### MiniMaxims
> Management expertise has become the creation and control of constants, uniformity, and efficiency, while the need has become the understanding and coordination of variability, complexity, and effectiveness.

Loss of the job was a crushing experience. Ferol and I were friendless in a massive city we hated, breathing air so polluted it seared the eye and blotted out everything beyond a few blocks—smog so thick we could see the bluish haze within our apartment. We had money for a week's groceries, no savings, considerable debt, two toddlers, and another baby about to be born. Pride prevented mentioning our plight to relatives, let alone seeking their help. We had been raised to believe that shame was the companion of need and pride the companion of self-sufficiency. We had worked for clothes and spending money since we were ten, thought nothing of it, in fact, derived our sense of self-worth from doing so. "Root, hog, or die," had set the tenor of our days.

One event is seared in memory. The feeling returns as sharp as a throbbing tooth. A few days after the severance, we were desperate to know what to do. We had no money, considerable debt, and no idea when I might find a job or receive another paycheck. We agreed I must apply for unemployment. The next morning, deeply depressed, I drove through massive traffic and blinding smog to the nearest unemployment office. A line of people extended out the door and down the sidewalk.

Sitting in the car across the street, looking carefully at the faces of the people, I could not make myself open the door. One moment, I would see myself in the line, the next, trying to explain to my frightened wife that I had not done what had been agreed. Refusal to get out of the car was preposterous. It was self-indulgent in the extreme, no more than false pride. I was entitled to the compensation. Moments after the application was filled out, the feelings would vanish, and I would realize how silly I had been. *But I could not get out of the car.* Something deep inside, from a source impossible to understand, said, "No! Not in that line. Take me there and I will die." I sat in torment for nearly two hours watching other discouraged faces take their place at the back of the line. Sick at heart, I drove slowly home to explain to a bewildered, pregnant, young mother that entering that line was something I could not do. I did not know why then. Still don't.

The next morning I began a frantic campaign to find employment of any kind, anywhere, doing anything. A $200 loan volunteered by a friend bridged the gap. Within the month, a miserable job at a pitiful salary appeared, and I grabbed it, giving us momentary breathing room. We were determined never again to be in such a vulnerable position. We swore that, with the possible exception of a home mortgage, we would never again have more debt than cash in the bank. Within a month, I took two more miserable jobs. None of the three required regular hours or confinement. Here, the sprawling city was an advantage. I could work three jobs without any employer knowing of the others. It is amusing now to remember how we shredded every credit card in our possession, swearing never to have another. And for the next fourteen years, we did not. Be careful! Vengeful spirits have an affinity for oaths.

With Herculean effort, we paid our debts in a year and a half and put a small sum in the bank. I abandoned two jobs to concentrate on the best of the three, a tiny investment company in serious trouble due to corrupt management, since departed. The sole shareholder, a wealthy, thin-lipped, dour man, refused much in the way of salary but gave solemn assurance of freedom to use unorthodox methods and a substantial share of the profits if success followed. He kept the first promise.

Five years later, the lamb sat down with the owner to divide a handsome profit from the sale of a successful company, only to come face-to-face with naked greed and an astonishing display of accounting and contractual legerdemain. Although worth millions from a variety of businesses, he claimed the profit he promised to share must include years of losses that preceded my arrival. Therefore, there was no profit to share, even though the company fetched a large premium when sold. He was adamant. If the lamb didn't like it, he could sue.

It was a severe dilemma. Throughout his years in the financial services business, the lamb had strong aversion to compulsion and litigation, taking great pride in never repossessing mortgaged property without the customer's consent, and never suing a customer to collect a debt or enforce a contract. Everything had been accomplished by collaboration and persuasion. But this was not corporate money lent to borrowers, this was money owed to the lamb for five years of grueling work. It was a defining moment.

It was no longer a lamb but no less a sheep that looked deeply into those dead, expressionless eyes, drew a deep breath, and with suppressed anger, a tinge of pity, and a mountain of contempt softly said, "Keep the money. You apparently need it a hell of a lot worse than I do!" The dead eyes did not blink. The thin lips never moved. The expressionless face was frozen. The Beast, Avarice, had devoured him completely. The sheep turned and walked out the door. They never saw or heard from one another again.

ℒ♥

The sheep wandered north to Seattle to supervise the entry of a financial conglomerate into the consumer lending business. Don't hold your breath. Yes, it happened again: conflict between iconoclastic, innovative concepts of organization and management and the iron fists of hierarchal power and orthodoxy, and with the same, painful result. Just another hunk of unemployed mutton bruised and bleeding on the sidewalk. After sixteen years of unorthodox management and unblemished results, the sheep, by the standards of Industrial Age command-and-control organizations, was a complete failure.

In truth, those with whom the sheep battled and lost were not without merit. Beneath the sheep's many scars was ample evidence that the words they used to inflict so many wounds were not without justification: stubborn, opinionated, unpredictable, unorthodox, rebellious. The power of those words to wound came from elements of truth each contained; their weakness from the fact that none contained the whole of it. There can be no doubt that the sheep's confrontational ways and inability to swallow whole or fully practice the gospel of Industrial Age management were invitations to battle.

It would be a comfort now to claim that the sheep never accepted or practiced Industrial Age beliefs and methods, but it would be a lie. He did so often and well. That, too, was part of the learning, for it inevitably brought distress and shame at the damage inflicted on self and others.

During those years the sheep was torn apart by internal conflict. He was filled with desire for acceptance in the world as he found it, for his piece of the American dream. He wanted to believe and belong; to rise to a place among the powerful, rich, and famous. But he was also filled with many things he would not do to get there. Side-by-side with a compelling desire to excel in the world as he found it was equal desire to behave in accordance with the world as he wished it to be. Shoulder-to-shoulder with desire for power, fame, and fortune was longing for solitude and contemplation. Hand-in-hand with the urge to excitement and action was the call to serenity and beauty.

The sheep did not fully realize how thoroughly he was being pulled apart by a society methodically pulling itself apart, or how rapidly that society was pulling apart the biosphere. Nor did he see clearly what was doing the pulling, or why. But he felt the pain and saw it everywhere around him. And he was slowly learning.

Through the sixteen years of successful failure, the sheep had continued to read avariciously—poetry, philosophy, biography, history, biology, economics, mythology—anything and everything that satisfied his curiosity about connectedness and relationship. He mastered nothing, nor did he wish to, but new ways of seeing old things began to emerge and new patterns to reveal themselves. The preoccupation with organizations and the people who hold power within them had slowly become an obsession. It was then, in the mid-sixties, out of the maelstrom of experience, study, and stress, that the three questions emerged vaguely, softly at first, then time after time returning, more demanding and compelling each time.

> *Why are organizations, everywhere, whether political, commercial, or social, increasingly unable to manage their affairs?*

> *Why are individuals, everywhere, increasingly in conflict with and alienated from the organizations of which they are part?*

> *Why are society and the biosphere increasingly in disarray?*

The vague shape of some answers had begun to form, but the sheep had no idea what to do with them. Sheared, bloodied, and once again unemployed, he lost heart and sank into the slough of despond.

CHAPTER FOUR

Retirement on the Job

*How can a part know the whole? Man is related to
everything that he knows. And everything is both
cause and effect, working and worked upon, medi-
ate and immediate, all things mutually dependent.*
— BLAISE PASCAL

*For prosperity doth best discover vice, and adversity
doth best discover virtue.*
— SIR FRANCIS BACON

It was 1965 when the heart went out of me. Four years before,
partially from concern we would never be able to educate
three children on my earnings alone and partially to fulfill a
thwarted dream, Ferol decided she would begin university. She
was the eleventh of twelve children raised in a three-room cottage on a small, hardscrabble farm. Only one child had gone
beyond high school. In spite of twelve years of perfect 4.0
grades, she had set aside dreams of university when her father
died of cancer during her final year of high school, taking work
as a seamstress in a clothing mill to support a widowed mother
and younger sister.

With Ferol at university, three young children, a heavily
mortgaged house, no job, and little money in the bank, it was
impossible to stay out of a dismal swamp of depression. Day
after day, while walking the woods alone in the misting

Northwest rain, my constant companion was an overwhelming feeling of failure. Something must be fundamentally wrong with me. Why constant inability to climb the corporate ladder? Others were able to do so. Why continual conflict with superiors? Extraordinary effort and exceptional results had come to nothing. It seemed impossible to act consistent with my beliefs and succeed in the corporate world. Yet, there seemed no way to escape it without putting the welfare of my family at risk. That I could not do.

Ferol was in her final year at the University of Washington, well on the way to a degree in education and speech and hearing therapy. Our children were doing well in school and community. Another move was foolish. We made a firm decision. Ferol would obtain her degree and take a teaching job helping children with speech and hearing impairments. I would make no more effort to climb the corporate ladder. I would make no more intense commitment to work. Instead, I would join the crowd and take up what may be the most common career in modern organizations: "retirement on the job." My victim would be one of the local banks where a modest living could be had at the cost of a pleasant demeanor, conformity, and fractional ability or effort. There would be no cheating. A creditable job would be done. But they would get no great bargain. Henceforth, my life would be family, books, oil painting, gardening, and nature. It must be a bank headquartered in the area so that a move would not be necessary. I began looking.

The Seattle First National Bank was disheartening. Endless, inane forms to be filled out. Interminable, officious interviews with officers housed in a rabbit warren of offices in a pretentious high-rise building. Years of interviewing people for loans had left me skilled at extracting information. In the midst of interviews filled with programmed praise of the bank, it was not difficult to induce several officers to confide a litany of complaint.

The National Bank of Commerce was different. On the fourth floor of a modest building, the elevators opened into a large, open space with windows across one wall. After stating my business to a gracious receptionist, I was quickly greeted by a man who rose from one of several desks spread across the room, Ron McDonald, senior vice president in charge of personnel. Soft-spoken and pleasant, he ushered me into a tastefully appointed sitting room. We were soon in a deep discussion ranging far beyond banking and finance. This was not an interview, it was an interesting conversation.

In a quiet way, he made it plain that the bank filled management positions from within. However, it was not a sacrosanct policy from on high. It was merely a sensible thing to do. Within the hour, after asking if I had time to meet the president of the bank, he escorted me to another of the desks in the open room, where a tall, thin man with a kind face and shy smile rose to greet me.

"Dee, this is Maxwell Carlson. Max, this is Dee Hock. Dee has interest in the bank. I thought you two should meet." McDonald excused himself and I enjoyed a pleasant hour with Maxwell Carlson. It was easy to forget my need of a job and become engrossed in conversation. An hour later, I left with nothing but assurance they would reflect on our conversations and call within the week. I was certain nothing would come of it, but such gracious treatment was nonetheless heartening.

Ron McDonald's call was unexpected and perplexing. There were no positions open at the bank. They had no idea when there might be. However, they felt the people at the bank might enjoy working with me, and I with them. They would be happy to have me join the bank. We could get acquainted through temporary assignments. In time, something consistent with my experience and interest might be found. No title was offered. No promises were made. The salary was little more than half of that to which I was accustomed. Not a scrap of paper had been filled out. Not a test had been taken.

But, Whoa Nellie! Back up a minute. For the first time in sixteen years, there would be nothing to manage. There would be no title. There would be no assurances of what the future might hold. At thirty-six, I would be a trainee, a nobody. We couldn't live on the salary. If nothing happened, our savings would be gone in a year. *But I really liked these decent people.* With hand over the telephone mouthpiece, the circumstances were quietly conveyed to Ferol. She urged me to consider my feelings about the people, not numbers and power. For the first time, I abandoned logic, tossed old barren reason in the trash, and made a career decision on intuitive feeling and faith. A deep breath! "Yes, I would be pleased to join the bank." Thus, loss of identity, uncertainty, and inadequate income were added to depression and gnawing self-doubt. It was not the best time in my life. The flames of self-respect guttered, but they didn't wink out.

The next year was worse than I had imagined. Shunted from one department to another—the credit department, a branch office, the real estate department, the commercial loan department—and given little of substance to do, there was nothing to challenge either mind or body. People were kind and considerate, but they didn't know what to make of the situation, let alone what to do with such a stranger. My days were filled with menial work that I could have done in my sleep. This was retirement on the job with a vengeance.

The marvelous part was time to read, reflect on the past sixteen years, and dive deeply into the obsession with organizations and the people who hold power within them. Old Monkey Mind and I found ourselves exploring simple words we thought we knew well, such as *lead, follow, manage.* They were not so simple after all, and the more we thought, the more we began to understand our constant conflict with institutions. As that year passed, and many years to follow, it became increasingly clear.

Leader presumes follower. Follower presumes choice. One who is coerced to the purposes, objectives, or preferences of another is not a follower in any true sense of the word, but an object of manipulation. Nor is the relationship materially altered if both parties accept dominance and coercion. True leading and following presume perpetual liberty of both leader and follower to sever the relationship and pursue another path. A true leader cannot be bound to lead. A true follower cannot be bound to follow. The moment they are bound, they are no longer leader or follower. The terms *leader* and *follower* imply the freedom and independent judgment of both. If the behavior of either is compelled, whether by force, economic necessity, or contractual arrangement, the relationship is altered to one of superior/subordinate, management/employee, master/servant, or owner/slave. All such relationships are materially different than leader/follower.

Induced behavior is the essence of leader/follower. Compelled behavior is the essence of all the others. Where behavior is compelled, there lies tyranny, however benign. Where behavior is induced, there lies leadership, however powerful. Leadership does not imply constructive, ethical, open conduct. It is entirely possible to induce destructive, malign, devious behavior and to do so by corrupt means. Therefore, a clear, meaningful purpose and compelling ethical principles evoked from all participants should be the essence of every relationship, and every institution.

A compelling question is how to ensure that those who lead are constructive, ethical, open, and honest. The answer is to follow those who will behave in that manner. It comes down to both the individual and collective sense of where and how people choose to be led. In a very real sense, followers lead by choosing where to be led. Where a community will be led is inseparable from the conscious, shared values and beliefs of the individuals of which it is composed.

True leaders are those who epitomize the general sense of the community—who symbolize, legitimize, and strengthen behavior in accordance with the sense of the community—who enable its conscious, shared values and beliefs to emerge, expand, and be transmitted from generation to generation—who enable that which is trying to happen to come into being. The true leader's behavior is induced by the behavior of every individual who chooses where they will be led.

The important thing to remember is that true leadership and induced behavior can be constructive or destructive, but have an inherent tendency to good, while tyranny and compelled behavior have an inherent tendency to evil.

Over the years, I have frequently had long, unstructured discussions with hundreds of groups of people at every level in diverse organizations about any subject of concern to them. The conversations most often gravitate to management; either aspirations to it, dissatisfaction with it, or confusion about it. To avoid ambiguity, I ask each person to describe the single most important responsibility of any manager. The incredibly diverse responses always have one thing in common. All are downward-looking. Management inevitably has to do with exercise of authority—with selecting employees, motivating them, training them, appraising them, organizing them, directing them, controlling them. That perception is mistaken.

> **MiniMaxims**
>
> Compelled behavior is the essence of tyranny. Induced behavior is the essence of leadership. Both may have the same objective, but one tends to evil, the other to good.

The first and paramount responsibility of anyone who purports to manage is to manage self; one's own integrity, character, ethics, knowledge, wisdom, temperament, words, and acts. It is a complex, never-ending, incredibly difficult, oft-shunned task. Management of self is something at which we spend little time and rarely excel precisely because it is so much more difficult than prescribing and controlling the behavior of others. Without management of self, no one is fit for authority, no matter how much they acquire. The more authority they acquire the more dangerous they become. It is the management of self that should have half of our time and the best of our ability. And when we do, the ethical, moral, and spiritual elements of managing self are inescapable.

Asked to identify the second responsibility of any manager, again people produce a bewildering variety of opinions, again downward-looking. Another mistake. The second responsibility is to manage those who have authority over us: bosses, supervisors, directors, regulators, ad infinitum. In an organized world, there are always people with authority over us. Without their consent and support, how can we follow conviction, exercise judgment, use creative ability, achieve constructive results, or create conditions by which others can do the same? Managing superiors is essential. Devoting a quarter of our time and ability to that effort is not too much.

Asked for the third responsibility, people become a bit uneasy and uncertain. Yet, their thoughts remain on subordinates. Mistaken again. The third responsibility is to manage one's peers—those over whom we have no authority and who have no authority over us—associates, competitors, suppliers, customers—the entire environment, if you will. Without their support, respect, and confidence, little or nothing can be accomplished. Peers can make a small heaven or hell of our life. Is it not wise to devote at least a fifth of our time, energy, and ingenuity to managing peers?

Asked for the fourth responsibility, people have difficulty coming up with an answer, for they are now troubled by thinking downward. However, if one has attended to self, superiors, and peers, there is little else left. The fourth responsibility is to manage those over whom we have authority. The common response is that all one's time will be consumed managing self, superiors, and peers. There will be no time to manage subordinates. Exactly! One need only select decent people, introduce them to the concept, induce them to practice it, and enjoy the process. If those over whom we have authority properly manage themselves, manage us, manage their peers, and replicate the process with those they employ, what is there to do but see they are properly recognized, rewarded, and stay out of their way? *It is not making better people of others that management is about. It's about making a better person of self. Income, power, and titles have nothing to do with that.*

The obvious question then always erupts. How do you manage superiors—bosses, regulators, associates, customers? The answer is equally obvious. You cannot. But can you understand them? Can you persuade them? Can you motivate them? Can you disturb them, influence them, forgive them? Can you set them an example? Eventually the proper word will emerge. Can you *lead* them?

> **MiniMaxims**
>
> *Lead yourself, lead your superiors, lead your peers, employ good people, and free them to do the same. All else is trivia.*

Of course you can, provided only that you have properly led yourself. There are no rules and regulations so rigorous, no organization so hierarchal, no bosses so abusive that they can prevent us from behaving this way. No individual and no organization can prevent such use of our energy, ability, and ingenuity. They may make it more difficult, but they can't prevent it. The real power is ours, not theirs.

There is an immense difficulty in this perception of things. Failure is constant and certain. If one's conduct, intelligence, and effort are deficient, as at times they inevitably must be, it is a failure of the first magnitude. If one fails to gain the confidence, consent, and support of superiors, it is a failure of the second magnitude. If one is subverted by peers, dominated by competitors, or hamstrung by mindless regulators, it is a failure of the third magnitude. If those over whom we have authority are not induced to understand, accept, and practice the concept, it is a failure of the fourth magnitude. One must look to self for every failure.

At first, it seems an impossible burden to bear. Upon reflection, it is neither to be dreaded nor feared. It is no burden at all. Success, while it may provide encouragement, build confidence, and be joyful indeed, often teaches an insidious lesson—to have too high an opinion of self. It is from failure that amazing growth and grace so often come, provided only that one can recognize it, admit it, learn from it, rise above it, and try again. There is no reason to be discouraged by shortcomings. True leadership presumes a standard quite beyond human perfectibility, and that is quite all right, for joy and satisfaction are in the pursuit of an objective, not in its realization. The only question of importance is whether one constantly rises in the scale.

It is easy to test this concept. Reflect a moment on group endeavors of which you are an observer rather than participant. If your interest runs to ballet, you can undoubtedly recall when the corps seemed to rise above the individual ability of each dancer and achieve a magical, seemingly effortless performance. If your interest runs to sports, the same phenomenon is apparent. Teams whose performance transcends the ability of individuals. The same phenomenon

> **MiniMaxims**
>
> *Success, while it may build confidence, teaches an insidious lesson: to have too high an opinion of self.*

can be observed in the symphony, the theater, in fact, every group endeavor, including business and government.

Every choreographer, conductor, and coach, or for that matter, corporation president, has tried to distill the essence of such performance. Countless others have tried to explain, and reduce to a mechanistic, measurably controlled process, that which causes the phenomenon. It has never been done and it never will be. It is easily observed, universally admired, and occasionally experienced. It happens, but cannot be deliberately done. It is rarely long sustained but can be repeated. *It arises from the relationships and interaction of those from which it is composed.* Some organizations seem consistently able to do so, just as some leaders seem able to cause it to happen with consistency, even within different organizations.

To be precise, one cannot speak of leaders who *cause* organizations to achieve superlative performance, for no one can *cause* it to happen. Leaders can only recognize and modify conditions that prevent it; perceive and articulate a sense of community, a vision of the future, a body of principle to which people can become passionately committed, then encourage and enable them to discover and bring forth the extraordinary capabilities that lie trapped in everyone struggling to get out.

> **MiniMaxims**
>
> The most abundant, least expensive, most underutilized, and constantly abused resource in the world is human ingenuity.

Without question, the most abundant, least expensive, most underutilized, and constantly abused resource in the world is human ingenuity. The source of that abuse is mechanistic, Industrial Age, dominator concepts of organization and the management practices they spawn.

In the deepest sense, distinction between leaders and followers is meaningless. In every moment of life, we are simultaneously leading and following. There is never a time when our knowledge, judgment, and wisdom are not more useful and applicable than that of another. There is never a time when the knowledge, judgment, and wisdom of another are not more useful and applicable than ours. At any time that "other" may be superior, subordinate, or peer.

Everyone is a born leader. Who can deny that from the moment of birth they were leading parents, siblings, and companions? Watch a baby cry and the parents jump. We were all born leaders; that is, until we were compelled to go to school and taught to be managed and to manage.

People are not "things" to be manipulated, labeled, boxed, bought, and sold. Above all else, they are not "human resources." They are entire human beings, containing the whole of the evolving universe, limitless until we start limiting them. We must examine the concept of leading and following with new eyes. We must examine the concept of superior and subordinate with increasing skepticism. We must examine the concept of management and labor with new beliefs. And we must examine the nature of organizations that demand such distinctions with an entirely different consciousness.

It is true leadership; leadership by everyone; leadership in, up, around, and down this world so badly needs, and dominator management it so sadly gets.

Retirement on the job at the National Bank of Commerce was not all reflection. One day stands out. I had been sent to a suburban office to learn branch banking. The manager turned me over to a crusty woman who was to train me to be a teller. The very soul of courtesy to customers and a genius at the work, she was, nevertheless, of choleric disposition, not at all improved by tenuous relations with men. When she turned away from attending to a customer, she could be a veritable bear, and

I was raw meat. At the close of a trying day she brought me to my knees.

The branch was closed for the day and empty of customers. The lady and I could not balance the day's activities. More than an hour passed as we checked everything time and again without success. Clearly, this was not something to which she was accustomed. The likely source of the problem was standing at her side. She turned to me with an order, beneath which there appeared a glint of sadistic humor.

"It must be a lost deposit. Go down to the basement, look through the garbage, and see if you can find it." Speechless, I descended to the basement visualizing a single can of crumpled paper. There, neatly in a row, were eleven fifty-five-gallon cans stuffed with far more than paper—cigarette butts, ashes, chewing gum, rotting remnants of leftover lunches, and other disgusting detritus.

My neck grew hot with anger. This ripped it! After managing businesses since the age of twenty, this was preposterous! Language learned working my sixteenth summer in a slaughterhouse poured out. Damned if I was going to spend the night grubbing though garbage for a lost deposit, and double-damned if a snotty bank teller was going to order me about, and triple-damned if I was going to spend another day at the #*X*X#* National Bank of Commerce. They could take this job and "put it where the sun don't shine."

At the worst and the best of times, the ridiculous has always tickled my funny bone. As anger and expletives diminished, in the dismal basement, laughter came pouring out. Sure, I'd been climbing the corporate ladder for sixteen years, but before that I'd done stoop labor, picked beans, thinned sugar beets, mucked out dairy barns, cleaned offal, and dumped slop. I'd been proud to be a boy able to do a man's work, and never felt demeaned by a minute of it. Hell, I'd worked for sadistic bosses who made this woman look like the tooth fairy. Words spoken a thousand times to employees came swinging back to clout me in

> **MiniMaxims**
>
> *There isn't any poor work; there's only work poorly done, poorly recognized, or poorly paid.*

the back of the head. "There isn't any poor work; there's only work poorly done, poorly recognized, or poorly paid."

Off came coat, tie, and shirt as I upended the first can. If there was a lost deposit I would find it if it took all night. *Then,* they'd learn what they could do with this job. The more I worked the more I laughed. Pride is pride. *This work* was not going to be poorly done. I dove into the garbage.

Within minutes, Old Monkey Mind took me happily into the magical forest of questions without answers, only more fascinating questions. What is pride? How can there be such a thing as pride without humility? How can there be such a thing as humility without pride? Humility would be impossible to conceive without the notion of pride. One defines the other. They are integral, one and the same, different faces of the same coin. Were not both pride and humility dancing simultaneously, seamlessly through me? What made me think of them as separate? What made me want to choose one and deny the other?

Was someone shuffling papers alone high up in a luxurious building at an expensive desk in a large room with a sign reading *President* a superior form of humanity to someone sorting trash in the basement? Whence came the craving for one rather than the other?

Where did all this superior, inferior nonsense come from? By what method could one possibly know—by what possible measurement and what standards could one judge the value of climbing a ladder of power, wealth, and fame, other than the pronouncements of those who lust after them? Could such desires amount to no more than a basement of trash? Isn't all life a seamless blending of all opposites? If so, why do we think to separate one thing from another and elevate it to the status of a deity? On and on the questions whirled and swirled as time lost all dimension.

Two hours and ten cans later, my "boss" came down the stairs to take away my desired victory, smiling smugly as she said, "I found the error. We're in balance. It wasn't a lost deposit after all." Had I been had by this diabolical woman? I could not know, but no matter, for if I'd been had, it was a masterful piece of work. The next day, equanimity restored, working frantically in the teller's cage to keep up with a flood of customers, she casually turned. As though it were a rhetorical question, she sweetly said, "Would you run down to the drug store and pick up a prescription for me, and bring a cup of coffee on your way back?"

I gave it to her like a man. "Run your own #X*&#*X errands. I'm not your personal servant."

She didn't take it like a woman, but gave it back in kind. "And I'm not here to clean up your *X#*X# mistakes." We stood nostril to nostril, eyeball to eyeball, breathing fire as we stared each other down. Later, in a slack half hour, both defeated and laughing, we went on the errands together.

It did not seem so then, but now it seems a matter of perspective whether sorting trash in the basement of the branch was the high or low point in my retirement on the job at the National Bank of Commerce. The year provided ample time for reading and reflection, along with days wandering forests, mountains, and ocean shores. Better yet was reconnection to the suppressed, yet incredible, spirit, will, and creativity of the managed—the many who day in, day out do the ordinary work of the world from which the wealth, power, and fame of the few is extracted. These were my people. It was where I belonged, although I denied it then, and longed to escape.

Years before, words by Emerson had leaped from the page to stick in my mind like a cockle burr in a long-haired dog. "Everywhere you go you take your giant with you." He was writing about the insatiable desire to escape the present and seek paradise in the new and different—new places, new stations in life, new possessions—a futile quest to escape self. No matter how hard I had tried to escape my giant, he always returned—the country kid, the two-room house, manual labor, no university degree, estrangement—the raging sense of inferiority. It was then that I had the guts to turn, look my giant in the eye, and say, "You're an ugly cuss and you scare the liver out of me, but if we're going to be together forever we might as well get to know one another and live civilly together." My giant and I are not yet buddies, but we're working on it.

In a strange way, every institution is the same. Everywhere they go they take their giant with them. No matter how much we shuffle control and responsibility back and forth from one Industrial Age form of organization to another—government or private enterprise, democracy or socialism, monarchy or republic, planned economies or free markets, national or municipal government, nonprofit or for-profit—our social and environmental problems continue to escalate. Everywhere our institutions go they take their giant—mechanistic, Industrial Age organizational concept—with them.

No matter how we try to suppress our problems with Industrial Age techniques, they reemerge in different dress or form, more complex and virulent than ever. Something is deeply, fundamentally wrong. No matter how many technological miracles we perform, no matter how sophisticated the virtual worlds we create, no matter how many atoms we crack, no matter how much genetic code we splice, no matter how many space probes we launch, things will get progressively worse until we discern and deal with that fundamental institutional problem.

In truth, there are no problems "out there." And there are no experts "out there" who could solve them if there were. The problem is "in here," in the consciousness of writer and reader, of you and me. It is in the depths of the collective consciousness of the species. When that consciousness begins to understand and grapple with the false Industrial Age concepts of organization to which it clings; when it is willing to risk loosening the hold of those concepts and embrace new possibilities; when those possibilities engage enough minds, new patterns will emerge and we will find ourselves on the frontier of institutional alternatives ripe with hope and rich with possibilities.

At bottom, it is a wrong concept of organization and leadership based on a false metaphor with which we must deal. Until our consciousness of the relational aspect of the world and all life therein shall change, the problems that crush the young and make grown people cry will get progressively worse.

Within days of my wrestling match with the garbage cans and crusty lady boss, Maxwell Carlson leaves a message saying he has something he would like to discuss with me. Well, here it comes. My vows of conformity and a pleasant demeanor have been broken and the consequences must be born. No matter, for this is not the kind of retirement on the job I had imagined. What's one more failure? Just another arrow to stick in my quiver of confrontation.

Mr. Carlson smiles and waves me toward the small conference room near his desk. When I am comfortably seated, he assumes his accustomed position, one leg wound around the other, toes hooked behind an ankle, thumbs parked in the pockets on either side of his vest, looking thoughtfully down. He is ever quick to the point, saying softly, "It was kind of you to arrange time to see me this morning. There are a few things happening at the bank which you may find interesting."

It breaks my stride. Kind of me to see Mr. Carlson? Does he mean it? This is a strange way to begin a termination. I hold my tongue as he continues. "Since you once lived in California you are no doubt aware of the credit card program of the Bank of America. You also know that Seattle First National Bank has entered the business with their 'Firstcard.' A good many of our senior officers think credit cards are unsound, and I'm not certain I disagree with them. Nevertheless, Bank of America has decided to franchise BankAmericard and we have agreed to take a license. We would like to be in business within ninety days. Bob Cummings is to head the program. He is a highly competent experienced branch manager, but has no experience with credit cards or unsecured consumer lending. He could use your help. We would like to borrow you to assist him. What do you think?"

What do I think? I think it is a very strange way to offer someone an assignment, or induce them to accept it—this is not why I came to the bank—who is Cummings?—ninety days is an impossibly short time to launch such a venture—senior officers don't wish it well and will undercut it—I'm fed up with the bank anyway—is this some sort of punishment? Might as well get it over with, but how to say no to a kind, gracious man without offense? Candor begets candor.

"Mr. Carlson, there are a couple things you should know. I've been managing businesses since I was twenty and would be a terrible assistant anything. And I have absolutely no use for credit cards. All I had were destroyed fourteen years ago. I've not had one since and want none in the future." Well, that should take care of that!

He reflects for a scant moment as a suppressed smile tugs at his face and wins. Grinning, he softly replies. "Well, young man, if that won't bother you too much, I expect it won't bother me a great deal either. Why don't you have lunch with Mr. Cummings and see if the two of you can work it out?"

What is left to be said after one has thrown his best verbal pitch and watched it effortlessly hit out of the ballpark? It will be another year before I realize Mr. Carlson never promotes anyone. He "borrows" them for new assignments so that they can withdraw without feeling a failure if the new situation is unsuitable. If it proves productive, titles and rewards follow.

But Cummings was something else again.

CHAPTER FIVE

Ordinary People, Extraordinary Things

I experienced under the sun that
The race is not to the swift,
Nor the battle to the strong;
Wise men lack an income,
Prophets do not have riches,
And the learned lack wealth,
And time and chance overtake them all.
— KOHELETH

Bob Cummings and I verbally circled and sniffed one another like two strange dogs deciding whether to fight or form a pack. We soon discovered four things in common. We didn't like one another. We didn't want the jobs we had been offered. We didn't know why we had been selected. And we had high regard for Maxwell Carlson.

Bob had come up through the ranks of commercial lending. He was a traditional, conservative bank manager. I knew that credit cards were nothing but high volume unsecured consumer lending. The thought of being burdened by an unimaginative, conservative banker boss was appalling. Bob knew that credit cards were nothing but another form of banking. The thought of being burdened with a consumer-credit, outsider assistant was appalling. I knew it wouldn't work. Bob knew it wouldn't work. In the end, it came down to Maxwell Carlson. Since we were both "borrowed to get it started," either or both could walk away when the inevitable rupture occurred. Right now, Mr. Carlson needed our help. Neither of us could deny him that. Reluctantly, warily, we agreed to give it a shot. Talk about archaic internal models, distorted perspectives, and bad perception.

Within two weeks, Bob and I were in San Francisco for training at the Bank of America licensing corporation, along with representatives of five other licensee banks. The first day left both of us extremely uncomfortable. As the meeting droned through presentation after presentation, it all boiled down to little more than "mass-issue hundreds of thousands of unsolicited cards, sign every merchant in sight, and all will come right in the end." Questions were either brushed aside or answered with another harangue. We were puzzled that the instructors were all marketing people, none of whom had experience in the Bank of America card operation. In the hotel that night, we shared our concerns.

"Bob, either I never learned anything about consumer credit in sixteen years or these people don't know what they are talking about. All they talk about is mass-marketing, mass-marketing, mass-marketing. It's individuals that earn income and pay debt, not mobs."

Bob was equally uncomfortable. "I've got the same feeling about their claim of how much banking business we can get from issuing cards to merchants and cardholders who deal with other banks, then selling them our bank services. When it's all over, I don't think much banking business will change hands."

I was inclined to openly challenge the training, but Bob disagreed. "We don't know enough to argue about what we're being told."

A small light came on. "Bob, I know a couple of people in the BankAmericard operating center. Why don't you attend the training sessions, while I quietly disappear and dig into operation of the center? At night, we can compare notes and see if what we're being told squares with what's actually being done, and if it makes sense." Bob agreed.

The next night as we shared experience of the day, little squared and less made sense. There was bad blood and limited communication between the BankAmericard center and the licensing corporation. They reported to different segments of the bank. Worse yet, the bank's own card center had no capacity to comply with rules prescribed in the licensing agreements. The National Bank of Commerce had already made a public announcement of its BankAmericard program. There was no way to reverse the decision. The bank had a forty-year correspondent banking relationship with the Bank of America. Founders of both banks had been close friends. Bob and I were in deep trouble, wondering how we might somehow get "unborrowed" by Maxwell Carlson.

> **MiniMaxims**
>
> *You can learn much from what people say, but more is revealed by what they do not say. Listen as carefully to the silence as the sound.*

On the flight home we cooked up a plan. The next day, in the midst of an airline strike, we set off across the country, flying catch-as-catch-can to spend each day at a different credit card company, cramming ourselves with their diverse experience. There was something to learn from each, yet none fit our circumstances well enough to emulate. We made deals to share experiences in the months ahead. Within a single week, our original belief that the BankAmericard franchise would provide a well-marked, expeditious road to the future had been shattered by what we learned.

There was no choice but to design a program out of our collective experience, knowledge of our market, and what we could glean from the diverse experience of others. When we returned to Seattle, most of the Bank of America training material was tossed into the trash. The bad news piled up. There was no empty space in our bank building, and none readily available in the vicinity. Preliminary calls to suppliers of imprinters, card stock, card embossers, point-of-sale material, and other essentials brought solemn warnings of limited capacity, and intense pressure to order immediately. Were we being honestly advised or hustled? There was no way to know.

The situation was screaming for the iconoclastic concepts of organization and management in which I deeply believed, but had tried to suppress. I had come to know Bob fairly well in the preceding two weeks. His mind was quick. He was decisive. Lurking below the surface was a quirky sense of humor. Hints had come along that "Bob is not your traditional branch manager." I could smell a closet rebel. Restraint went into the garbage can, and I pleaded with Bob to abandon tradition, throw detailed planning to the winds, rely on a clear sense of direction, a few simple principles, common sense, ingenuity, and let the answers emerge.

"Bob, we only have ten weeks. We'll make endless mistakes, but if they're mistakes of commission, they can be fixed. But there will be no remedy for mistakes of omission. You know banking and the Washington State market cold. I know consumer credit and unorthodox management. If we ask enough crazy questions, the answers will emerge." It took little persuasion. He was already there.

The next day we picked up the telephone and ordered thousands of imprinters. Another two calls, and we were on the hook for two hundred thousand plastic cards and several card embossers. I don't remember the sum, but it was huge for the time and circumstances. The same day we commandeered the bank auditorium.

Within the week, we had rifled bank departments and storage warehouses for spare file cabinets, massing them on the stage. We "liberated" all the desks we could find, rented others, lining them end-to-end across the floor of the auditorium in rows four feet apart. Electrical and telephone cords were taped to the floor along the front edge of each row of desks. We "borrowed" all willing, unassigned employees, and all those who could be spared for ninety days, no questions asked. Ads went in the paper for credit analysts, merchant sales representatives, collectors, and other essential personnel not readily available in the bank. It wasn't quite "send me the miserable refuse of your teeming shores," but it was similar.

Within two weeks, the auditorium was a beehive of people, laughing, interviewing, ordering supplies, planning advertising, and attending to hundreds of other tasks. It was out of control. It was chaos. But bit by bit, order was emerging. Word had moved like lightning through the bank. No one passed on their way to lunch without poking their head in the door to observe the frenzy, shaking their head and laughing as they walked away. Within days, we were dubbed "The Zoo." Not inappropriate, for it was pure lamb's milk and Monkey's bananas.

Three days and you were trained. A week brought competence. Two weeks produced an "expert." A month made an "old hand." Hours became meaningless as the days swept by. Each week knocked eight percent off the time to launch. We tried to keep the executive office informed but it was difficult, for we often surprised ourselves. We kept an eye out for the corporate iron fist. It rarely came down. When it did, we ducked. The staid old bank seemed unusually malleable. Either that, or everyone was happy to stand aside while Cummings and Hock dove off the bridge into a few inches of water. We became blood brothers on a crusade. The Zoo was only the beginning.

Within the month we are in Yakima, Washington, in the last of many grueling meetings across the state in an effort to qualify 120,000 bank customers for credit cards within weeks. In front of us are several dozen veteran commercial bankers, not at all thrilled with the notion that the bank is entering the credit card business. The room reeks of skepticism and hostility. By now, our act is well rehearsed. Bob begins the meeting, grumbling about his new assignment, drawing on his credibility as a branch manager to gain sympathy and confidence. The veteran bankers are not reluctant to unload. "Ridiculous business—unconscionable to lead people into continual debt—our customers don't need or want credit cards—only irresponsible people use them—this is worse than financing cars—credit cards should be outlawed—the bank will lose its shirt." The litany pours out while we nod and sympathize. We've heard it all before.

Suddenly, Bob throws both arms in the air and stops the meeting abruptly. "Hold it! Hold it!" I choke off a grin as he continues. "Get out your wallets. Come on, all of you. That's right, get them out and lay them on the table. Now open them and take out everything other than checks and cash that you use to buy stuff—come on, out with them—all your charge cards—gas, merchandise, airline tickets, entertainment—all of them." The room begins to look like a giant poker game as cards cover the tables.

"Good! Now fan them in your hand like a deck of cards—go ahead—use both hands if you're having trouble. Good! Now hold them over your head." A few faces break into grins as they glance around the room. It looks like an overplanted flower garden in the summer sun. There is not an empty hand in the room.

"Wonderful! Now, while you hold them up, we'll talk as long as you like about the evils of credit cards and the irresponsible people who use them!" The room erupts in laughter. Arguments begin about who is the most reckless spender in the crowd. "OK," Bob continues, "now, let's get down to it and figure out how the National Bank of Commerce is going to enter this business in a sensible, responsible way. You're the people that can make that happen, and we're going to rely on you."

We already know that branches will come up with different but similar plans. Every employee with lending authority in every branch will work together reviewing a computer printout of every checking account, savings account, and loan customer of the bank. A "yes" from any office without dissent and a card will be issued with no further investigation. A "no" without dissent and a card will not be issued. We will rely entirely on the integrity of our people and their knowledge of customers. If a customer is not well known one way or the other, a credit report will be drawn and a decision made later. Every customer selected will receive an advance mailing so that they can accept or decline a card.

We will make the same careful preparation for enrolling merchants. No major promotions outside the bank will be made until our own customers have been properly served. The results are spectacular. The people in each branch self-organize the work, and within the month, letters are on the way to 120,000 customers, offering them a card.

As the ninety days we had been given to launch the card program flew by, Old Monkey and I never stopped thinking about the nature of organization. The Yakima branch officers were only one of dozens of groups of people coming together, agreeing on things to be done, doing them, and vanishing into other sets of relationships. The National Bank of Commerce was the explicit organization, but we were the implicit. What we were doing had little resemblance to the way the bank had operated before. Its normal processes and procedures had little effect on what was happening. They certainly did not cause or design it. Nor did they prevent it. When Bob and I met over a plate of smoked oysters and agreed to work together, did that act alone constitute an organization?

Is it possible the most concise definition of organization is simply "agreement"? Wherever there is need for agreement, there is either ambiguity or differing points of view. There is also desire for reconciliation. When two people engage in such reconciliation, is that the essence of organization, however small in scale and transitory in time? Such a moment contains both the essence of conflict and of resolution. There is desire to prevail and willingness to compromise. Even the words *will* and *willing* are revealing. *Will* implies self-interest and desire; the ability to formulate an objective and realize it. Yet *willing* implies ability to set aside self-interest and compromise. Thus, the will can be used to realize diametrically opposed objectives.

Agreement contains the essence of both difference and commonality. If there is no difference, there is nothing about which to agree. With agreement comes at least some degree of commonality. If two individuals meet and agree, the agreement contains the essence of organization. They are, no matter how briefly or for what purpose, "organized." That agreement also contains the essence of self-governance, for each must rely on the self-induced behavior of the other to act in accordance with the understanding.

Agreement is always dynamic, imperfect, and malleable. Language, with all its vagaries and nuances, is our primary tool with which to reach agreement. Its use is complicated by the fact that every word uttered or written is conditioned in the mind of the originator by one set of beliefs, emotions, expectations, and experiences, and conditioned in the mind of the recipient by quite another. Reaching agreement is a continual process, as alive as the people involved. It does not admit of certainty or perpetuity, especially in the particulars. Relationships between even two people who live or work together are far too complex to allow agreement much beyond intent, sense of direction, and principles of conduct. This reveals another essential element of agreement: tolerance and trust. One must accept that the behavior of another can never be reduced to the kind of specificity that science proposes and contracts attempt to provide, or ever conform entirely to any single understanding of words, sentences, and paragraphs. No agreement can provide for all particulars, and particulars will never conform to any agreement, yet certainty and conformity are what present institutions—in fact, the whole of society—have been organized to try to create.

In the constructive sense of the word, governance can only be based on clarity of shared intent and trust in expected behavior, heavily seasoned with common sense and tolerance. This is not to say that contracts, laws, and regulations do not serve a purpose. Rather, it is to point out that they can never achieve the mechanistic certainty and control we crave. Rules and regulations, laws and contracts, can never replace clarity of shared purpose and clear, deeply held principles about conduct in pursuit of it. Principles are never capable of ultimate achievement, for they presume constant evolution and change. "Do unto others as you would have others do unto you" is a true principle, for it says nothing about how it must be done. It presumes unlimited ability of people to evolve in accordance with their values, experience, and relations with others.

True governance is based on understanding that even simple societies are far too complex to expect that there can be agreement in the particular. Systems of self-governance, in the individual and at every scale beyond, are based on understanding that ordinances, orders, and enforcement deal with an absence of true governance. They are an attempt to compel the kind of behavior that organizations fail to induce. Ordinances, orders, and enforcement are simply different words for control, command, and tyranny. The ultimate sanction of control is force. Force is the tool of tyranny. Those who rise in a tyrannical world are those least capable of self-governance or inducement of it in others, else they would not engage in tyranny. And when they rise, it is axiomatic that self-governance will decline and government will gradually be for the benefit of the few and not the many. It will inexorably become destructive. Ultimately, there will be no limit to that destruction, for there appears to be no limit to the ability of the rational mind to create devices to alter and manipulate all life forms and all aspects of the physical world.

There is no way to give people purpose and principles, nor can there be self-governance without them. The only possibility is to evoke the gift of self-governance from the people to themselves. It is in that process that a true leader may be useful. Nor can self-governance occur if the principles do not deal with such fundamental issues as the locus and exercise of power, and the distribution of rewards.

True self-governance requires freedom from physical necessity. If people lack the basic necessities for sustaining life—clean food, water, and air, adequate shelter and clothing—they are enslaved as surely as if their master was standing above them with a whip, even though their masters be multiple, separated from them by continents and countless government, corporate, and monetary veils. If people lack either a physical environment or a society that allows a basic measure of dignity, meaning, and security, behavior is compelled. Physical violence is but the most visibly shocking end of a chain of other violence. If we choose to engage in ecological violence, economic violence, social violence, spiritual violence, and psychic violence, how can we expect to live free of physical violence?

We now live in a world of such complexity, diversity, and multiplicity of scales that there is little possibility of achieving constructive, sustained governance with existing concepts of organization. People, everywhere, are growing desperate for renewed sense of community. Shared purpose and principles leading to new concepts of self-governance at multiple scales from the individual to the global have become essential.

It is nearing the end of 1966, and we are but two weeks from launch, faced with major problems and no margin for failure. One hundred thousand card mailers in huge rolls arrived today, along with special machinery for feeding them into computer printers and cutting and folding them as they emerge. The printing contractor is standing to one side, admiring the gleaming new machinery he has installed to the front and back of the bulky printer. To the side is the large mainframe of the IBM 1401 computer. A long row of tape drives, each as tall as a man, stare at us with plate-sized eyes of spooled magnetic tape. A labyrinth of cables connects them to punch-card readers and high-speed printers, each the size of three desks. Dozens of spools of magnetic tape lie waiting, filled with the names, addresses, and essential data of a hundred thousand bank customers who are to receive a small rectangle of blue, white, and gold polyvinyl chloride emblazoned *National Bank of Commerce, BankAmericard*. No one there can imagine that all the power in that room will, in three decades, reside in a five-pound laptop computer costing a few thousand dollars.

We have carefully calculated the ten hours required to print, cut, and fold the card mailers. Processing of all other bank work has been suspended at great risk to give us sole use of the computers until seven in the morning—twelve hours. Two hours to spare. No more time available. It's now or never.

I am awed, almost worshipful in this temple of technology. The past two and a half months have again inflamed the obsession with institutions. The grinding work of entering the card business occupies only part of my mind. Imagination is seething with what this all means to the world of organizations. It has pushed me into computer and programming classes, a few dozen books, and led to crazies on the fringes of the computer world willing to share their dreams. Giving people another way to borrow money interests me not at all. What credit cards might become is something else.

What is the meaning of the marriage of money and computers? How does that meaning change, if they get a bit polygamous and also wed telephone lines, radio, and television? Where does software fit in? What is the nature of money in computer memory? What is the difference between the "bone boxes" running about on every pair of shoulders in the computer room and the "black box" of the computer immobile on the computer floor? Aren't both processing information? Is there some cosmic beat to all this?

Awareness rises. This whole thing is not about banks or merchants or credit or cardholders. It's not about data or information or computers. It's about connections! No, no, it's about more than connections. It's about massive change in interconnectivity. No, no, it's got to be deeper than that. It's about dissolution of the notion of boundaries between separate, connected things—it's about—it's about—it's about—there are no good words. Could it be about relationships and growth; about all things growing from one another and everything growing from some indefinable *essence that is*; about all things inseparably interrelated? Could it be about some flaw in the very concepts of separability, particularity, and linearity? Is there some analogy between the industrialized machine age as an extension of muscle and the computer age as an extension of mind and memory?

Old Monkey loves these questions, but we are rudely jerked back into the computer room. Something is sadly awry. The form-feeder cannot be synchronized with the printer. Both machines constantly jam. As mailers flow erratically from the printer, cutting and folding machinery slices some in half and crumples others. Technicians are bent over, heads and hands deep in the machinery. The supplier soon confesses. The whole setup is untested. They've never used it before, and it's an abysmal failure.

Bob and I walk away to a quiet corner near a supply closet to console one another. There is no possibility of another block of time on the computer. Without mailers by morning, the whole thing is off. How can we explain our failure to Maxwell Carlson, a hundred thousand customers waiting for their promised cards, and merchants waiting for those customers? Bob is idly leaning on the handle of a push broom. Inspiration is the child of desperation. Could he be leaning on the answer? We quickly unscrew the handle, rush to the stack of mailers, and shove it through a roll. With a heave we lift it—might even be able to hold it for half an hour at a stretch, maybe more, or prop it on cabinets. The broom handle makes a decent axle. With a third person to guide mailers into the printer and alternating crews, it might work. Other crews could wind mailers on broom handles as they come from the printer. If we can get mailers printed, we'll worry about cutting and folding another day.

We call everyone together, printing company executives, bank officers, programmers, operators, janitors—everyone. Will they work the night—no bosses—no procedures—just grab a piece of the problem and get it done—need help, ask—want to help, offer? Yes? Good! Two people lift a roll of mailers and the printer begins to chatter. Two others grab a second broom handle and begin to roll up forms as they emerge. Suggestions pour out and someone is instantly on the way to attend to each. "Search the building and steal broom handles." "Get food and drinks sent in." "We'll need gloves." "Round up relief crews." "Rig a backup printer." No one knows all that is happening and no one has time to care. We must trust.

The last roll comes off the printer at six in the morning. An exhausted, happy band of brothers and sisters heads home to catch a few hours' sleep before the next ordeal begins. As we labored through the night, someone had claimed ownership of every aspect of the printing as well as future work separating and folding the mailers to get the project back on track. Is that how the future happens? Ingenuity? Passion? Spontaneous order out of chaos? It seems so, as long as control is kept on a leash.

With but days left until launch, there remains one immense problem to which we have no answer. More than a hundred thousand mailers are ready to receive newly embossed NBC BankAmericards. Each card must be proofread against the printed mailer, hand-inserted, and bundled for delivery to the post office. It must be done in three days. It is far beyond the capacity of the small staff of the card center. We need a mass of clerical workers motivated to do an excellent job. The ingenious solution is Bob's.

Who are the best at the work to be done—the real experts? Clerical employees and keypunch operators on the bottom rung of the bank ladder. Good! They will be the "leaders." The ingenious part we explain to Andrew Price, Maxwell Carlson, and Robert Faragher, chairman, president, and executive vice president, respectively. It is fiendishly simple. They "borrowed" Bob and me to help get the card program launched in an impossibly short period of time. Now we need to "borrow" them. If each of them will come to the center at 4:30 for three days, report to their leader, and work the evening proofreading and stuffing their share of the cards, other executive officers will be invited to share in the work. With those acceptances in hand, we will offer the same opportunity to every officer and manager in the bank. No pressure, first come, first served, no records kept. The marvelous part is that all are exempt employees, not hourly workers subject to overtime. Meals will be catered by the bank cafeteria. Aside from extra compensation and overtime for the "leaders," it will cost almost nothing. It is outrageous. It is common sense. It catches fire.

One after another, executive officers agree to be "borrowed." Within a day of the bankwide communication, we are oversubscribed. Everyone wants to see the brass doing clerical work and taking direction from ordinary folk. No one wants to miss this upside-down party. We have to ration time, allowing no officer more than a single night. Those late in calling are put out at being rejected.

It is some party, not without lighter moments. In the midst of fifty intensely concentrating people, there is a crash and all eyes turn to stare. Bob Faragher, executive vice president, has knocked his tray of cards off the desk, scattering them across the floor. With a laugh, he is down on his knees while his boss, little Nancy Smilinich, card embossing operator, kneels by his side, helping and consoling. "Never mind, it could happen to any of us." At the end of three nights, more than a hundred thousand cards are in the mail, and the program is launched.

During the next year, Bob grew to love his job and he was loved by the people. I thought he would be there for years, if not the remainder of his career. I expected to work until the center was well established, then get back to retirement on the job.

A couple of months after the first anniversary of the launch, Ron McDonald asked if I could come by to speak with him. I assumed I would be assigned elsewhere in the bank. To my surprise, he told me there was a need to "borrow" Bob for another assignment, which he was eager to accept. That would not be possible unless I was open to becoming head of the credit card department at a significant raise in pay. It appeared Bob would be denied something he wanted if I were to decline, nor did our family finances make it prudent to say no. Yes, of course I would accept.

Bob pulled it off to perfection. It was years later, at his retirement party, when I finally learned the truth. He had walked into Ron's office and abruptly announced, "Get me out of this job. Dee needs and deserves it. I'm just in his way."

If Bob Cummings had not made such an extraordinary gift, the events of the next chapter would not have occurred.

CHAPTER SIX

The House of Cards

*The ideas of the past, although half destroyed,
being still very powerful, and the ideas which are
to replace them being still in process of formation,
the modern age represents a period of transition
and anarchy.*
— GUSTAVE LE BON

*Taking a new step; uttering a new word is what
people fear most.*
— FYODOR MIKHAILOVICH DOSTOYEVSKY

Early in 1966, within months after Bank of America let it be known that it would license its BankAmericard program and five California banks announced a joint Mastercharge program, the banking industry was seething with speculation and rampant with rumors: "Citicorp has committed millions to develop proprietary card technology to force an industry standard controlled by them"—"American Express is buying a bank and will blanket the country with American Express bank cards"—"Bank of America's licensing program is a cover-up they will use to promote deposit accounts nationwide"—"Citicorp and Chase Manhattan are going to license proprietary cards"—"Banks in a dozen different regions are forming groups modeled after the California Mastercharge association"—"Independent bank cards are forming a network using a common interbank logo"—

"Legislation will give the Federal Reserve system a monopoly for the clearing of sales drafts between banks"—"The federal government is going to pass a usury law to preempt all state laws governing credit card rates"—"The federal government is going to forbid mass-mailing of unsolicited cards"—"There is a shortage of polyvinyl chloride to make cards"—"There is a shortage of imprinters."

Bankers found the rumors hard to believe. But that changed when many rumors vehemently denied were confirmed by surprise announcements and aggressive marketing. Thousands of vendors, suppliers, and consultants leaped into the feeding frenzy, playing one bank against the other, exaggerating everything, and dreaming up credit card marketing and operating schemes, none so bizarre that it failed to find takers.

Within months, there was no rumor so wild and no claim of success so exaggerated that it was without believers. It was the great Oklahoma land rush magnified a thousandfold. Whoever got there first and got their stake in the ground would win. Whoever got there last would come home in a broken wagon with empty hands. Fence-sitting bankers did an about-face. The risks of getting into the business seemed insignificant compared with the risks of staying out. Doubts were swept under the rug and the panic was on.

Stories of the banking madness of the time are legendary. In the beginning, there was no magnetic strip on the card and no electronic card readers at point of sale. Cards were placed in the bed of a manual imprinter, a four-part sales draft placed on top, and a lever pulled or pressed to create an impression. They were dubbed "zip zap" machines. Imprinters were purchased by banks for a few dollars and rented to merchants for handsome monthly fees. Many banks were incensed when imprinters they had supplied were used to serve cardholders of competitors.

Determined to stamp out this injustice, one major bank reissued all its cards with a hole in the center and installed a steel peg in the bed of its imprinters to shatter the card of other issuers. No sharing of point-of-sale devices for this rabid competitor.

Merchant service representatives of a Southern bank engaged in creative marketing. They leased imprinters to merchants at a reduced rate and carried away imprinters of their competitor with assurance to the merchants that all was understood between the banks. Where the liberated imprinters went was a bit murky. The bank's market research proved faulty, for the local sheriff turned out to be a loyal customer of the bank's competitor. He swiftly rounded up the innovative merchant representatives and threw them in the slammer. It set off a feud between the rival bankers that, ten years later, resulted in a VISA board member—an officer of one of the banks—being unseated by an officer of the other in a bitterly contested election.

Advertising slogans knew no bounds. "The Card With A Heart." "The Captain America Card." "The Everything Card." A prominent bank in a southeastern state entered the business with a huge mass-mailing of cards, plastering its market with billboards and saturating it with television screaming, "THE CARD YOU WON'T GO BERSERK WITH," a challenge the public accepted with enormous enthusiasm. The earnings of the bank were soon sadly depressed and shareholder dividends suspended.

The system for clearing sales drafts between banks was primitive. There were no electronic data entry or clearing systems. Each merchant-signing bank accepted all transactions regardless of the issuing bank, crediting the merchant account for the total, manually sorted the transactions by issuing bank, and reimbursed itself by drawing a draft on each issuing bank through the Federal Reserve system. When the clearing draft reached the issuing bank, it was posted to a suspense ledger while waiting for the merchant bank to keypunch the sales drafts and send them through the U.S. mail.

Meanwhile, the merchant bank, having already been paid and under immense pressure to handle its own cardholder transactions, had no incentive to process the transactions and get them to the issuing bank for billing to the cardholder. Since every bank was both a merchant-signing bank and a card-issuing bank, they began to play tit-for-tat, while backrooms filled with hundreds of millions of unprocessed transactions, customers went unbilled, and suspense ledgers swelled like a hammered thumb. It became an accounting nightmare.

Criminals sensed a bonanza. Within two years, large quantities of plastic cards not yet embossed with cardholder names and numbers began to disappear from manufacturers' warehouses, shipping companies, and bank storage facilities. A few thousand dollars for embossing machines, some organized pilferage of account numbers from discarded copies of sales drafts, and crooks were "in business." Counterfeit cards were soon more than matched by cards stolen wholesale on their way through postal departments, pilfered from mailboxes, snatched by pickpockets, and "forgotten" by customers with assistance from conniving store clerks. Thousands of counterfeit and stolen cards were soon on the black market, selling for as little as $50, each card swiftly used to purchase and resell thousands of dollars of merchandise, then abandoned.

Sham merchants appeared, depositing large quantities of fraudulent sales drafts during the two months it took banks to process them through the system, then vanishing with the money as complaints piled up.

There were no electronic systems for authorizing transactions. Each merchant had a floor limit, beneath which no authorization was required. It took criminals no time at all to pattern such limits and accurately assess the degree of risk in each merchant location. A transaction over the floor limit required that a merchant employee telephone the bank with which they had contracted. An employee of the merchant bank then made a

> **MiniMaxims**
>
> *Haste never made time, and waste never made abundance.*

long-distance call to the card-issuing bank, where an employee manually looked up the customer's account in huge, computer-printed paper ledgers, determined if the sale could be authorized, and gave an authorization number to the inquiring bank, who passed it along to the merchant. Meanwhile, the customer waited angrily or was required to return later. The card-issuing bank posted a hold on the customer account for the amount of the sale, to be released when the sales draft appeared weeks, often months, later.

Merchants realized it was prudent to obtain an authorization in advance for every potential sale, however slight the chance it would be completed. Cardholder lines of credit were swiftly absorbed by holds for sales never completed. They were denied credit they should have had. System authorization costs soared, since merchants made local calls, while banks absorbed all long-distance, bank-to-bank calls.

There was no Internet, no electronic entry of data, no CRT screens for electronic examination of accounts, and no dispersed computing power. All data entry required keypunching each digit of information (every letter and every number) into a four-by-six-inch piece of cardboard by a clunking mechanical punching typewriter the size of a large refrigerator. The punched cards were then put through an elongated card reader twice the size of the keypunch machine to capture the data on magnetic tape, then fed into a van-sized computer for posting to customer accounts. The data was returned to tape and finally sent into a large mechanical printer to produce huge binders of customer records.

Primitive and cumbersome as the system was, it performed well enough to allow massive outpouring of cards to gain considerable consumer and merchant acceptance. As acceptance skyrocketed, the number of transactions flowing between banks exploded and the clearing system rapidly disintegrated under the volume.

There were not many bankers with sound experience in the management of unsecured consumer credit, and fewer with knowledge of credit cards. The most experienced and best qualified people outside the banking industry were repelled by the methods and madness of the industry, nor did they find the mediocre salaries common to banking attractive. However, there was no shortage of those with questionable ability and experience. They came forward in droves. Most were quickly snapped up.

Within the banks, similar problems appeared. Most bankers looked down their noses at the card business, placing it lower on the scale of respectability than auto dealer financing, only then gaining scant acceptance by banks. Few banks really wanted to be in the card business. Few bankers wanted to be assigned to it. Card operations were located in the least desirable part of the bank premises and staffed with employees who did not fit comfortably elsewhere.

It was both curse and blessing. Most credit card departments were filled with an eclectic mixture of bankers and outsiders, pragmatists and dreamers, liberally laced with iconoclasts, renegades, and incompetents. Isolated and disdained, they were lashed by top management to launch a poorly understood, massive business in an impossibly short time in the midst of competitive frenzy. Strangely, however, it contained just the kind of innovative, adventurous spirits that the resulting disaster required. Those who survived would later emerge as a major force in bank management.

By 1968, the fledgling industry was out of control. No one knew the extent of the losses, but they were thought to be in the tens of millions of dollars, a huge sum for the time and for the size of the system. Drawing on Greek legend, *Life* magazine, then in its glory days, ran a cover story depicting banks as Icarus flying to the sun on wings of plastic, one a BankAmericard, the other a Mastercharge. Below was a blood-red sea labeled "losses." The magazine predicted banks would soon plunge down, wings melted, and drown in a sea of red ink.

In the midst of the credit card maelstrom, Old Monkey Mind and I could not escape the three questions that had emerged from our sixteen years of institutional life. The difference between our experience creating the National Bank of Commerce card program and the disaster the industry had become increased our obsession with institutions and the people who hold power within them. Again and again the same questions returned, demanding an answer:

> *Why are institutions, everywhere, whether political, commercial, or social, increasingly unable to manage their affairs?*
>
> *Why are individuals, everywhere, increasingly in conflict with and alienated from the institutions of which they are part?*
>
> *Why are society and the biosphere increasingly in disarray?*

Slowly, bit by bit, our old perspective dissolved, new perceptions arose, and a pattern began to emerge. The answer to those questions was deeply embedded in compression of time and events. Some readers may recall the days when a check took a couple of weeks to find its way through the banking system. It was called *float* and many used it to advantage. One might even think of it as a primitive form of free venture capital. Today, we are all aware of the incredible speed and volatility with which money moves throughout the world and the profound effect it has on us all. However, we ignore vastly more important reductions of float, such as the disappearance of *life float*.

The first life forms appeared approximately 4.5 billion years ago. It took evolution about half that time, 2.2 billion years, to make the first tiny step from the nonnucleated cell to the nucleated cell. It took only half that time, another billion years, to create the first simple vertebrate, then only a half-billion years to produce the first fish, reptiles, and forests. Then, in only 200 million years, it produced dinosaurs, birds, and complex plants, then mammals in only 100 million years. Each change reducing by more than half the time required to produce the next exponential leap in the diversity and complexity of organisms, right on through to the creature reading this book. There is no reason to believe this exponential reduction of time to create more complex, diverse organisms will not continue. In fact, with the advent of genetic engineering, the time required for creation of new species (life float) may literally collapse.

The same pattern is apparent with respect to information float. As the futurist James Burke pointed out, it took centuries for information about the smelting of ore to creep across a single continent and bring about the Iron Age. During the time of sailing ships, it took decades for that which became known to become that which was shared. When man set foot on the moon, it was known and seen in every corner of the globe 1.4 seconds later. Yet that is hopelessly primitive. Today countless events anywhere can be instantly heard and seen everywhere.

Even more important is the disappearance of scientific and technological float: the time between the discovery of new knowledge, the resultant technology, and its universal application. It took centuries for the wheel, one of the first bits of technology, to gain universal acceptance—decades for the steam engine, electric light, and automobile—years for radio and television. Today, countless microchip devices sweep around the earth like the light of the sun into universal use.

The same is true of cultural float. For the better part of recorded history, it took centuries for the customs of one culture to materially affect another. Today, that which becomes popular in one country can sweep through others within weeks. Nor is language an exception. Words from one language used to require generations to take root in another. Common words now emerge from the global culture simultaneously in all languages, while English is rapidly becoming a universal tongue, as anyone who has listened to pilots and controllers at any airport in the world is bound to note.

It is no different with space float. Within a couple of long lifetimes we went from the speed of the horse to the speed of interstellar travel. Men and material now move in minutes where they used to move in months, while services based on information do so in a fraction of a second.

> **MiniMaxims**
>
> *The past is ever less predictive, the future ever less predictable, and the present scarcely exists at all.*

This endless compression of float, whether of life forms, money, information, technology, time, space, or anything else, can be combined and thought of as the disappearance of change float: the time between what was and what is to be, between past and future. Only a few generations ago, the present stretched relatively unaltered from a distant past into a dim future.

Today, the past is ever less predictive, the future is ever less predictable, and the present scarcely exists at all. Everything is accelerating change, with one incredibly important exception. There has been no loss of institutional float.

Although their size and power have vastly increased, although we constantly tinker with their form, although we constantly change their labels, there has been virtually no new idea of organization since the concepts of corporation, nation-state, and university emerged, the newest of which is several centuries old. Much as Old Monkey and I loved such ideas and wished every moment was free to pursue them, events would not leave us alone. It was good that they did not, for they were shattering our old perspectives, emptying us of much that we had accepted as true, and allowing space for new thoughts to rush in.

In the midst of the credit card mess, the Bank of America Service Corporation called a meeting of licensee card program managers to discuss operating problems plaguing the system. Jim Cronkhite, operations officer of our card center, and I flew to Columbus, Ohio, to join 120 others from across the country. We were surprised to find that top officers of the BofA Service Corporation had apparently not thought it important to attend. Other licensees were no less surprised. The meeting was to be conducted by Hal and Don, both pleasant and capable bank operations officers assigned to the Service Corporation to work with licensee banks.

The meeting droned on for most of the first day, many licensees sharply critical of what they perceived as the Bank of America's lack of awareness of the problems and inability or unwillingness to deal with them. The bank's representatives were no less critical of their licensees. By the end of the day, accusations, denials, and counteraccusations were flying about the room. Licensees were attacking one another as well as the Bank of America. Jim and I debated whether to return to Seattle rather than waste another day in the midst of the squabble, but decided to remain.

The next morning was worse. By midday, the meeting disintegrated in acrimonious argument. Shortly before lunch, in evident desperation and without prior discussion with those named, Hal and Don announced appointment of a committee of seven licensee card-center managers, of which I was one, to which they intended to refer a couple of the more critical problems. We were to study the problems and suggest solutions, which Bank of America would attempt to impose on licensees, providing it found the suggestions agreeable.

I thought such a committee would be an exercise in futility and during the lunch break asked Hal and Don for a few moments in private, thinking to persuade them to appoint another in my place. Hal, sweating and face flushed beneath his shock of red hair, was angry and beleaguered. Don, tall and reserved, was nonetheless disturbed. Both listened defensively.

"Look, I don't want to make things more difficult than they already are. If you insist, I'll do this committee thing, but I'd rather not be involved. It would be a big favor if you'd get someone else."

Hal's reply is abrupt and sarcastic. "You guys seem to think everything we try to do is wrong, so here's your chance to do it right."

Don is a bit more reserved but equally concerned. "Dee, why not? Do you have a problem with the idea of the committee itself, or is there some other reason?"

There is no reason to hold back. "Don, it's a waste of time. By the time the committee can meet and agree on anything there'll be a dozen more problems. No one really knows how many problems there are or how serious they might be. Nothing a committee could suggest would satisfy everybody. The way your license agreements are written, if a licensee refuses to go along with the rules your only choice is to kick them out of the system. BofA won't do that and we all know it. It would jeopardize too many banking relationships. I just don't want to waste my time."

Hal and Don stare at me in silence. What the hell, they are friends and we are speaking in private. It might as well be on the table. "Don," I continue, "you can't renegotiate every license every time you want to change operating procedures, and that's essentially what your licensing agreements require. Besides, this mob hasn't the chance of snow in the desert of reaching agreement on anything, let alone sticking to it. And if you think you can renegotiate all the licenses to get licensee banks to surrender enough authority to the Bank of America to let you make rules and enforce them, you've fallen down the rabbit hole with Alice. We all know that BofA would swallow our banks like a snake swallows a mouse if branch banking law didn't prevent it." Neither Hal nor Don can prevent a grin.

Don gives it back in kind. "Yeah? Well, I'm not a snake and you're not a mouse, so what do you suggest?"

"If you're going to form a committee to do anything," I reply, "why not give it responsibility for creating some way to examine all problems in a systematic, continuous way? What's the point in trying to correct any problem if we're constantly guessing about its importance, what else needs to be done, and how they all connect and affect one another? And why mill around yapping at one another out of ignorance?" We're soon in intense discussion. The more we talk, the more they warm to the idea, but not without reluctance.

Don explains. "Even if we agree with you, we have no authority from the bank to set up such a committee. Even if we did, there's no way we're going to suggest it. If it comes from us, it'll be suspect."

"Don, I don't think so. Most licensees would welcome such a suggestion from the Bank of America. We all know the system is in trouble and any coordinated, self-organizing effort would be welcome, even if it came to nothing."

"Dee, we can't do it without approval from the bank."

"Why not? You called the meeting and asked us to come to discuss system problems. Didn't the bank trust you to run the meeting? Don't they trust you to act in their best interest and the interest of the system? All I'm suggesting is that you ask the committee you've appointed to find the best method to do just that. There's no risk. The committee has no authority. It can't commit the bank to anything."

Hal and Don are obviously on the horns of a dilemma. I know their difficulty without asking. They like the idea and know they should support it. They don't want to say no, but they clearly don't want the responsibility. They're trapped by the same old paradigms of predictability and control. They want to know how things will end before they begin. They don't want to create the conditions for solutions to emerge without being able to control what the solutions might be. They're enmeshed in a command-and-control organization and fear how it will respond if they obey their own common sense, creativity, and judgment.

I try to ease them off the horns of the dilemma. "Look, I don't want to put you on the spot. You asked and I answered. It's not my affair. Just announce that I have other commitments, appoint someone in my place, and get on with it. I think it's a mistake, but so what? I'm not going to say anything unless someone asks, and they won't."

But Hal and Don won't let it go, puzzling over what to do. I offer them a way off the hook. "Is this a Bank of America meeting, or is this a licensee meeting that the bank just happened to convene? Is there anything in the license agreements that forbids licensee banks to meet any time they want, anywhere they want, to talk about anything they want? If the idea makes sense, maybe you have an obligation to tell the group about it. You don't have to take a position. Attribute the idea to me, if you want. Just give them the option and ask them what they want to do. What's the big deal? Just do it or let it die."

It's plain their decision is reluctant as Hal responds. "Well—OK, but we won't suggest it. It's your idea and you'll have to present it."

"Look, it's your meeting and I don't want to mess with it. If it's the right thing to do, you should take the lead. That's what the group will expect." But Hal and Don become adamant both ways. The suggestion must be made, but I must make it.

It is a perplexed group that assembles after lunch to find one of their own on the stage. They listen to Hal's preamble, then my concerns about the system and suggestion that the committee address a single problem—how to create a cohesive, coherent, self-organizing effort involving all licensees to examine the problems plaguing the system. It should be an open effort committing no one, including BofA, to anything other than participation.

"How much will it cost?" someone in the audience asks.

"Nothing but some of your time and an occasional airplane ticket."

"What will it commit us to?"

"Nothing."

The audience, in the way of all disorganized groups faced with a proposal creating the illusion of progress but requiring no money or commitment, swiftly agreed. The meeting disbanded and the committee of seven met. Fred James, a soft-spoken, laconic man of considerable influence from Memphis, Tennessee, was the first to speak. "Well, I don't know what you got us into, but this is sure your idea. Unless somebody wants to argue, looks like you're the chairman. Any you other folks contrary-minded?"

And just so, I was elbowed into the chair with no intent but to do a bit of civic duty, never suspecting I had stepped on another of those tiny, jeweled bearings on which the future turns.

CHAPTER SEVEN

Nothing to Lose

*To be free is precisely the same thing as to be
pious, wise, just and temperate, careful of one's
own, abstinent from what is another's and thence,
magnanimous and brave. . . . To be an opposite of
these is the same thing as to be a slave. . . . So it
comes to pass that the nation which has been incapable of governing and ordering itself and has
delivered itself up to the slavery of its own lusts is
itself delivered against its will to other masters, and
whether it will or not, is compelled to serve.*
—JOHN MILTON

There was no time for the new licensee committee to do more than get acquainted and agree to meet two weeks hence. On the flight home, Jim Cronkhite and I ripped a map of the United States from the airline magazine and began dividing the country into sections, minds buzzing with a multitude of questions. What might best define areas of operational, political, cultural, and banking interests? What might provide equitable balance of number of licensees and volume of BankAmericard business? What might keep travel time and costs to a minimum? What might include a healthy mix of differing interests, yet not be so diverse as to make agreement impossible?

We arrived in Seattle with a rough concept of multiple, self-defined regions with operating, marketing, credit, and systems committees within each region. Every card-issuing bank within each region would have a right to appoint a representative to its regional committees. A regional executive committee would be composed of the chairmen of the functional committees and any other individuals the executive committee selected. Comparable national committees would be composed of the chairman of each committee in the seven regions. Everyone would be heard but no one would dominate.

Within the week, the concept was expanded to a set of proposals. The appointed licensee committee met in Atlanta, Georgia. After a day of discussion and modification, agreement was reached. The seven regions became eight. Each member of the group would return to his region, host a meeting of all licensee banks to share the concept, and if successful, coordinate self-organization of regional committees. In the event the concept was not acceptable to all regions, the effort would be abandoned. If the effort was successful, the regional committees would elect their respective chairs, which would automatically determine composition of permanent national committees. The present committee, selected by the Bank of America, would be replaced by the national executive committee.

It was a cumbersome concept but it had the advantage of including every card-issuing licensee bank. Each would not only be acting on its own behalf, but on behalf of hundreds of merchant-signing banks that it had sublicensed in accordance with rights granted in its license from BofA. We identified issues to be addressed. A tentative schedule of meetings was set for the national committee meetings, at which regional information and suggestions would be synthesized into a comprehensive picture of the whole.

It was our hope that the committee structure would not only develop preliminary data about fraud, credit, operating, and technology problems, but assign priority to them and propose solutions to the most vexing. Bank of America would have an ex officio member on each national committee. As sole owners of the service marks and the franchising company, BofA would have responsibility for implementing any proposals, providing it was in agreement with them. Whether BofA could or would, and how, was anyone's guess.

Within six months, the complex of regional and national committees had self-organized. In the process, I was asked to serve as chairman of the Pacific Northwest regional executive committee, and chairman of the national executive committee as well. It was thankless, unpaid, often unpleasant work that added substantially to the time already heavily committed to the management of the National Bank of Commerce card operation, and I loved it! So much for retirement on the job!

The complex of committees had but one redeeming quality: it allowed organized information about problems to emerge. It took only two cycles of meetings to realize they were enormously greater than anyone imagined—far beyond any possibility of correction by the existing committees or licensing structure—and growing at an astonishing rate. Losses were not in the tens of millions, as everyone had thought, but in the hundreds of millions and accelerating.

Suddenly, like a diamond in the dirt, there it lay. The need for a new concept of organization and a precarious toehold from which to make the attempt.

The thought was enough to send Old Monkey Mind and me leaping joyously among our endless thoughts about institutions. In an effort to understand what is happening in the institutional world we often found it profitable to turn to history and philosophy. More

than four centuries ago, in his classic book, *The Prince*,
Machiavelli wrote:

> As the doctors say of a wasting disease, to start with, it is
> easy to cure but difficult to diagnose. After a time, unless it
> has been diagnosed and treated at the outset, it becomes easy
> to diagnose but difficult to cure. So it is in politics.

It is no different for societal institutions. Biological and social
evolution have several things in common. Neither is static or predictable. Both are constantly in motion, constantly evolving. An
organism is a manifestation of and inseparable from the physical
environment from which it emerged, and on which its health and
existence depend. An institution is a manifestation of and inseparable from the social environment from which it emerged, and on
which its health and existence depend. Every organism is interdependent with every other organism and with their physical environment. Every institution is interdependent with every other
institution and with their social and physical environment.

The trick for a biological organism in a changing physical
environment is to evolve into whatever form best serves function.
The trick for each part of the organism is to assume a form useful
to the evolving whole. It is no different for organizations. The trick
for an organization in a changing social environment is to continually evolve into whatever form best serves function. The trick for
each part of the organization is to assume a form useful to the
emerging whole. Healthy biological organisms and healthy organizations alike are an ever shifting panoply of relationships
exhibiting characteristics of both *chaos* and *order*. So is the earth
itself, and the universe as well. They are all *chaordic*.

A principal thing they have in common is penalty for failure
to evolve. Organisms resistant to a changing physical environment
are biologically obliterated; they physically die out. Organizations
resistant to a changing social environment are economically
destroyed; they socially die out. In truth, organisms and organiza-

tions are not separable. Nor can the physical world be separated from the social. In the deeper, larger sense, distinctions such as "physical, biological, and social" or "organism and organization," however useful for insular, limited purposes, are deceptive in the extreme. All things are irrevocably interconnected in a cosmic dance drawn on by energy in the form of light from the sun.

Whether biological or social, whether organism or organization, all things are living processes, not constructed mechanisms, and none can be made to behave as though they were machines, in spite of all our illusions to the contrary. None, at bottom, are controllable, and science, mathematics, and measurement can

> **MiniMaxims**
>
> *Life will never surrender its secrets to a yardstick.*

never bring them to compelled behavior. We may damage them severely. We may destroy them utterly. But we cannot change or compel their essential nature or behavior. Life will never surrender its secrets to a yardstick.

Old Monkey Mind and I were fascinated. We returned to an ancient bit of philosophy which had served us well. Understanding requires mastery of four ways of looking at things—as they *were*, as they *are*, as they *might become*, and as they *ought to be*. We knew a thing or two about the financial services industry and credit cards. *How they were* we had pretty well mastered. *How they are* was literally killing us. We knew a fair amount about *how they might become*. But what about *how they ought to be?* Was that fun house of mirrors, *perspective*, which experience indelibly implants in everyone, warping our *perception?*

Could this be an opportunity to *reconceive*, in the most fundamental sense, the very ideas of bank, money, and credit card—even beyond that to the essential elements of each and how they might change in a microelectronic environment? Over the next few weeks Old Monkey and I went happily swinging through a forest of past and present and possible futures, not only as they might become, but as they ought to be.

Imagine yourself a *Homo sapiens* in that shadowy world which preceded corporations, institutions, tribes, perhaps even family. A thinking animal in a world teeming with carnivores rich in tooth and claw, seeking to fill their bellies with tender flesh. Experience would soon teach you, if common sense did not, that failure to differentiate between the nature of a cobra and a rabbit, a lion and a gazelle, would result in a short and nasty life. If you did not understand *the nature of the beasts*, it would be of little use to know the mechanics of their anatomy.

Today, we are all living in a world in which the filling of bellies by tooth and claw has been enormously diminished through the use of institutions—family, city, county, state, nation, church, corporation, school, association—millions of every size and description, accepted with as little thought as we accept the changing seasons. Yet, institutions can demean, damage, or destroy us as certainly and capriciously as any saber-toothed tiger. And they do so with technological, psychological, and economic instruments infinitely more destructive than tooth and claw.

Institutions are not a law of nature, nor did they spring full-blown from the head of Zeus. In the great sweep of history they are, for all their size and complexity, newly born, primitive, aberrant, and often uncivilized. People are not the creatures of institutions, institutions are the creations of people, yet they increasingly seem as much beyond our control as the turning of the earth and the burning of the sun. We endlessly tinker with their anatomy and bear up under their abuse, but how well do we understand *the intrinsic nature of the institutional beast?*

Not well at all. The problem arises from the pervasive habit of perceiving an institution as a tangible, physical reality, such as a building or a machine. So, when anyone began to talk or act as though a company had such reality, I would assure them that it was a fiction, that it did not exist. Most would argue vociferously that it certainly did. I would test their convictions with a simple exercise in which you, the reader, can easily engage. Fix firmly in your mind the company you work for, or any other organization of which you are part. Not its physical manifestations such as its name, employees, or offices, but the company itself. Put all other thoughts aside and concentrate on that organization you know so well.

Surely you have seen it. What color is it? No? Well, then, you must have smelled it from time to time. Describe its odor. No? Then surely you've tasted it. Is it sweet or sour, tart or bland? You don't know? Well, you must have touched it often. Is it hot or cold, hard or soft? No? Then, without doubt you have heard it. Make its sound. No? Can you perceive the company you work for, or any other organization, whether political, social, or commercial, with any of your senses? Obviously not. If you can't perceive an organization with any of your senses, does it have any reality at all? Perhaps it's a fiction. Perhaps it doesn't exist at all. But you're not going to accept that explanation.

The truth is that a commercial company, or for that matter, any organization, is nothing but an idea. All institutions are no more than a mental construct to which people are drawn in pursuit of common purpose; a conceptual embodiment of a very old, very powerful idea called *community*. All organizations can be no more and no less than the moving

> **MiniMaxims**
>
> *Healthy organizations induce behavior. Unhealthy organizations compel it.*

force of the mind, heart, and spirit of people, without which all assets are just so much inert mineral, chemical, or vegetable matter, by the law of entropy steadily decaying to a stable state.

Healthy organizations are a mental concept of relationship to which people are drawn by hope, vision, values, and meaning, and liberty to cooperatively pursue them. Healthy organizations induce behavior. Induced behavior is inherently constructive.

Unhealthy organizations are no less a mental concept of relationship, but one to which people are compelled by accident of birth, necessity, or force. Unhealthy organizations compel behavior. Compelled behavior is inherently destructive.

Since the strength and reality of every organization lies in the sense of community of the people who have been attracted to it, its success has enormously more to do with clarity of a shared purpose, common principles, and strength of belief in them than with money, material assets, or management practices, important as they may be. When an organization loses its shared vision and principles, its sense of community, its meaning and values, it is already in the process of decay and dissolution, even though it may linger with the outward appearance of success for some time. Businesses, as well as nations, races, tribes, die out not when defeated or suppressed, but when they become despairing and lose excitement and hope about the future. Without a deeply held, commonly shared purpose that gives meaning to their lives; without deeply held, commonly shared, ethical values and beliefs about conduct in pursuit of purpose that all may trust and rely upon, communities steadily disintegrate, and organizations progressively become instruments of tyranny.

To the direct degree that clarity of shared purpose and principles and strength of belief in them exist, constructive, harmonious behavior may be induced. To the direct degree they do not exist, behavior is inevitably compelled. It is not complicated. The alternative to shared belief in purpose and principles is tyranny. And tyranny, whether petty or grand, whether commercial, political, or

> **MiniMaxims**
>
> *People deprived of self-organization and self-governance are inherently ungovernable.*

social, is inevitably destructive. *People deprived of self-organization and self-governance are inherently ungovernable.*

Old Monkey and I, then in our middle years, were off on an extraordinary adventure. It was necessary to rethink the very nature of the institutional beasts in which we were enmeshed. To examine in the most fundamental way the functions of a bank, of money, and of a credit card; even beyond that to the essential nature of each and how it might change with full application of emerging electronic technology. We must get beyond *how things had been* and *how they were* into *how they might become,* and even beyond that into *how they ought to be.* It was slow. It was painful. It was frustrating. Several convictions slowly emerged. They were enormously exciting.

First: such zealously protected things as branches, deposits, loans, and investments were the anatomy, not the nature of banking. They were form, not function. The nature of a bank, its essential function, was the custody, exchange, and loan of money. But what was money? More digging. Money was not coin, currency, or credit card. That was form, not function. Money was *anything* customarily used as a measure of equivalent value and medium of exchange. But what had that *anything* become?

Coin had long since been debased. It no longer contained more than a trace of precious metal. Melt a few hundred pounds of coin from any country and you would be fortunate to get a few pennies for the resulting blob of metal. Certainly the paper on which currency and checks were printed had no significant value, nor did the ink. A barrel of ink and a few pulped trees costing little would print billions of dollars worth of currency. Old

Monkey Mind and I continued to peel our onion of under-standing looking for the essence of money.

The realization slowly dawned that money had become alphanumeric symbols recorded and transported on valueless metal and paper. This still left a gap in understanding, for symbols themselves had no value. Anyone could write down letters and numbers; printing presses and computers could spew out infinite quantities. It eventually emerged. *Money had become guaranteed alphanumeric data expressed in the currency symbol of one country or another. Thus, a bank was no more than an insti-tution for the custody, loan, and exchange of guaranteed alphanu-meric data.*

Even this did not satisfy us. It was necessary to know what that data might become. What actually happened when a com-puter was injected into the process? Certainly the metal of the coin and paper of the currency played no part in the bowels of a computer.

What was the essence of what happened when we used the telephone to authorize a credit card transaction? That was cer-tainly a guarantee. Certainly data of some sort was being trans-ferred by voice—by sound. But no sound was passing down that wire. The voice saying "five hundred dollars" was being turned into electronic signals and those signals were turned into sound on the other end. Such signals could pass through wires or through broadcast waves. Nothing was passing but disturbance of electronic particles—waves of energy.

Peeling this onion of understanding was enough to make us cry. The essence of money seemed to be everywhere, yet nowhere. But we had to understand. More research, more dig-ging, more connections. What was the essential nature of the computer, of the communications systems rapidly emerging, and what would happen if they became ubiquitous, as many sci-

ence fiction writers were speculating? What if most data began
to move as electronic impulse—radio waves—even beams of
light? Certainly everything seemed headed in that direction, and
at an ever accelerating pace. Our old perspective began to evap-
orate. Our perception began to change. It was as though we
could now see with different eyes. Even more, with a different
mind. Even beyond that: *with a different consciousness, and it was
incredibly exciting.*

Money would become nothing but alphanumeric data in
the form of arranged energy impulses. It would move around the
world at the speed of light at minuscule cost by infinitely diverse
paths throughout the entire electromagnetic spectrum. *Any
institution that could move, manipulate, and guarantee alphanumeric data in the form of arranged energy in a manner that individuals customarily used and relied upon as a measure of equivalent value and medium of exchange was a bank. It went even
beyond that. Inherent in all this might be the genesis of a new form
of global currency.*

Old Monkey and I were stunned. If electronic technology
continued to advance, and that seemed certain, two-hundred-
year-old banking oligopolies controlling the custody, loan, and
exchange of money would be irrecoverably shattered. Nation-
state monopolies on the issuance and control of currency would
erode. It mattered little that traditional banks or government
might be the settlers of last resort—the ultimate handlers of
huge, accumulated transfers of monetary value. The vast preponderance of the system would fall to those who were most
adept at handling and guaranteeing alphanumeric value data in
the form of arranged particles of energy.

We continued to peel the onion. Just what was the nature
of the business in which we were engaged? Was credit really the
nature of our business? What was the essence of the transaction

when a customer presented a sliver of plastic to a merchant? Clearly, it introduced a merchant willing to sell something to a prospective customer who might wish to buy it. In that regard, it was a substitute for a driver's license, social security card, government identity card, or other means of identification. *Thus, the first primary function of the card was to identify buyer to seller and seller to buyer.*

Clearly, it guaranteed that they could safely exchange value, the merchant delivering goods or services, and the customer signing a draft that the merchant could deposit for monetary credit. The seller would receive good funds in local currency and the buyer would be billed later in the currency of their country. *Thus, the second primary function was as guarantor.*

Clearly, it warranted to both buyer and seller that the system would attend to the mechanism of exchange without either having to know the language, laws, currency, customs, or culture of the other. The fact that many card issuers allowed the customer to pay for the transactions over a period of time ("extended credit," in the jargon of banking) was really an ancillary service and not the primary function of the card. When the card was put through the imprinter, it merely created a financial message in the form of alphanumeric data—it was a substitute for pen and paper. *Thus, the third primary function was origination and transfer of value data.*

As we abandoned our old perspective and challenged our mechanistic model of reality, we ceased thinking of the jargon of banking and payment systems. We thought in a more holistic way and another change of consciousness occurred. It seems ordinary and obvious now. It was a revelation then. We were not in the credit business. "Credit card" was a misnomer based on banking jargon. The card was no more than a device bearing symbols for the exchange of monetary value. The fact that it took the form of a piece of plastic was no more than an accident of time and circumstance. *We were really in the business of the exchange of monetary value.*

Old Monkey Mind and I began to race to put more of the pieces together. If our business was to guarantee and process the exchange of value between a buyer and a seller, where at any moment in time might the buyer and the seller be? With modern transportation and the collapse of time, the buyer might be anywhere, any time, around the globe, around the clock. With evolution of catalogue sales and electronic marketing, any seller might be able to present themselves to any buyer, anywhere, at any time, without being present. The demand for the exchange of value in the form of energy impulses would be around the clock, seven days a week, at every point on the globe.

Exhilarating realizations followed one after the other. Any organization that could guarantee, transport, and settle transactions in the form of arranged energy impulses twenty-four hours a day, seven days a week, around the globe, would have a market, every exchange of value in the world, that beggared the imagination. The necessary technology had been discovered and would be available in geometrically increasing abundance at geometrically diminishing cost. But there was a problem. No bank could do it. No hierarchal stock corporation could do it. No nation-state could do it. In fact, no existing form of organization we could think of could do it. On a hunch I made an estimate of the financial resources of all the banks in the world. It dwarfed the resources of most nations. Jointly, they could do it, but how? It would require a transcendental organization linking together in wholly new ways an unimaginable complex of diverse institutions and individuals.

At the time, did I think it could be done? No! It was impossible! Did I think the Bank of America would give up ownership of the program? No! Did I think banks worldwide could be brought together in such an effort? No! Did I think laws would allow it? No! Did I think anyone would seriously listen to such notions or allow them the light of day if they did? No! *But did I believe it was what ought to be?* Ah, that was another question indeed! Powerful enough to draw me on.

Absurd as it seemed, might this be an undreamed-of opportunity to experiment with my beliefs about organizations and management? It seemed beyond imagining. But what could be lost by the attempt? Oh, how well I knew the answer to that one. And I was sick of being a bloodied sheep. This time, I was not going to shoot off my mouth about my beliefs, nor would I force them on others. They would guide what I did. To the best of my ability, I would act in accordance with them. But if nothing came of the effort, let them die a quiet death. If people should come to the ideas, let it be in their own time, in their own way, for their own reasons. If something of substance should result, let it emerge in the fullness of time.

One thing was certain; it was time for a talk with the boss.

CHAPTER EIGHT

The Impossible Imagined

To be confused about what is different is to be confused about everything. Thus, it is not an accident that our fragmentary form of thought is leading to such a widespread range of crisis, social, political, economic, ecological, psychological, in the individual and in society as a whole. . . . To develop new insights into fragmentation and wholeness requires a creative work even more difficult than that needed to make fundamental new discoveries in science, or great and original works of art. Suddenly, in a flash of understanding, one may see the irrelevance of one's whole way of thinking . . . along with a different approach in which all the elements fit in a new order and in a new structure.

—DAVID BOHM

"Mr. Carlson, I'm in trouble. When I shot off my mouth at the meeting in Columbus I had no intention of getting so involved. I agreed to serve on the committees with the thought of setting things in motion and stepping aside. Problems are much worse than we imagined. People across the country have become deeply concerned and are looking to the committees as a possible solution. There is growing expectation I'll continue to lead the effort. I have a few ideas about how to proceed, but no way of knowing what might result. I'm continually being drawn deeper into the situation and should either make a serious commitment or step aside. I'm torn between the two."

Conversations with Mr. Carlson are never long. The most patient, intense listener I know, his questions are inevitably short, penetrating, and singularly to the point, although often softened by looking down or away. His manner induces others to listen intently and give short, clear answers. In the habit of referring to me as "young man," that is how he begins.

"Well, young man, how much of your time do you think this might take?"

"I honestly don't know. In the beginning, perhaps a quarter or more, but if something comes of the effort, it might be more than full time. There's simply no way of knowing."

"I see. If something is not done what will happen?"

"Again, there's no way to predict. If the BankAmericard system fails, we'll either have to convert to a private card program or make an affiliation with another system. Either would be costly. If the industry fails, our program will be dragged down with it. Worst case, we would have to call in all cards and discontinue business at substantial loss. In any event, we can't isolate our reputation from the reputation of BankAmericard or the credit card industry. It's all interconnected."

"Yes, yes, I see. Well, what about the people you work with? Could they manage without you?"

"They're good people who know how to take care of themselves and help others do the same. They don't need direction; they need reasonable resources, encouragement, and recognition from time to time. I don't think the center would lose a tick. It might do better without me."

Mr. Carlson suppresses a smile. "I understand. Would your salary and expenses be paid by the committee?"

"To this point, every bank has paid its own way. It's possible it could be turned into a paid position funded by the banks. At the moment, there is no entity to receive or disburse money, but that could easily be remedied. We have been working as equals, and I'm comfortable with that. Working for the others would be quite different."

"Well, young man, what will this effort commit us to?"

"Again, I don't know, Mr. Carlson. But I do know that it can't succeed if any bank has a preferred position. The job can't be done properly unless the National Bank of Commerce is in the same position as all others. It should receive information, be involved, and function on the same basis as any other licensee bank. Whoever does this job must be above reproach with respect to openness and fairness. It simply can't be done without a great deal of trust and confidence, and that will be hard to develop. I don't want to attempt the work if this bank receives preferred information or treatment."

"Yes. Yes. Even if that were the case, would others believe it if you were still connected with the bank?"

"That's not the point. What others believe is their own affair. In time, I expect most would prefer the truth."

There is a long pause as he looks intently down, deep in thought, thumbs hooked in vest pockets, legs intertwined with one another as is his wont. His next words will become engraved in memory and in my heart. Smiling gently he looks up.

"I think I understand. Well, young man, sometimes we just have to be good citizens. Go where you have to go and do what you have to do. Treat us as you would the others. We will ask no more. The resources of the bank are at your disposal. You must have a place and position from which to do this work. You will continue as vice president of the bank and head of the credit card department with full salary and all expenses paid. Arrange things there as you think best."

Dumbfounded, I watch as he leans back in his chair and asks the question with which he closes all meetings. "Did the meeting serve your purpose?" Did it serve my purpose! I have never been so treated in my entire life. For this man, I would do anything. Such an obligation as he has just given me is a joy that should come to everyone. Did the meeting serve my purpose? Well, well—almost.

"Mr. Carlson, there is one other matter. We're going to need legal advice and there's no money for lawyers." Without a word he picks up the telephone and dials a number. The managing partner of the bank's outside law firm answers. Maxwell Carlson is ever to the point.

"Mr. Hock is doing some work that is in the public interest. He needs legal assistance that we would like you to provide. If the costs are not paid by others, they will be paid by the bank. Please tell no one in the bank what you are doing, including me. This is a private matter between you and Mr. Hock." He listens intently for a moment, says, "Yes. Yes. Thank you kindly."

Returning the receiver to the cradle, he turns to ask once more, "Did the meeting serve your purpose?"

"*Yes, sir!*" And it served my spirit, my confidence, my need for understanding, my belief in humanity, and—well, what didn't it serve? He rises, shakes my hand warmly, smiles, and says, "Thank you so much for coming to see me. Please let me know if I can be helpful at any time."

I floated out of the place—*can't even remember if I thanked him*—determined this man should never have cause to be disappointed in what he had done. In the next two years, through some incredible events, of which you shall learn more in the next few chapters, Maxwell Carlson never once asked where I was or what I was doing, nor did others in the bank. I hope with all my heart he never had cause to be disappointed. If he did, not a whisper came back to me.

❧

With compelling need for a new organization, a precarious toehold from which to make the attempt, and the liberty to try, I suppressed my perspective of what the future might be and tried to create the conditions by which new concepts could emerge. How that might happen, I did not know. My learning would have to evolve in concert with the others. I thought long and hard about each member of the national executive committee, settling on three, each of whom seemed to have a good sense of who he was, an open, curious mind, generous spirit, and keen sense of humor. More important, none seemed inclined to either follow or lead a mob. Each moved to a rhythm of his own making.

Sam Johnson was a big, bluff, Boston Irishman with a ready smile and a thousand ideas that spilled from him like iridescent marbles from a bowl. His enthusiasm was contagious, and his huge capacity for friendship had wrapped me in its arms.

Jack Dillon was a veteran of World War II who for years had remained in the army reserve. He loved to talk of army life, though long removed from it. A thirty-year employee of the Bank of America, raconteur extraordinaire, connoisseur of fine food and wine, he was delightful to be around.

Fred James, from Memphis, Tennessee, was a fine storyteller in the droll southern manner. Often, in the middle of intense discussion, he would shake his head and say, "Well, now, that's shore mighty interestin', and I don't doubt it for a minute, but I do wonder what that little old lady in Calico Rock's gonna think about it." Whether "that little old lady in Calico Rock" owned the bank, was an archetypal customer, or just a clever way to get our attention, I never knew.

After sharing belief about the opportunity that might be hidden in the problems of the system, I asked if they would be willing to take a week or more of their time, isolate themselves completely, set aside all thought of the problems of the system, and address a single question based upon a single assumption: *If anything imaginable was possible, if there were no constraints whatever, what would be the nature of an ideal organization to create the world's premier system for the exchange of value?* After a bit of head-shaking and rolled eyes, they became intrigued and agreed—providing I would join them. It would have been a bitter disappointment had they not asked.

Sausalito was a small, quaint town a mile or two beyond the north end of the Golden Gate Bridge. Houses tightly tucked together cascaded down a steep hillside facing the north arm of San Francisco Bay. A narrow band of funky shops and houseboats lined the shore. It was a complex place, at one time noted for the variety of its wildlife—mostly *Homo sapiens*. Many remain today as respectable, gray-in-the-muzzle remnants of the "love bead" generation of the sixties. It catered as well to conservatives wanting magnificent views and proximity to San Francisco. Tourists, intellectuals, and an eclectic host of others of the live-and-let-live variety found it attractive. It was, altogether, a charming place. Still is.

The Altamira Hotel, tucked on a hillside in Sausalito, was as long in the tooth and charming as its surroundings, with a thriving business in tourists, weddings, honeymoons, and enamored couples not yet ready for matrimony. The restaurant and ample outdoor dining deck provided a panoramic view across the bay to cities and hills in the east and central San Francisco to the south. It was there we hid out for more than a week.

We argued over every conceivable kind of organization for three long days and agreed on nothing. Frustration increased. Tempers flared. It would be difficult to imagine a more unlikely group in a more unlikely place addressing a more unlikely question, but there we were, and there it happened. For three nights, Old Monkey and I woke often and thrashed about, trying to see a way forward. It took us deeply into things we had been struggling with for many years.

Over the years of reading and thinking about organization, thoughts from some long forgotten source in Eastern philosophy had formed and fixed themselves in Old Monkey Mind. If one is to properly understand events and to influence the future, it is essential to master four ways of looking at things: *as they were, as they are, as they might become,* and *as they ought to be.* It is no less essential to synthesize and hold them in mind as a single perspective. Not "ought" in the compulsory sense of an instructive command, but in the inductive sense of a preferred, ethically better condition.

Mastering all four perspectives—how things were, how they are, how they might become, and how they ought to be—and synthesizing them into a compelling concept of a constructive, peaceful future is the true work of the genius that lies buried in everyone, struggling to get out. And the world is crying out for it.

In our frantic attempt to know everything through use of the rational mind alone, we have fractured knowledge into hundreds of incestuous specialties and fragmented those specialties into thousands of isolated, insular trades and disciplines.

> **MiniMaxims**
>
> *Perspective is the Achilles heel of the mind, distorting everything we think, know, believe, or imagine.*

The world is filling with people who know more and more about less and less. Within each specialty, we dismiss as largely irrelevant all things, events, and ways of understanding outside the ever narrower boundaries of our discipline. We can ignore all relationships not essential to our ever narrowing perspective. We can ignore all consequences not immediately affecting or affected by our ever more constricted pursuit. We can abdicate responsibility for even thinking about them. We can each decide and act within our ever smaller intellectual prisons and narrower mental cells, and defend our acts with logical, efficient, methodical rationality. Never mind that the sum of the whole is social, commercial, and biological madness.

Since the past can never be more than preparatory and the present no more than a point of departure, it is the future that should have our best thoughts and energy, though it seldom does in the stress and strain of modern life. If one examines organizations *as they might become* or *as they ought to be*, the specifics of that which we know must yield to the abstracts of that which we can conceive. Perception is the primary means by which we cast up such concepts. Therein lies a serious problem.

Somewhere in the middle of perception is the fun house mirror of perspective. It distorts and discolors everything we know, think, believe, or imagine. Therefore, when considering the future, one's viewpoint, one's frame of reference, one's internal model of reality, in a word, the *perspective* that experience indelibly implants in each of us is all-important. Out of the lumber of things we are taught, the gravel and cement of our experience, the nails of the externalities we observe, and the blueprint we imagine, we slowly erect an internal edifice, our internal temple of reality, gradually filling it with the furniture of habit, custom, preference, belief, and bias. We get comfortable there. It's our sanctuary. Through its windows, small and warped though they may be, we view society and the world. Our internal model of reality is how we make sense of the world. And it can be a badly built place indeed. Even if it is magnificently constructed, it may have become archaic. Everything that gave rise to it may have changed. Society and the natural world are never stagnant. They are constantly becoming.

When it becomes necessary to develop a new perception of things, a new internal model of reality, the problem is never to get new ideas in, the problem is to get the old ideas out. Every mind is filled with old furniture. It's familiar. It's comfortable. We hate to throw it out. The old maxim so often applied to the physical world, "Nature abhors a vacuum," is much more applicable to the mental world. Clear any room in your mind of old perspectives, and new perceptions will rush in. Yet, there is nothing we fear more.

We *are* our ideas, concepts, and perceptions. Giving up any part of our internal model of reality is worse than losing a finger or an eye. Part of us no longer exists. However, unlike most organs of the physical body, our internal model of reality can be regenerated but never as it was. And it's a frightening, painful process. It is our individual perspective, the view from our internal temple of reality, that often so discolors and distorts perception that we can neither anticipate what might occur nor conceive what ought to be. Perspective is the Achilles heel of the mind. And the bloodied sheep had been a long time even realizing he had one.

Lying awake the fourth night, Old Monkey Mind and I knew that no bank could create the world's premier system for the exchange of value. No hierarchal stock corporation could do it. No nation-state could do it. In fact, no organization we could think of could do it. But what if a fraction of the resources of all the financial institutions in the world and a fraction of the ingenuity of all people who worked for them could be applied? Jointly they might do it, but how?

It was beyond the power of the imagination to understand the complexity of such an organization and the diversity it must embrace, let alone the variables it would encounter. It was equally beyond the power of reason to design such an organization, even if the diversity and conditions could be imagined. It was impossible to perceive the rate and extent of change it would encounter. Yet, lying there, Old Monkey Mind kept poking me in the ribs, reminding me how evolution routinely, effortlessly tossed off countless varieties of much more complex organisms and organizations—rain forests, marine systems, weather systems, cheetahs, whales, body, brain, immune system—with seeming ease. The puzzle gradually dissolved my brain, and I fell into deep sleep.

With the dawn, half-awake and surfing the shores of consciousness, came a fascinating question. Could such an organization be patterned on biological concepts and methods? The question seemed to contain its own answer. Such an organization would have to evolve, in effect, to organize and invent itself. It was not enough to reconceive the nature of the business, we must try to reconceive the very nature of organization itself. More questions came tumbling one after the other. What if we quit arguing about the structure of a new institution and tried to think of it as having some sort of genetic code? How does genetic code in individual cells create recognizable patterns— platypus and people—palm tree and pine—minnow and mouse—yet never duplicate a single creature, leaf, blade of grass, or even snowflake? How does nature create infinite diversity within infinite patterns of infinite complexity?

If institutions have no reality save in the mind, might their genetic code have something to do with purpose and principles? What's the nature of a principle? Does "Honor thy father and mother" tell us how to do anything, or just what *ought to be* done? Does it prescribe behavior, or merely describe it? Aren't there infinite ways to honor a father or mother? Does it induce behavior or compel it? Whoa Nellie! Back up a minute. What was that word? *Ought? Ought to be?* Do pure principles deal with *how things ought to be?* What if we set aside all discussion of things *as they were, as they are,* and *as they might become,* and immersed ourselves in *how they ought to be?* What if—what if—?

I raced into the fourth day of meeting with no recollection of showering, shaving, or dressing. Nor do I have recollection of the details of the following three days. In that deeper level of thought and discussion about purpose and principles we began to discover that we shared many fundamental beliefs, although we had never experienced an organization in which we could act in accordance with them. Nor did we believe that there ever might be such an organization. But I was beyond the rational mind, scratching at heart and soul, and it was exciting. At the time, we made no attempt to reduce them to writing. It was difficult enough to shape them in the wholeness of our being and give them a bit of verbalization. Precise language could come later. It was a degree of common understanding we were after. Slowly, painfully, a number of principles began to emerge. More than enough for a beginning. A few examples may help.

IT SHOULD BE EQUITABLY OWNED BY ALL PARTICIPANTS.

It should be owned by, not own, its participants. No participant should have an inherently greater or lesser ownership position, or be able to negotiate, buy, or sell their position. Every participant should be able to trust that it would not be subordinate to any other, and accept that it could not be superior.

PARTICIPANTS SHOULD HAVE EQUITABLE RIGHTS AND OBLIGATIONS.

It must not attempt to impose uniformity. Equity would require many types of participation with differing rights and obligations, but within each type, they should be common, and everyone should have the right to change their type of participation.

IT SHOULD BE OPEN TO ALL QUALIFIED PARTICIPANTS.
While it must be able to create standards for eligibility, once those standards were established, it should be open to all interested participants meeting the standards.

POWER, FUNCTION, AND RESOURCES SHOULD BE DISTRIBUTIVE TO THE MAXIMUM DEGREE.
No power should be vested in any part and no function performed by any part that might reasonably be exercised by any more peripheral part. All revenue should flow to the most peripheral participants and only that amount essential to joint activities, as determined by the participants, be surrendered to any core governing entities.

AUTHORITY SHOULD BE EQUITABLE AND DISTRIBUTIVE WITHIN EACH GOVERNING ENTITY.
Governing entities should be composed entirely of affected participants and constituted to equitably represent the interests of all relevant and affected parties. No interest should be able to dominate deliberations or control decisions, particularly management.

NO EXISTING PARTICIPANT SHOULD BE LEFT IN A LESSER POSITION BY ANY NEW CONCEPT OF ORGANIZATIONS.
Existing rights and obligations of each licensee should be respected and honored, whether or not they elected to participate. Should its formation require material change in any licensee position, the change should be equitably phased in over a reasonable period of time.

TO THE MAXIMUM DEGREE POSSIBLE, EVERYTHING SHOULD BE VOLUNTARY.

Persuasion, not compulsion, should be fundamental. Participants should have perpetual rights of participation, but be free to leave at any time without penalty or sanction. They should have the right to utilize any commonly held properties, products, services, or assets in an equitable manner at any time for any reason connected with the purpose, but should not be compelled to do so.

IT SHOULD BE NONASSESSABLE.

Revenues obtained from participants should be prospective, not retrospective. Prospective fees should be set by the governing entities composed of participants, but if the governing entities failed to operate within the constraints of revenue and budget and created a deficit, participants should have the right to withdraw without obligation beyond fees already paid.

IT SHOULD INDUCE, NOT COMPEL, CHANGE.

It should attract people secure and productive when moving from the known to the unknown; people expert at managing the very process of change itself. It should liberate and enhance their creativity and ingenuity.

IT SHOULD BE INFINITELY MALLEABLE YET EXTREMELY DURABLE.

It should be capable of constant, self-generated modification of form or function without sacrificing its essential nature or embodied principle.

It took months to develop and gain acceptance among licensees of these conceptual ideas. They were never explicitly codified, but they underlay every discussion. The concepts were accepted, in part, because no one, self included, thought it likely that such an organization could be brought into being. We could not change the banking laws of a single state, let alone laws of nations. We could not change the structure or management of a single bank, let alone thousands in the United States and tens of thousands throughout the world.

We had no money with which to purchase the system from the Bank of America, no money to hire consultants, advisors, or other "experts," no money to engage in research or hire employees. We had no power to influence regulators, legislators, or others in political power. Traditional means of approaching the problem were closed to us. But we were enamored of the emerging concepts, for there seemed no better alternative. I was more than enamored. As one of the participants put it twelve years later in a Harvard business case study, "He had a passionate commitment to the ideas that bordered on zealotry."

It is only in hindsight that it becomes clear as the dawn that the need to rely entirely on the power of ideas, concepts, and beliefs was what brought VISA into being. It was no stroke of genius. It was plain old necessity. Had we power, capital, position, or influence, we would undoubtedly have used them in the command-and-control style in which we had been so admirably indoctrinated. Without them, we were forced to a change of consciousness; to conceiving larger, better ideas that could transcend and enfold existing institutions and practices. Four vice presidents of four modest banks could not dominate or compel anyone. They could only persuade and induce. And so they did. Bit by bit, though we could not know it at the time, we were building a foundation on

> **MiniMaxims**
> *True power is never used. If you use power, you never really have it.*

which an extraordinary enterprise would self-organize and evolve, unfinished to this day.

In retrospect it seems extraordinary. What was taking shape in our minds and hearts ran contrary to conventional wisdom. At the time, there was no complexity theory, there was no Internet, there was no World Wide Web, there were no alliances, there was no information society. The Soviet Union was the evil empire to the United States—the United States was the devil incarnate to the Soviet Union. Both professed to have all the answers. IBM, General Motors, ITT, and other such hierarchal giants were the epitome of management and the shining path to a bright commercial future. Science and technology, with a few tens of billions more dollars, would see us to the promised land. A bigger, more powerful, central government would solve all our social problems. The world was an ideological battleground contesting which kind of massive, centralized power and wealth best solves societal problems. Only a handful of people questioned whether they could, ever would, or should.

During the next year and a half, the effort grew steadily as hundreds of minds and dozens of disciplines became intrigued and were applied to it. In the beginning, none of the licensees thought that the Bank of America would surrender ownership of a trademark and licensing system that assured them, in perpetuity, a quarter percent or more of the sales volume of every participant. No one thought that banks would voluntarily surrender a portion of their autonomy and act together for a common purpose. No one believed that such a horizontal grouping of competitors could exist within the spirit and constraints of antitrust laws. And no one dreamed the emerging ideas would bring together in common ownership and enterprise people and institutions of every race, language, custom, and culture—every economic, legal, philosophical, and religious persuasion in the world.

In the beginning, few paid the effort much attention. As it advanced and gained attention, it was subjected to much ridicule. As it approached success, bitter opposition emerged from many sources. Many times, the best abilities and worst behavior of command-and-control organizations and powerful disciples devoted to that way of thinking were brought to bear against it. Yet, each time, it had enough vitality to survive. As it advanced, the purpose, principles, and people, tempered by the fire of each ordeal, grew stronger.

There were dozens of times when I longed to quit. What prevented me is not entirely clear. All that is clear was stubborn conviction that the ideas that had been forming over the years were sound. They had to be tried. The possibility of that which has never occurred cannot be determined by opinion. Attempting the impossible is not rational, though reason may play some part in it. It is beyond reason. It is a matter of hope, faith, and determination.

Each time I fell into despair and wanted to give up—and it happened often—something softly whispered, "Not now. Not while you still believe and cannot know. If you can see the next step, go on, go on!" It really wasn't courage. It wasn't compulsion to succeed. It wasn't fear of failure. More than enough failure had come my way to create healthy respect for and strong aversion to it. Failure hurts worse than a rotten tooth, but it's not fatal. What kept me going remains a mystery. It doesn't really matter, for there was an inexpressible, compelling sense that in some profound, nonphysical way, existence would lose meaning if I did not persist.

> **MiniMaxims**
>
> *If you think you can't, why think?*

Jack, Fred, and Sam were dear friends and stalwarts through the next year and a half of trial and trauma. They received nothing for all their commitment and labor except the joy and satisfaction it brought. Well after life led them in other directions, we met one last time in Sausalito to honor them as progenitors of VISA. Our paths drifted apart over the years and I do not know where they are today, but one thing I do know. Without Jack, Fred, and Sam, VISA would never have come to be. Bless them one and all.

CHAPTER NINE

The Next to the Last Word

What is a good man but a bad man's teacher?
What is a bad man but a good man's job?
If you don't understand this you will get lost,
However intelligent you are.
It is the great secret.
— LAO-TZU

Trust thyself; every heart vibrates to that iron
string!
— RALPH WALDO EMERSON

The weeks after the Sausalito meeting were filled night and day by work with lawyers, accountants, and members of the various committees as we struggled to translate the principles into a conceptual structure. Dozens of working groups formed, dissolved, or combined as question after question was posed. No ultimate answers emerged, only better questions. If this institution were to self-organize—in effect, to design itself—what we had thought of as answers must become no more than consensus. Not consensus in the shallow, modern meaning of unanimous agreement, but in the original, deeper sense of solidarity. A place where all could agree that they could stand comfortably together to act in accordance with purpose and principle, learn from the acts, reflect upon the learning, and formulate the next step. This would require placing innovation above engineering—synthesis above analysis—understanding above knowing. Another of the MiniMaxims was slowly form-ing, although he could not artic-ulate it then. In lighter moments I now refer to it as the theology of chaordic organization writ simple. Heaven is purpose, prin-ciple, and people. Purgatory is paper and procedure. Hell is rules and regulations.

> **MiniMaxims**
>
> *Heaven is purpose, principle, and people. Purgatory is paper and procedure. Hell is rules and regulations.*

In an early meeting with Bank of America officers, we had gained assurance that they would neither oppose nor endorse the committee's intent to explore alternatives to the licensing program. They would participate in those efforts, reserving the right to act unilaterally as events unfolded. Top management of the bank would not be directly involved. Jack Dillon would con-tinue to work with the committees on a day-to-day basis, along with representative of the Licensing Corporation. Policy deci-sions would rest with Kenneth Larkin, senior vice president of the bank, who would seek approval from higher authority as required.

Ken Larkin was a man not easily overlooked. A former foot-ball lineman at Hofstra University, over six feet tall and mas-sively built, he was a good many years and a great many pounds past his playing days. But there was nothing ponderous about his intellect. Deliberate and soft-spoken, he would often lean back, impassive, eyes closed, as people spoke. He would come out of what appeared to be deep sleep, alert and articulate, with every nuance in mind. Casual acquaintances were inclined to describe him as a giant, temperate, teddy bear of a man, and so he usually was. But there were hidden depths to him not often discovered. Come hard up against his desire to win and temperate teddy bear are not words you would use. Come hard up against his temper and giant would do fine.

In June 1969, the committee met in San Francisco for two days of intense work shaping the concept. Fred, Sam, Jack, and I, newly designated as the organizational subcommittee, met with Ken Larkin the third day to review our work, since an early response from the Bank of America was important to its continuation. Although casually acquainted with Ken—Sam, Fred and I had never dealt with him on substantive matters.

It was not an auspicious beginning. Ken rose, greeting us with a derisive, "Well, well, well. Here they are—the leaders of the revolution!"

Among licensees, the prevailing view was that the condition of the system was largely the result of failure on the part of the Bank of America. The licensees did not see themselves as revolutionaries, but as people with programs at risk volunteering to clean a stable fouled by other people's horses. It was an incendiary situation, to say the least.

I could literally hear the hair rising on the back of Sam and Fred's necks. Mine was certainly bristling. Jack merely grinned. Fortunately, no one responded in kind as we began to explain in considerable detail the work already done, the emerging conclusions, and the direction in which the effort appeared to be heading. Near the end of the discussion, Fred, in his polite, southern way, put a point he was making vigorously and without equivocation. Ken rose bolt upright in his chair. His face grew red. His neck swelled. Veins in his forehead stood out. His anger fed on itself as he bellowed, *"We own the *#~*'d system! We invented the system! We produce 40 percent of the system volume! *#*d if we will be pushed around!"*

Shocked and embarrassed into silence, Sam, Fred, and I watched the performance. Jack said nothing, a touch of a grin teasing the corner of his mouth. As abruptly as the explosion came, it vanished. In an impressive exhibition of self-control, Ken settled back in his chair, took a deep breath, and without apology or comment, resumed as though nothing had happened. He assured us the bank would give careful consideration to our recommendations and formulate a prompt response.

After the meeting we separated, Jack, noncommittal, returned to his duties at the bank, while Sam, Fred, and I shared a cab to the airport. It seemed as though the bank had little understanding, appreciation, or sympathy for what was being attempted. Were they merely creating a façade of cooperation, waiting to see what benefit might accrue while looking for an opportunity to put the upstarts in their place? Fred was furious and Sam was girded for battle. No less angry, I nevertheless felt it would be foolish to allow emotions to distract us from our objective.

For a month, we heard nothing one way or the other, only that the matter was "under consideration at the highest levels of the bank," presumably, the board of directors. Near the end of July, the reply came. The bank "is in sympathy with the avowed aims of your executive committee, namely to form a national association responsive to the collective needs and desires of the licensees but. . . ." The bank then laid out its position.

They must have representation on the board equal to their percentage of the sales volume. That would violate our fundamental principle: governance not dominated by any institution or interest. They must be retained as managing partner of the association for a minimum of five years. This violated nearly all of the principles and would leave the system subject to the same management that was responsible for the current situation. The bank, as managing partner, must retain ownership and control of all trademarks and remain as exclusive licensing agent, which they would exercise with dispassion and objectivity (presumably, an equitably elected board of a new organization could not do so). Again, it was contrary to all our principles. They must retain ownership of the goodwill, trademarks, and properties. Again, contrary to all principles. The letter continued at some length in the same vein. It appeared to be a complete impasse. A call to Ken Larkin revealed it was the best the bank would do. The decision had been carefully considered at the highest levels and would not be changed.

The licensee executive committee assembled to consider whether to proceed with the reorganization in view of the bank's position. We thought such an imposition by BofA would ensure the failure of the organization. Everything it did would be suspect. It might be somewhat better than the present situation, but far short of our intent. It was abysmally short of my dreams. It put us in the same position as the prominent politician who received an excoriating letter from Tom Paine shortly after the American Revolution. I shared the final line with the committee.

> As to you sir, history will be hard put to it to decide whether you abandoned principle, or ever had any.

Were we going to abandon principle, or did we really have any? It was a tough question. Some were inclined to stand on principle and abandon the effort. Others thought the bank's position was better than the present situation and should be accepted. BofA hadn't exactly slammed the front door in our faces, but they had certainly told us to use the servants' entrance. Would they answer the front doorbell if we rang again?

With the committee's consent, I called Ken Larkin informing him the committee was in session and, before making a decision, would like to go over the bank's position to be certain it was not based on their misunderstanding of our work, or our misunderstanding of the bank's intent. We went over each point in the bank's letter. He was adamant. "The decision has been made after careful consideration at the highest levels of the bank—it is generous, proper, and fair—it should be accepted—there is nothing further to negotiate." We had no reason to doubt his word.

Another defining moment. Each member of the committee would have to decide in accordance with their personal convic-tions. If the committee capitu-lated, I must step aside, for my convictions were unshakable. But were the bank's? Only one way to find out. During my years of high school and college debate, I had held fast to the notion that until someone categorically said "No!" and adamantly refused to have another word on the subject, they were in the process of saying "Yes" but just didn't know it.

> **MiniMaxims**
>
> *Until someone has repeatedly said no and adamantly refuses another word on the subject, they are in the process of say-ing yes and don't know it.*

"Ken, let me repeat the position of the Bank of America so that I can get it down precisely." My voice gradually slowed to writing speed as I improvised a word here and there for effect. "Ken Larkin, Senior Vice President of the Bank of America, said, 'The Bank of America will not agree to an organization equitably owned by all banks . . . unless . . . it . . . can . . . unilater-ally . . . control . . . management . . . for—'"

He abruptly interrupted. "What are you doing?"

"Ken, I understand and respect the bank's position. I can't speak for the committee and don't know what decision they will make. However, my strong recommendation will be to abandon the effort. If the committee agrees, we have no choice but to immediately inform all licensees and the media of our decision, along with the reason. It is essential we convey the bank's position fairly and accurately. I want to quote you with precision."

The silence was long and profound before his voice came back over the line. "Maybe you should come to San Francisco and meet with Sam Stewart, vice chairman of the board." *So, it wasn't their last word on the subject.*

ℒ❤

In San Francisco, I crossed the cold, windswept plaza adjoining the towering Bank of America high-rise, pausing momentarily to glance at the huge, polished blob of black granite sculpture. It was fondly known by half the city's cab drivers as "The Banker's Heart" and by the other half as "The Last Deposit." After ascending the express elevator to the executive offices near the top, I was promptly ushered through a palatial executive floor to shake hands with an impressive man with a booming, bass voice so deep it seemed amplified. It emerged from a barrel chest below a generous smile and an engaging face. Lawyer, litigator, general counsel, and now number two in the largest bank in the world, he had it all: polished hardwood floor—antique Oriental carpet—cases of rare books—fine art—breathtaking 220-degree views of city, bay, and hills. An aircraft carrier moved imperceptibly down the bay, a child's toy under a bridge crawling with eight lanes of metal ants.

After a gracious few moments, he began to set forth the position of the bank. It was apparent I was there for correction, not conversation. I sat quietly, listening intently. The bank had pioneered the bank card business—they had created BankAmericard—they had suffered through huge losses to make it profitable—they had created the licensing structure—major problems were normal in such an expansion—banks had taken licenses in reliance on the Bank of America's experience and expertise—the name BankAmericard, the name of the bank, and the goodwill of both were at stake—they had been cooperative throughout the effort—they had made many concessions—it was unreasonable to expect them to subject themselves to a new, untested concept with unknown management—it was unreasonable to abandon the effort and blame the bank—we should accept their proposal and work in good faith to resolve system difficulties.

He fell silent, waiting for a reply. It was all true. There was nothing with which to argue—*from his perspective.*

I instinctively liked this man. He was without guile. I was not being manipulated. What he said was honest, to the point, and articulated with all the logic and force of a powerful man of strong convictions. And yet—and yet—something was missing. What he said was about *how things were, how they are,* and *how they might become.* He had said nothing about *how they ought to be.* The future is not about logic and reason. It's about imagination, hope, and belief. I did not believe his perception was right. His candor and sincerity deserved as much in return. With a deep breath and great trepidation, the sheep went off the high dive.

"Mr. Stewart, it's not politic or sensible for a vice president of a modest bank in Seattle to tell the vice chairman of the largest bank in the world that he is mistaken, but I believe you are." The silence was deafening. I plunged on, "What you propose is not in the interests of the Bank of America, the licensees, or the industry." He stared at me intently, soberly, over his half-lens reading glasses for a very, very, *very* long moment, while I got loose in my chair. This meeting was about to end abruptly.

"You really believe that, don't you?"

"Yes, sir, I really do."

"Then tell me why." He tipped his chair back, folded his hands across his stomach, stared into my eyes, and said not a word as I loosed conviction and belief.

Control of management would ensure the failure of a new organization—it was contrary to all the principles we had worked so assiduously to develop, in which we deeply believed—the new organization would have no heart, no spirit if they were abandoned—truly honest people would not work under such controlled conditions—the licensing structure could never compel cooperative behavior—licensees would never surrender autonomy to an organization controlled by one bank—reconceiving product and organization could expand markets far beyond anything now imagined—the Bank of America would benefit far more from its share of that market than it ever could from royalties in the present market—the bank should be the leader of a movement, not the commander of a structure.

It was certainly not a performance up to Sam Stewart's level, but it was not bad for a bloody sheep. He asked a few questions for clarification, then boomed, "Will you put your thoughts in writing and send them to me? Can you come again in two weeks?"

"Yes, sir."

A day later, a three-page letter was in the mail. Two weeks later, Sam met me at the door with a warm smile, settled us in comfortable chairs, and in that magnificent bass voice I grew to respect, then to love, bowled me over in ten seconds.

"We've thought very carefully about what you said and have come to the conclusion that, in the main, it is right. There are many things to be better understood and some to be negotiated, but you'll have our full support in the attempt to form a new organization and our good faith in negotiating terms and conditions for transfer of ownership." Although there were a great many differences to be overcome in the months ahead, although some people within the bank never quite got the message, from that day forward the support of Sam Stewart and the Bank of America never wavered.

To this day, the explosion of Ken Larkin at our early meeting remains a mystery. It was not the last conflict we would have over the years, but out of it came great admiration and trust. Ken became a longtime director of VISA, an honest critic, a staunch supporter, and a wonderful friend.

✍♥

It was a mammoth undertaking. After the purpose, principles, and concepts were clear and general consent obtained, laws had to be analyzed, a corporate charter and constitution quite unlike any that had ever existed had to be crafted, initial operating procedures written, a jurisdiction found where such an entity could be brought into legal existence, consent from the Department of Justice obtained, contracts with the Bank of America for licensing of the service marks constructed, compensation negotiated, money for organization expenses obtained, and hundreds of other complexities analyzed and understood. One after the other, seemingly insurmountable obstacles were encountered and overcome.

Understanding of the opportunities and excitement about the concepts were soon contagious. Hundreds of talented, dedicated people from more than one hundred banks volunteered their time, self-organized, and worked assiduously to understand and anticipate legal, marketing, operating, financial, and technological problems and opportunities. Virtually everyone had full-time jobs in their card centers as well. It had to be done with no assurance the organization could ever be brought into being, for no one could be certain what would emerge.

Commitment was only to the process. Commitment to the eventual result could not be asked from any bank, not even the Bank of America, until the final result was fully known and carefully documented.

Early in 1970, it appeared everything was falling in place and the greatest obstacle of all could no longer be ignored. There were nearly two hundred full-licensee card-issuing banks. Each had the right to contract with other banks as agents to enroll merchants and solicit consumers for cards. Nearly twenty-five hundred agent banks had been sublicensed, bringing each licensee bank as much as a quarter million dollars a year in franchise fees and service income, with prospects of much more.

Meanwhile, the frenzy had not subsided. Banks continued to flood into the business, fearing their traditional banking business would be eroded. More banks were being licensed every month and the problems continued to accelerate. Three thousand banks must be induced to surrender their license for cancellation to Bank of America and simultaneously bind themselves to membership in the new organization: National BankAmericard Incorporated (NBI), a Delaware, nonstock, for-profit, membership corporation. An initial meeting must be organized to elect the first governance board, but no one could know which banks might be eligible to attend and vote until the actual membership agreements were signed.

All banks would sign an identical membership agreement. In a couple of paragraphs, each would acknowledge receipt of the NBI certificate of incorporation, bylaws, and operating procedures, and agree to abide by them "as they now exist or are hereafter modified." It was a surrender of autonomy to their collective selves, since they would be the owners, members, and governors of the new organization. Never before had banks voluntarily surrendered autonomy to any organization. It may have been taken from them by government or regulatory authorities, but voluntarily surrendered—never. Inducing three thousand banks to surrender their licenses and become owner-members of a new, untested concept of organization was no job for a sheep.

In the comfortable sitting room near his desk, Maxwell Carlson, as always, settles into his chair, hooks both thumbs in the small pockets of his vest, winds one leg around the other, and looking down, listens intently to an explanation of the problem. His reply is concise.

"Go directly to the top, young man, or the decision will become hopelessly mired in middle management. Such a decision will not be made in any bank without approval of the chief executive officer and, quite likely, the board. Start with ten or fifteen of the most influential, highly respected chief executive officers whose lead will be followed. Gain their consent, and ask their help in persuading others." He mentions several names. They might as well be Jesus and the Twelve Apostles for all the influence I would have.

"Mr. Carlson, would you help form such a group?"

"Young man, that would be a mistake. The National Bank of Commerce is not a large, money-center bank, nor do I have the personal influence you need. If asked, we will be pleased to participate; however, it would do you and the effort a disservice if we were to take the lead. The man who could do this without difficulty is Tom Clausen, president of the Bank of America. You should speak with him."

"But, I've only said hello to him once in passing. If I should try to speak with him he may refer the whole thing to someone who knows nothing about the situation. I don't want to start over."

"You seem to have gained the confidence of Sam Stewart. He might do as well as Clausen. Why don't you start with him?"

He rises, smiling, to bid me farewell. "Did the meeting serve your purpose?"

"Yes, sir."

A day later, it was a lucky sheep who flew from one statesman and wonderful human being to another. Sam Stewart had graciously crowded me into his schedule. He listened carefully, thought it a good approach, and agreed to take the lead. We drew up a list of twenty or thirty chief executive officers, selecting thirteen, making certain there was one from each of the regions in which committees had been formed. Sam felt it would be unlikely we would get all CEOs on short notice. If not, he would ask that another top officer with full authority to act for the bank be designated to participate.

Each would be asked to become a member of an executive officers' organizing committee to meet for a half-day in New York and listen to an exposition of problems, opportunities, and essential elements of the new organization. Each would receive complete documentation in its present stage of development, return to their bank, have it analyzed by appropriate people, and suggest improvement for consideration by the working committees, which would accept only those suggestions that met the test of purpose and principle.

Thirty days after their first meeting, the CEO committee would meet again for a final discussion. Each would then either commit to support the reconception of the system or decline to participate. If two-thirds or more agreed to the program, each would continue to serve for six months and support an effort to bring NBI into being. Sam agreed to make calls to induce them to participate, and if they agreed, to arrange a meeting.

Sam was a powerful persuader. Within the week he called to say all had agreed. We would meet a week hence in New York. Sam would open the meeting, indicate that the Bank of America thought the proposals had merit, and thereafter act only as one member of the committee. The rest was my responsibility. Frightening, but fair enough.

✍

It was an impressive group that met February 8, 1970, in New York, in an awesome board room near the top of another towering bank headquarters. They greeted one another as old friends, comparing private jet flights, golf scores, and banking deals made. It was an intimidated sheep who sat silently, wondering if they were people behind corporations that bloodied the hide of obstreperous sheep. Nothing had prepared me for this, save a few conversations with Sam Stewart and Maxwell Carlson. I'd never before been in a corporate board room. Little more than a year before I had been sorting trash in the basement of a bank branch.

I silently repeated a small mantra devised years before. It is the only human equation that has ever made sense to me. Whenever approaching someone with greater wealth, power, and position, I silently repeat, "*I am as great to me as you are to you, therefore, we are equal.*" When approached by those with less power, wealth, or position, I silently repeat, "*You are as great to you as I am to me, therefore, we are equal.*" It doesn't always work, but it never fails to help.

> **MiniMaxims**
>
> I am as great to me as you are to you, and you are as great to you as I am to me, therefore, we are equal.

Sam opened the meeting, made it clear the Bank of America was receptive to the concepts but would act only as one of the group. Thereafter, he seemed content to sit quietly listening to others and observing their reaction, forcing me to handle the discussion and respond to concerns. Once in a while, when I became tangled in my own verbal underwear, he would inject a few thoughts to untie the knots.

It was clear the bank wanted freedom to act as it thought best after knowing the reaction of others. While he made no effort at persuasion, his mere presence and leadership in calling the meeting was enough to ensure a fair hearing from everyone. They were uniformly courteous, interested, perceptive, but non-committal. Questions were to the point, and discussion centered on substantive issues rather than detail. My tension melted as I got out of myself and into the ideas that meant so much to me.

They left with the package in hand, committed only to meet sixty days later in Chicago. At that time, after having received a final set of documents and another round of discussion, they would be asked to commit their bank or withdraw. If committed, they would agree to serve for another six months, sponsor meetings of CEOs of full-licensee banks in their area at which the same presentation would be made. The proposal would live or die on its merits. Momentum was building.

✑

It is a raw, windy day in Chicago, March 11, 1970, as the executive officers' organizing committee gathers for the second time. Another towering bank building, another awesome board room, another splendid lunch. It's hard to imagine these folks ever meeting in a stock room to sit on a box and laugh together over a sandwich. They are really comfortable in such posh places. I'm sure as hell not, but this is where life has led and there's nothing to be done about it except endure.

The meeting begins with sharp, penetrating questions, constructive and informed. No one appears to have taken the proposal lightly. I have no time to coddle my discomfort.

"What happens if a bank decides not to join?"

"The organizing principles require that such banks not be left in a lesser position. Their license with Bank of America will remain in full force and effect. Members of the new organization will be obliged to interchange with them on the same basis as they would with members. The Bank of America will apply all regulations adopted by NBI to the licensees. However, they will have no voice in the new organization."

"What if a bank decides not to join and does not wish to continue in the system?"

"They will be free to surrender their license, have ample time to discontinue operations, sell their program to another licensee, or convert their BankAmericards to a competitive program of their choice."

"What if a bank wants to enter the program with a license from Bank of America rather than through the new organization?"

"NBI will have an exclusive, perpetual license covering the United States. There will be no further licensing by Bank of America and none by NBI. Participation will require becoming an owner-member with equitable rights and obligations."

"What about banks in other countries?"

"Creating such an organization in the U.S. alone is difficult enough. If it can't be done in one country, it can never be done at greater scale. Attempting to create such an organization among nations with different cultures, languages, laws, currencies, and economic systems could jeopardize the U.S. effort. The Bank of America will continue the licensing program overseas, and NBI will act on behalf of its members in relations with foreign licensees."

"How can NBI ensure equity and fairness between hundreds of U.S. banks operating under different laws in different markets?"

"If you conceive of NBI as nothing but its core board and employees, it can't. But that's a misperception. There will be no negotiated contracts. Each member will sign an identical agreement acknowledging that they have received a copy of the certificate of incorporation, bylaws, and operating procedures and agree to abide by them as they now exist or are hereafter modified. Modification can only be made by governance bodies and methods that ensure that all views will be heard and decisions are not dominated by anyone. Think of it as a reverse holding company. The regulations to which each party must submit are created by them. Any time a member does not like what has been created, they are free to walk away without obligation. It is an open, enabling, self-governing organization."

"Will NBI be brought into operation if only a small percentage of banks join?"

"No. If two-thirds commit it will become operational. We believe NBI is important enough to risk losing participants that produce a third of the volume of the system, but not more. If members producing two-thirds of the volume do not join, the effort will be abandoned."

"What if the owner-members want to make major changes, such as selecting a new name and abandoning the name 'BankAmericard?'"

"There will be no restrictions on the power of the board to act in any manner within the constraints of law. However, the constitution of the new organization requires higher percentages of approval on critical matters. The name can be changed if 80 percent of the banks approve."

"Doesn't the antitrust law forbid the formation of an organization composed of competitors?"

"Normally, yes. But there is a provision that allows such formation if it can be demonstrated that the service or product is impossible to provide without joint action. The Justice Department will then issue a letter that does not release the organization from its obligations under the antitrust laws, but gives assurance the department will not act against them unless anticompetitive effects are observed. We have had extensive advice from antitrust lawyers, as well as many discussions with the Department of Justice, and have received such assurance."

"What assurance do we have that NBI can resolve present problems and create the kind of markets you envision?"

"None! It's a matter of judgment and trust."

The questions come fast and intense, hour after hour, through the morning and into the afternoon. These people are being asked to put their reputations on the line for a concept that bears little resemblance to organizational concepts with which they are familiar and adept. It is one thing for card-center managers who are being torn apart by present problems and have little to lose to support the concept. It is quite another for the people who hold power and responsibility and are asked to surrender a portion of it, no matter how small.

In the middle of the afternoon, the questions dwindle and come to an end. Finally, the moment of truth. Will they commit their banks? Will they put their individual power and prestige behind the effort? They hesitate, then, surprisingly, ask if I will leave the room so they can have a half hour in private. There is no choice but to accede to their wishes. It is a half hour of torment.

The door finally opens and the reason is revealed. They have one condition without which none are prepared to make a decision. There must be no change of leadership at this critical juncture. Will I commit to continue to head the effort? It is puzzling. Why in the world would I not? Why should it require private discussion?

"Yes, of course. There is no way I will walk away until the job is done, even if it takes a year or more."

One of the more outspoken interjects.

"I don't think you understand. We want a commitment that you are prepared to move to San Francisco and head NBI. You've led the effort since the beginning and brought it this far. We don't want to risk a change of leadership during the remainder of the process, or for several years thereafter. If you are willing, Sam will negotiate terms and conditions. Only the board of the new organization can appoint officers of NBI, but if they select you, we want to be certain you will accept. If you will make that commitment, you have our commitment."

"All of you? Everyone?"

"Yes."

Thoughts race through my mind as I fall silent. Had I wanted to be asked to lead the new organization if it came into being? Yes, of course. I would have cursed them if they had not. Had I expected them to? No! I didn't fit the mold—had no credentials—was not a member of the club—carried no recommendation from previous employers—had been savaged often enough to expect no better.

Had I any intention of accepting if asked? None! I was exhausted. The work had taken every moment of my waking hours for a year and a half. Both sons were to graduate high school in four months. Both had been accepted at the University of Washington. Our daughter was a freshman in high school. Ferol was a year out of university and well established as a speech and hearing therapist. I loved the mountains, forests, and lakes of the Pacific Northwest. There was a great sense of obligation to Maxwell Carlson. What I desperately wanted was my life back—to bring this dream into being, return to the Northwest, and perfect my retirement on the job.

I explained my position and desires. It made no difference. They would like a decision within the week. It was unreasonable. They were asking me for commitment to a job they could not offer, working for a company not yet fully structured, for owners yet to be determined, and governed by an unknown board. But they were adamant. No commitment, no commitment. As simple as that. I was gibbeted, swinging in the wind.

CHAPTER TEN

The Corporation or the Cane?

Man is not born evil. Why then are some of them infected with this plague of malevolence? It's because those who are at their head have the malady and communicate it to the rest of mankind.
— VOLTAIRE

It is a ridiculous thing for a man not to fly from his own badness, which is indeed possible, but to fly from other men's badness, which is impossible.
— MARCUS AURELIUS ANTONIUS

The next two days in Seattle were miserable as I alternated between the multitude of things needed to keep the organizational effort moving and wandering the woods seeking solace and equanimity. Near the end of the second day, notebook and pocketknife in my jacket, I slipped away for a long walk in woods filled with slanting shafts of light from a spring sun sinking slowly in the western sky. A few yellowed pages of notes survive from that day, resurrected from an old file where they remained unseen and forgotten these thirty years past. The flood of feeling they evoke is impossible to describe.

I walked to the hill, sat on a fallen tree in the edge of a thicket and leisurely whittled a crooked, maple walking stick. It came to me that forming and building NBI, or anything of worth, is much the same. It requires sound material, a good tool, a capable hand and, most important, a clear vision of things to come. It requires patience and persistence to pursue the vision chip, by chip, by chip, and willingness to change the vision as the nature of the material is revealed.

What foolish logic would rationalize becoming president of NBI? It means giving up grass, rain, trees, birds, insects—all the natural living things. It means dirty air, city jungles, confinement in steel and concrete boxes, conniving people, and fussing, futile work. It means living where I do not live, liking what I do not like, and working how I work not. Perhaps I can hang on to reality if I remember that, and simply write off the next three years for education of the children and my desire to provide Ferol with freedom and some of the finer things she so richly deserves. Will I prefer the corporation to the cane? Somehow, I doubt it.

As Old Monkey Mind and I struggled with our personal dilemma, we could not avoid our endless effort to understand the nature of organizations, particularly the concept called "corporation." Like all organizations, corporations have no reality save in the mind. They are no more than mental concepts; manifestations of the ancient idea of community. Corporations have become so ubiquitous, so much a part of us from the moment of birth, that we accept them with as little thought as the air we breath and the water we drink. But they are not natural phenomena. They are creations of man. Old Monkey and I knew we could never understand corporations unless we followed the advice of ancient, Eastern philosophers and examined them *as they were, as they are, as they might become, and as they ought to be.* NBI would certainly be incorporated in one legal jurisdiction or another. If it was to be truly different, we must peel the corporate onion to its essence. We began with the dry skeletons one finds in the dusty closets of dictionary and encyclopedia.

Black's Law Dictionary tells us that a corporation is "an artificial person or legal entity created by or under the authority of the laws of a state or nation . . . ordinarily consisting of an association of numerous individuals. Such entity . . . is regarded in law as having a personality and existence distinct from that of its several members . . . vested with the capacity of continuous succession irrespective of changes in its membership, either in perpetuity or for a limited term of years"—et cetera. Mr. Black was obviously struggling, along with the rest of us, to make something understandable out of the mental abstraction called "corporation."

Corporations *as they were* bear little resemblance to corporations *as they now are.* The original concept of corporation was a collective entity intended to attract people and resources needed to realize a desired social objective beyond the ability or resources of a single individual. It was created through the power of government and authorized to exist as a pseudoindividual with limited, carefully prescribed rights and obligations. It was to be chartered for a limited time, function in a limited area to realize a public purpose open to rigorous social and governmental surveillance. Its "natural" death in time was specified in the charter. Actions in excess of, or inadequate to the purpose, would be punished by social death through revocation of the charter.

The proliferation of the corporate concept of organization as a pseudoperson was given great impetus in the sixteenth and seventeenth centuries by the huge, imperialist expansion of Western nation-states through subjugation of people on other continents. The increase in geographic scale, attendant risk, and capital that imperialist expansion required fueled the desire for limited personal liability and responsibility for risk, and for unlimited opportunity for gain. The corporate form of organization became a useful instrument for government plunder. It is not to be wondered that it soon had a tendency to become an instrument for private plunder as well. Pursuit of limitations of personal liability and unrestrained opportunity for gain became a conflagration burning ever hotter from the seventeenth century to the present day.

In the United States, the first general for-profit corporation statute was enacted by New York State in 1811, with other states gradually following its lead. The corporation as a business mechanism came into prominence during and after the Civil War, again as an instrument of government for achieving its purpose in a time of great civil strife and expense. The statutes covering such entities have been liberalized, broadened, and made more detailed in their provisions ever since, gradually moving away from the interests of government and society to the interests of monetary shareholders and management.

In the beginning, no one dreamed that a small aggregation of wealth and power legalized in the form of a pseudoperson to achieve a social purpose would not only be used in pursuit of the purpose, but to persistently grind away social and legislative mandates that defined corporate purpose, restricted its territory, controlled its growth, and curbed its behavior. But it did.

The for-profit, monetized shareholder form of corporation has demanded and received perpetual life. It has demanded and received the right to define its own purpose and act solely for self-defined self-interest. It has demanded and received release from the revocation of its charter for inept or antisocial acts. The roles of giant, transnational corporations and government have slowly reversed. Government is now more an instrument of such corporations than the corporations are instruments of government. They are no longer, not even indirectly, an instrument of the populace they affect, but an instrument of the few who control the ever increasing power and wealth they command. The inevitable tendency of wealth is to acquire power. The inevitable tendency of power is to protect wealth. The tendency of wealth and power combined is to acquire ever more wealth and power. The use of commercial corporate form for the purpose of social good has become incidental.

The monetized commercial form of corporation has steadily become an instrument of those with surplus money (capital) and those with surplus power (management) to reward themselves at the expense of the community, the biosphere, and the many without surplus wealth or power, commonly called "consumers" and "human resources." (Demeaning but revealing phrases.) "Human resources" are mined, smelted, shaped, made into products, worn out, and discarded with little more consideration on the part of monetary stockholders and management than they might give to a load of ore or a pile of lumber.

Nor is corporate power restricted to power over the employed. Global corporations now have implicit sovereignty over people throughout the world, since they are beyond the reach of any nation-state. They hold government and its instrumentalities to ransom for use of land, for reprieve from taxation, for access to natural resources far below cost, for direct monetary subsidization, and for use of land, air, and water as a repository for refuse; all by the simple expedient of bargaining one government against another for the claimed economic benefit of their presence. Global corporations are creating a market for government in which they are the sole buyers. They can move their money, their operations, their products, and their management at will worldwide. No government can do so. No community can do so. Few individuals can do so.

Such corporations are gradually becoming superb instruments for the capitalization of gain and socialization of cost. When a corporation rips from the earth irreplaceable energy or resources, no matter how much it pays for them, or any resources more rapidly than they can be replaced or at less than full replacement cost, it has socialized a cost and capitalized the gain. When it "downsizes" workers, abandons a community, or pays less than a living wage; when it creates and disposes of waste in the process of manufacturing or marketing a product, or at the end of its useful life; when it receives a subsidy, guarantee, or relief from taxation by government, it has socialized a cost and capitalized the gain.

When a corporation utilizes highways, railroads, airlines, postal departments, or other public infrastructure at less than their full cost; when it uses the military, the CIA, or any other government instrumentality to protect its interests; when it diminishes topsoil, depletes the water table, or pollutes and poisons any biological system on which life depends, it has socialized a cost and capitalized the gain. When a corporation engages in unsound lending or currency speculation and looks to government, the World Bank, or the International Monetary Fund to bail out its customers, public or private, in order that they may repay their debt; when a corporation is awarded scarce portions of the electromagnetic spectrum to market its ideology and wares, it has socialized a cost and capitalized the gain. The possibilities for socializing cost and capitalizing gain are endless, as those who hold power or wealth within monetized corporations have discovered to their endless benefit.

> **MiniMaxims**
>
> *Corporations are a great place to make love to capitalization of gain in one bedroom and socialization of cost in the other.*

This effect of this vast corporate socialization of cost and capitalization of gain is no longer limited to the current generation. Liability for the socialized cost is transferred to the unlived life of the young and to generations yet unborn through countless government guarantees, instruments of long-term debt, and depletion of natural resources that require centuries for regeneration. Interest is added to such debt and, when collected, paid to the same people who hold most shares in corporations, for it is their surplus wealth that is borrowed to fund government or private debt future generations must pay.

Round and round the merry-go-round, as fewer and fewer get richer and richer and ever more powerful, while more and more people fall into poverty and despair, and generations unborn are placed deeper in bondage to the appetites of the moment. The fascinating thing about the whole of it is that there are no evil people who wish it so, or who have conspired to make it happen. All are victimized by a false metaphor, a wrong concept of organization, an internal model of reality that is flawed; a consciousness of reality neither whole nor wholesome. The excuses we give, receive, and too often believe ring hollow. "That some have is evidence that all may get." "Power and wealth are the result of superior intelligence, effort, and ability." "Poverty is the result of a lack of determination and character." "That some rise from the bottom to the top is proof that all others could, if they had sufficient intelligence and will." "There is fault at the bottom and virtue at the top." "Unlimited pursuit of self-interest (the 'invisible hand') will result in the greatest good for all." "A rising tide lifts all boats."

When we trumpet the glories of monetary capitalism and praise the fiction of free markets while decrying the evils of socialism we are engaging in cant and hypocrisy. Clearly, we make love to socialism in the balance-sheet bedroom called cost, and make love to capitalism in the bedroom called gain. It is tearing the physical world apart and most of us as well. If the purpose of each corporation is not primarily the health of the earth and well-being of all life thereon, if its principles are not based on equitable distribution of power and wealth, if it avoids responsibility for the sustenance of family, community, and place, if it has no belief system, or one devoid of ethical and moral content, it is difficult to see why it should have the sanction and protection of society through government.

We know *how monetized corporations were*. We know *how they are*. We know *what they are becoming*, and it is not a happy prospect for the vast majority of people. It is far past time to examine how corporations *ought to be*. There can be no doubt that the people who control corporations should lead this odyssey in the most profound way. If they profess to be leaders, they should "go before and show the way."

꧁

Our obsession with numbers and measurement brings into being the phenomenom of accounting, a profession and practice that plays a dominant role in our present societal structures. In the deepest sense, there is no such thing as "accounting." Accountants are merely a modern version of the tribal storyteller, whose role was to accurately portray their tribe as it was, as it is, as it might become, and as it ought to be, thus informing its evolution and future. That the tribes are now called corporation, nation, university, church, county, partnership, or any other appellation is irrelevant. That the primary language used to inform those tribes is now mathematics, and accounting is relevant only to the degree it accurately explains how the tribe was, how it is, how it might become, and how it ought to be.

It was well put by H. Thomas Johnson, an economic historian, CPA, and former president of the Academy of Accounting Historians. He wrote:

> The Cartesian/Newtonian worldview has influenced thought far beyond the physical sciences, and accounting is no exception. Double entry bookkeeping and the systems of income and wealth measurement that evolved from it since the sixteenth century are eminently Cartesian and Newtonian. They are predicated on ideas such as the whole being equal to the sum of the parts and effects being the result of infinitely divisible, linear causes. . . . Quantum physicists and evolutionary biologists, among others, now believe that it is best to describe reality as a web of interconnected relationships that give rise to an ever-changing and evolving universe of objects that we perceive only partially with our limited senses. In that "systemic" view of the world,

nothing is merely the sum of the parts; parts have meaning only in reference to a greater whole in which everything is related to everything else. . . . Why should accountants continue to believe that human organizations behave like machines if the scientists from whom they borrowed that mechanistic worldview now see the universe from a very different perspective? . . .

The language of financial accounting merely asserts answers, it does not invite inquiry. In particular it leaves unchallenged the worldview that underlies [the way] organizations operate. Thus, management accounting has served as a barrier to genuine organizational learning. . . . *Never again should management accounting be seen as a tool to drive people with measures. Its purpose must be to promote inquiry into the relationships, patterns, and processes that give rise to accounting measures.*

In more precise terms, in the years ahead we must get beyond numbers and the language of mathematics to understand, evaluate, and account for such intangibles as learning, intellectual capital, community, beliefs, and principles, *or the stories we tell of our tribe's value and prospects will be increasingly false.*

We must understand, evaluate, and account for wholly new, nonmonetary forms of ownership, assets, and liabilities of great value that have extraordinary effect but no tangible market price or mathematical means of measurement, such as participatory rights, alliances, systemic interdependence, and defined relationships, *or the stories we tell of our tribe will be increasingly archaic and misleading.*

> **MiniMaxims**
>
> *You can't count the steps to heaven, or calculate the slide to hell.*

We must understand, evaluate, and account for the full cost of *everything* removed from or returned to the earth, the biosphere, or the atmosphere, including reversion to natural elements in the original proportions and balance, *or our stories will result in increasing environmental catastrophe.*

We must conceive of and help implement wholly new forms of ownership, financial systems, and measurements free of the attempt to monetize all values which bind tribes to next quarter's bottom line, gross maldistribution of wealth and power, degradation of people, and desolation of the ecosphere, *or our stories will be increasingly immoral and destructive.*

And we must interconnect our stories with those of all other tribal storytellers in order to integrate them into a new, intelligible, larger story to inform the global community now emerging, *or our stories will continue to set tribe against tribe in ever accelerating economic, social, and physical combat.*

We are not helpless victims in the grasp of some supernatural force. We were active participants in the creation of our present consciousness. From that consciousness we created our present internal model of reality. From that internal model we created our present concepts of organization. With those organizations we created our present society. We did it. All of us. We know that we must do better. We know that we can do better. We know it must be done together. And we know that "together" must transcend all present boundaries and allow self-organization at every scale, from the smallest form of life to the living earth itself. It is not a journey. It is an odyssey. It will take time. It will require great respect for the past, vast understanding and tolerance of the present, and even greater belief and trust in the future. It calls out to the best in us, one and all.

As Old Monkey and I walked out of the woods with the crooked, maple cane and the journal, the choice was extremely difficult, yet simple. Either say no, abandon the dream, and incur economic risk for the family, or say yes and wholeheartedly accept the consequences, whatever they might be. With a heavy heart, but convinced it was the right decision, I returned to write the letter to Sam Stewart, mentioning but two needs: a salary small in relation to the responsibility and difficulty of the job ahead, but a bit more than Ferol and my combined salaries, and three years' salary guaranteed should they wish me to step aside, or move the headquarters east of the Rocky Mountains.

The three years was based on conviction that if I faced without equivocations the decisions and acts necessary to restore stability to the system I would so alienate members that continuance beyond three years would be impossible. The modest salary was suggested to make it clear this was a labor of love, not a matter of money. I fully expected that Sam and the committee would insist on more generous terms. Remaining west of the Rocky Mountains was pure personal indulgence. I was western bred and born and could not imagine living elsewhere.

Sam Stewart was an integral part of the culture of the Bank of America. A. P. Giannini, the founder of Bank of America, gained fame by living in the same modest, suburban house throughout his life and paying himself a small salary. Since he was founder and president of the bank, the salary scale went down from there. Whether he did so from conviction, or as a means of keeping costs low, was never known. At the very least, it was disingenuous, for he enjoyed vast wealth from his shares in the bank and a host of amenities from organizations and foundations he controlled, while the employees had none. Whatever A. P.'s motives, as the growth of California in the first half of the century pushed the bank to prominence as the largest, most profitable bank in the world, it was equally prominent for abysmally low salaries. Once again, I traveled to San Francisco to ascend the towering, palatial headquarters of the Bank of America.

Sam is blunt. "Dee, as president and CEO of NBI, your salary will be public information. There are only a half-dozen people in the Bank of America who make more than the sum you suggest. If NBI pays that salary it will become known in the bank, causing considerable discontent, and personal difficulty for me. We would be comfortable with a salary of $44,000 a year, beginning with the formation of NBI. We are also prepared to make a one-time payment of $10,000 in recognition of all that you have done in the past year and a half and must do in the months ahead to persuade the banks to join NBI and bring it into being."

I wait for him to break into a grin and explain the joke. He does not. He can't be serious! Forty-four thousand dollars, no benefits, and no equity to straighten out a $2 billion mess? Ten thousand dollars for two years of innovation and grinding work against impossible odds? Only a half-dozen people in the Bank of America who make more than $60,000 a year? Even if true, what of stock options, other perquisites, and lifetime security? But Sam is serious. He senses my distress and tries to ease the situation.

"Dee, these things take time. There was a period, earlier in my career with the bank, when I went for several years without a raise. It wasn't easy, but it worked out in the end."

"Sam, if that's true, the bank was undoubtedly in error the second year, the third year, and every year thereafter. Have you discussed the terms you're suggesting with other members of the CEO committee?"

"No. They authorized me to handle the matter. It should be settled here and now if we want their commitment."

Have I misjudged this man? Is this some sort of ploy to induce angry refusal and undercut the effort? What possible motive could underlay this absurdity? Even if what he says is true, why should my compensation be determined by the bias of a single man in a single bank?

How can I undertake such a commitment if it begins with conflict, suspicion, and mistrust? I can't! This is my dream. This work contains the meaning of my life. I'm not going to muddy it with distrust and suspicion, muck it up with a haggle over money, or be distracted from the pursuit. Not now, not ever! I refuse to believe this man dishonest or insincere. Mistaken, yes! Deceitful, no! I had not expected unpleasant circumstances to arrive so quickly or my convictions to be so unjustly tested, but my decision had been made without equivocation. And so it would remain.

"Sam, we'll do as you wish. But don't ask me to agree with you. You're wrong again, but this time it only compromises my pocketbook and I can live with that. Tell the committee yes and accept their commitment. I'll be back in a week with a plan." His pleasure is genuine and immediate.

It was with an extremely heavy heart and troubled conscience that I entered the sitting room in which I had spent three of the best moments of my life, to be greeted by Maxwell Carlson in his gentle, kindly manner.

"What can I do for you, young man?"

"Mr. Carlson, what I have to say is extremely difficult. You know how deeply I believe in the formation of NBI. The executive officers' organizing committee, which you suggested, has unanimously agreed to support the formation of NBI and committed their banks to membership. They have one condition. They insist I continue to lead the effort through the organizational phase and for the first three years of operation. I don't want to leave the National Bank of Commerce or the Northwest. The travel, notoriety, and stress of the NBI job is not pleasant to contemplate. The pay is poor. Yet, it's a concept in which I deeply believe and I desperately want it to succeed. A host of people have worked hard to bring it about and are depending on its success. It is not a happy choice, but I must leave the National Bank of Commerce and can't make return for all that you have done."

There is the usual, thoughtful moment of silence as he looks down; the inevitable gentle smile as he raises his head to reply. "Well, young man, I rather thought this might happen. Put your mind at rest. We have been amply repaid by doing as we thought best. If the new venture succeeds, we will be repaid time and again, both in material and more important ways. If it doesn't, there will always be a place for you at the National Bank of Commerce. Good luck, and if I can ever be of assistance, please let me know. Did the meeting serve your purpose?"

There isn't the slightest doubt about it. If Maxwell Carlson had been a lesser human being, VISA would never have come to be.

CHAPTER ELEVEN

And Then There Was One

Iron rusts from disuse; stagnant water loses its purity. . . . Even so does inaction sap the vigor of the mind.
— LEONARDO DA VINCI

Nothing is possible without individuals; nothing is lasting without institutions.
— JEAN MONNET

When I returned a week later with the promised plan, Sam did not like it.

"Dee, it's impossible. There is absolutely no way three thousand banks can be persuaded to surrender their licenses, become members of such a different organization, hold an annual meeting of members, elect a board, and have the whole thing in operation in ninety days. It can't be done."

Sam doesn't understand. Impossibility can only be determined by the attempt.

"Sam, you can't know that without making the attempt. We have the support of thirteen powerful people. We have the interest and participation of dozens of others who have worked on it for a year and a half. The concepts are sound. The need is compelling. Momentum is building. If we link people in the right relationships, challenge and free them, they'll perform miracles.

I've seen it happen before. Never on this scale, but we've got to try. If we drag it out it may never happen." Sam begins to waver.

"What would you need from the bank?"

"Six or eight dedicated people for sixty days to process the surrender and cancellation of all licenses."

"It would not be easy but it might be done. What else?"

"A management agreement under which NBI can borrow up to a dozen experienced, willing people from your card, legal, marketing, and systems departments, for six to eight months, to work solely in the interests of NBI and its prospective members. They will need the kind of independence I've had from the National Bank of Commerce. NBI to pay the bank 150 percent of all salaries and benefits. The people must be assured they can return to the bank at comparable jobs."

"That would be difficult, but it might be arranged."

I plunge ahead. "We'll need a $200,000 line of credit at market rates for organizational expense, to be repaid from service fees of members once NBI is operational, or divided among the banks represented by the executive officers' organizing committee and written off as expense if the effort fails."

"We could look into that. What else would you need from us?"

"Assistance from your personnel department in recruiting, investigating, and hiring a small initial staff should the effort succeed."

"That would be possible."

"Temporary space in the vacant part of your old building across the street at reasonable month-to-month rent, and the loan of some old desks, files, and typewriters."

"We can look into that as well. Anything else?"

Do I know him well enough? Can I take the risk? It's irresistible. I give his own words back. "Sam, there is no time to 'look into' these things. The operating committees authorized me to handle the matter. It should be settled here and now if we want their commitment."

He laughs, and gives me my own words in return. "OK, we'll do as you wish. I'll accept and never say more—but don't ask me to agree with you. You're wrong. There is no way this will be done in ninety days. Tell your operating committees yes and accept their commitment. I'll be back with a plan for our part in a week."

Within a day, I had called each member of the executive officers' organizing committee (EOOC) with an impossible request, but it caught their fancy and they agreed. Each would arrange a half-day, morning meeting with senior executive officers of each full licensee bank in their region. Each would attend the meeting they had arranged, explain the work the EOOC had done and its commitment to the concept. The chairman of the regional working committees and I would attend each meeting and present the proposal. Each member of the EOOC would accept an equal share of the organizational expense if the effort failed.

They were as good as their word. Within ten days, they had coordinated with one another, and twelve meetings were arranged, each on consecutive days at locations less than two hours flight time apart on well-traveled air routes. Those same ten days produced offices and "borrowed" employees from the Bank of America. Every prospective attendee had been sent a complete package of material. Every member of every working committee had been briefed and was in touch with the executive officer from their bank who was scheduled to attend the regional meeting.

There was no one with authority to command or control anyone else. What needed to be done was discussed and agreed; each person to take responsibility for any part was to coordinate with others, decide how best to proceed, and get it done. There was excellent communication and growing trust. Order, coherence, and cohesion emerged.

In another ten days, I lifted off from the Seattle airport on the first leg of an impossible schedule. It's all a blur now—intense questions, skepticism, enthusiasm, criticism, confusion, persuasion—mad dashes to airports—catch-as-catch-can sleep—no time, no time—twelve days, twelve cities, two hundred banks, hundreds of people. The sheep's first principle was burning hot. *Given the right circumstances, from no more than dreams, determination, and the liberty to try, quite ordinary people consistently do extraordinary things.* It didn't feel extraordinary; it felt extremely painful.

The executive officer of each licensee bank was to take their copy of the certificate of incorporation, bylaws, license cancellation agreement, membership agreement, and operating material, review it with anyone they chose, and send suggestions for improvement to the executive working committee, which would make final decisions for incorporation of *essential* changes. A final owner-member charter package would then be created and sent to each bank containing a provision for acceptance within thirty days. Not a sentence, not a word, not a comma of the final charter package would be changed. Accept or reject—no other alternative during the charter period, although membership would be open to any qualified bank at any time thereafter.

Every bank electing to join would sign an identical, brief agreement in duplicate original, acknowledging receipt of the material and committing to abide by all provisions of the documents "as they now exist or are hereafter modified."

A threshold of acceptance was specified. If reached, all charter member agreements and all contracts between NBI and the Bank of America would immediately be in full force and effect. If the threshold was not reached, membership agreements and contracts would be null and void. A first meeting of owner-members was scheduled shortly after the deadline for acceptance of charter members, at which the governing board would be elected and officers appointed, providing the effort was successful.

Each member would have one vote for every thousand dollars of sales volume transacted by their BankAmericard customers in the preceding year. Service fees would be one-quarter of one percent of that same sales volume. Thus, taxation and representation would be linked. Dividends or distributions, if any, would be on the basis of that fraction of the service fees paid by any member to that paid by the total membership, *in perpetuity*. There would be no need for endless negotiating, endless contracting, endless disputes and legal battles. Essential rights and obligations, as well as the structure itself, would be self-organizing and self-governing in perpetuity.

Memberships would be nontransferable and disconnected from cards and receivables. Portfolios of business could be sold, but not owner-membership in the organization or rights to the use of service marks or other properties. Those rights could only be acquired by eligibility, application, and acceptance to membership. However, it would be no closed club. Directors could determine general eligibility for membership, but would have no power to decline any applicant meeting those requirements, or any power to accept an applicant who did not.

Although voting rights would be related to size of the program, there would be a one-bank, one-director rule. No matter how many votes a member acquired as a result of their sales volume, once an employee of that bank was elected to the board, votes could not be used to elect another. Once elected, each director would have legal and fiduciary responsibility to the whole of the system, not to their bank or to the constituency from which elected. Each director would have a single vote with respect to board decisions.

There would be different types of directors. The country was divided into regions, each of which would elect a director. Only members headquartered in that region could vote for regional directors. One at-large director would be elected solely by banks having less than a minimal percent of the volume. Five at-large directors would be elected by the entire membership under cumulative voting procedures. Any bank having more than 15 percent of the sales volume of the system could appoint a director.

Every director must be reelected every year. The board could appoint a nominating committee to suggest candidates for election. However, if any other individual was nominated by a member and seconded by another, that person must be put on the ballot and given equal treatment with board nominees. Elections for regional directors could be by mail, but if a single member requested a meeting for purposes of election *it must* be held. Nominations could be made by any member from the floor at any meeting.

The president, appointed by the board, would be the chief executive officer and a member of the board by right of that appointment, but could not hold the chairmanship. The chairman would be elected by the board, but would have no executive or operating authority. The president would be responsible for preparing the agenda for board meetings. Any matter could be put on the agenda by any director. The chairman would preside at all board meetings, make certain all views were openly, equitably heard and that decisions were in accordance with all provisions of the bylaws and policies of the organization and relevant laws and regulations. The chairman would be free of any responsibility to support the views of management, but would have no right to suppress them.

Once the organization came into being, the board could amend the bylaws, but they were carefully crafted to require votes as high as 80 percent to protect provisions essential to the organizational principles on which the bylaws were based. Essential provisions required approval by 80 percent of the board and 80 percent of the membership.

Over and over again I explained the purpose, principles, concept, and structure, and repeated my mantra. "You will not like everything about the organization and you will not like everything it does. But one thing on which you may depend is that it can be trusted. No member of any class will have greater or lesser rights than any other. No director will have a greater or lesser voice. Management will have no control over composition of the board. The minimal autonomy necessary to the common good will be surrendered to yourselves as a cooperative whole. You, the participants, and you alone will make all decisions through the most open and equitable structure that hundreds of participants could devise. Deliberation and debate will be open to all and controlled by none, particularly management."

Many were skeptical, but as the days wore on they could find nothing in the charter documents to the contrary. Suggestions of all kinds flowed in. Some reflected misunderstanding. Some were self-serving, couched in terms of "we will only join if you change this or that." Some were clearly improvements. Every suggestion was carefully examined by a legal committee composed of counsel for a representative group of banks and by the operational committees. Final decisions for inclusion were made by the licensee executive committee.

Two months after Sam's consent to try, a final package of charter owner-member materials was on the way to all licensee banks and the commitment period was under way. It was highly likely the thirteen banks represented by the executive officers' organizing committee would accept the final package. Another fifteen or twenty banks had indicated strong intent to do so. Many had expressed reservations. Some were strongly opposed.

Needing undisturbed time, and every minute of it, a tiny, unused bedroom of our house was emptied, a small table moved in, and two telephones installed. On the table was a large spreadsheet with the names and telephone numbers of every bank officer who had attended any of the meetings or worked on any of the committees. There were brief notes about the interest or opinions each had previously expressed. With no commute, it was possible to be on the telephone to East Coast bankers by 5:00 A.M. "Did you receive the charter member package of materials? Do you have any questions? When might you have time to finish their review? When would it be convenient to call again to discuss any matters that might arise in the process?" "You can't locate the material? Another package will be sent by courier immediately. We'll call in two days to make certain it's been received." "He's gone for two weeks? Would you put me through to whoever is handling the matter in his absence?" "Can she call me back; anytime from five in the morning until ten at night."

Hour after hour, day after day, bank after bank, person after person, over and over, cajoling, sympathizing, explaining, appealing, thanking—all the while making a careful record of the needs, desires, and position of each. Not a day was free of demands, anger, patronization, and occasional abuse flowing back through the line. The temptation to agree to minor modifications was almost overwhelming. But there was much generosity, understanding, appreciation, and trust as well. By the middle of the second day, the small bedroom was stifling, the confinement unbearable. The table was moved to the garden and long telephone extension cords strung through the window. There, under a flowering pear tree, next to a tiny pool and waterfall surrounded by rhododendrons, the work went on into the dark of the evening, illuminated by light from the window.

The commitments began to come in, accelerating each day. If anyone had major problems and seemed on the verge of refusal, excuses were made to end the conversation and resume it another day; meanwhile committed banks who might be influential were induced to call the reluctant, who thus became aware of respected friends who were committing to the concept. Within three weeks it appeared likely we would reach the threshold that would automatically trigger formation of the organization. A day or two later it was certain.

But certainty was not enough. Fewer than twenty banks remained uncommitted, a half dozen were adamantly opposed. But none were refusing to have another word on the subject. We had come so far, overcome so many obstacles, maybe, just maybe! Back to the telephone, this time digging to know much more about the individuals and institutions involved, trying to understand their perspective and discover something that might help them to a different conclusion. One by one, they began to waver as the deadline approached. If so many banks whose judgment they respected were committed, could they have been wrong?

> **MiniMaxims**
>
> *Never confuse activity with productivity. It's what comes out the other end of the pipe that's important, not what you push into it.*

As the number of uncommitted banks dwindled, realization dawned that refusing to join and retaining their license would be a lonely place indeed. Even though they could continue with full rights of interchange, they would have no participation in future decisions. Although they could join at any time after the charter period expired, they would have no voting rights, or eligibility to serve on the board during the first year. Was it better to become an owner-member of NBI and influence its direction, or remain carping on the outside? As the mass of committed banks grew, so did enthusiasm for what the new organization might be able to achieve. It was infectious.

Two days before the deadline, I made the call I had longed for. It was to a senior officer of a responsible, capable bank, whose convictions I respected. I liked him a great deal, for he was open, honest, and intelligent. But he was convinced that such an unusual organization would not succeed, and had the courage of his convictions.

"Nolan, we greatly appreciate the time you've given this matter and truly understand your position. We have too much respect for your decision to make another appeal. On the other hand, the present situation is so unusual, I felt you should be aware of it."

"Dee, I'm aware that we're in a minority and that the organization will be formed. What is the situation that concerns you?"

"It's difficult to know how to put it, but you should know that every licensee card-issuing bank, save one, has committed to the new organization."

There was a long moment before he replied, "You're not joking with me? We're the only licensee who will not be a member?"

"I'm not happy to say as much, but, yes. You'll be the only one."

Another moment of silence before his reply. "No, we will not be the only one. We may have been the only one this morning, but we'll not be the only one tomorrow morning. Count us in."

"Nolan, there are moments when great gifts arrive and you've just given us one. We're deeply grateful."

"Thank you for letting us know. We're grateful as well."

✑

Today, before any audience in the world, I can hold a VISA card overhead and ask, "How many of you recognize this?" Every hand in the room will go up. When I ask, "How many of you can tell me who owns it, where it's headquartered, how it operates, or where to buy shares?" a dead silence comes over the room. The audience realizes something extraordinary has occurred, and they haven't a clue how it happened. Nor, in my judgment, should they. The results of the best organizations are apparent, but the structure, leadership, and process are transparent.

In 1968 the VISA community was no more than a set of beliefs and a vague concept. In 1970 it was born. Today, twenty-nine years later, its products are created by 22,000 owner-member financial institutions and accepted at 15 million merchant locations in more than 200 countries and territories. Three-quarters of a billion people use VISA products to make 14 billion transactions producing annual volume of $1.25 trillion—the single largest block of consumer purchasing power in the global economy. VISA has grown a minimum of 20 percent and as much as 50 percent compounded annually for three decades, through the best and the worst of times, with no end in sight.

But numbers reveal very little about the nature of organizations. What VISA was, I knew well. What it is today, I do not know. What it may become is no longer my affair. But what it ought to be is another matter. So I shall write about it as I experienced it, and believe it ought to be.

VISA was a quasi-governmental, quasi-for-profit, quasi-not-for-profit, quasi-consulting, quasi-franchising, quasi-educational, quasi-social, quasi-commercial, quasi-political alliance. It was none of them, yet it was all of them. It was chaordic.

In the strict legal sense, VISA was a nonstock, for-profit, membership corporation. In another sense, it was an inside-out holding company in that it did not hold, but was held by its functioning parts. The financial institutions that create its products were, at one and the same time, its owners, its members, its suppliers, its customers, its subjects, and its superiors. It existed as an integral part of the most highly regulated of industries, yet the core of the organization was not subject to regulatory authority, since it made no loans, had no stock, and engaged in no external business. The core was an enabling organization that existed for the sole purpose of assisting owner-members to do what they wished with greater capacity, more effectively, and at less cost.

It could not be bought, raided, traded, or sold, since ownership was in the form of perpetual, nontransferable, rights of participation. However, that portion of the business created by each member was owned solely by them, was reflected in their stock prices, and could be sold to any other member or entity eligible for membership—an extremely broad, active market.

VISA espoused no political, economic, social, or legal theory, thus transcending language, race, custom, and culture to successfully bring together people and institutions of every political, economic, social, and religious persuasion. It went through a number of wars and revolutions, the belligerents continuing to share common ownership and never ceasing reciprocal acceptance of products, even though they were killing one another.

Within a decade of its formation in 1970, it transformed a troubled product with a minority market share into a majority market share and the most profitable consumer service in the financial services industry, and at the same time reduced, by more than half, the cost of unsecured credit to individuals and the cost to merchants of handling payment instruments. Through this new concept of relationships, participants distributed a substantial amount of their expense at the cost of a minuscule amount of income. It spawned new industries and new ventures in the tens of thousands, creating conditions by which members can connect with them without permission or limitation. Since it had no interest in controlling or owning technology or participants, the unlimited ingenuity and creativity of thousands of external entities was freely brought to bear on the needs and opportunities of the system.

Its products were among the most universally used and recognized in the world, yet the organization was so transparent its ultimate customers, most if its affiliates, and some of its members did not know it existed or how it functioned. At the same time, the core of the enterprise had no knowledge of, information about, or authority over a vast number of the constituent parts. VISA had multiple boards of directors within a single legal entity, none of which could be considered superior or inferior, as each had irrevocable authority and autonomy over geographic or functional areas. *No part knew the whole, the whole did not know all the parts, and none had any need to.* The entirety, like millions of other chaordic organizations, including those we call body, brain, forest, ocean, and biosphere, was largely self-regulating.

A staff of fewer than five hundred scattered in more than a dozen countries on four continents coordinated this system as it skyrocketed past a hundred billion dollars, providing product and systems development, global advertising, and around-the-clock operation of two global electronic communication systems with thousands of data centers communicating through millions of miles of communications lines. Today, those systems clear more electronic financial transactions in a week than the U.S. Federal Reserve system does in a year.

Its employees received mediocre salaries by commercial standards, and could never be compensated with equity or acquire wealth for their services. Yet those people built the archetype of the present electronic system in ninety days for less than $30,000. And when it came time to do so, they selected the VISA name and completed the largest global trademark conversion in commercial history in a third the time anticipated.

Time and time again, they demonstrated a simple truth we have somehow lost sight of in our mechanistic, Industrial Age, command-and-control organizations: *The truth is, that given the right chaordic circumstances, from no more than dreams, determination, and the liberty to try, quite ordinary people consistently do extraordinary things.*

> **MiniMaxims**
>
> *Given the right circumstances, from no more than dreams, determination, and the liberty to try, quite ordinary people consistently do extraordinary things.*

Chaordic concepts of organization are immensely more powerful than even the success of VISA might suggest. There were many weaknesses in the VISA version of the concepts, as well as external conditions it could not overcome. Commercial law did not anticipate, thus could not prevent, but did not fit the concepts. Like a dead tree lying on a sapling, the law continually warped and constricted the natural evolution of the concepts in ways beyond correction. Today, the law is beginning to understand and accept such concepts.

Although the core and concept of VISA were chaordic, most members remained mechanistic and linear. They did not fully understand and exploit the concept. Many continually tried to reimpose on it old structure and management practices with which they were comfortable. As its growth exploded, managers brought into the organization did not properly understand and practice the beliefs and concepts on which it was based. Consciously and unconsciously they brought their old mental baggage and installed it in the new organization. I did not realize the immense cultural change required of each person if they were to fully understand, develop, and implement the concept. Today, such cultural change is emerging in many places.

I could think of no way to fully realize the concept by including merchants and cardholders as owner-members. The slightest hint in that direction raised a storm of opposition. We should have included them. Perhaps, with more time, tenacity, and ingenuity we could have. But that can never be known.

I had neither the experience nor strength of character to hold my convictions inviolable or develop them fully. I never ceased to try but failed to keep properly at bay the Four Beasts that inevitably devour their keeper: Ego, Envy, Avarice, and Ambition. Today, as I continue to struggle with those same

> **MiniMaxims**
>
> *Beware the Four Beasts that inevitably devour their keeper: Ego, Envy, Avarice, and Ambition.*

beasts, hundreds of thousands, perhaps millions of others have done and will do better.

Had such constraints not existed, it is impossible to know what the VISA community might have become. Within the next decade, such constraints will be greatly diminished, and the opportunity for chaordic organization will expand enormously.

ℒ♥

The end of the beginning was drawing to a close. The first annual meeting of members of National BankAmericard Incorporated was at an end. All business on the agenda had been covered. Sweating and relieved to have survived the ordeal, I asked the rhetorical question, "Is there any other business to come before the meeting?" Sam Stewart rose to his feet, stern and unsmiling. His booming voice filled the auditorium.

"Yes, there is. I have some unfinished business."

"Oh my God, what now?" I thought, as Sam faced the audience and began.

"When the Bank of America agreed to support the attempt to form NBI, we were convinced a quarter of the licensees might drop out. When Dee insisted we must perfect the new organization and convert the entire system in ninety days, I told him there was absolutely no way it could be done." He paused, and with great emphasis boomed, "I just want you to know I haven't changed my mind one bit!" The room dissolved in laughter. The meeting ended. The newly elected board met, elected Sam chairman, and appointed me president and chief executive officer.

Thus began what I expected would be a three-year commitment before I could regain a measure of freedom and return to a more private life. Had I an inkling those three years would become fourteen I would have walked away on the spot.

CHAPTER TWELVE

Quite Ordinary People

*If you have built castles in the air your work need
not be lost: that is where they should be. Now put
the foundation under them.*
— HENRY DAVID THOREAU

*This spreading radiance of a True Human Being
has great importance.
Look carefully around you and recognize the lumi-
nosity of souls.
Sit beside those who draw you to that.*
— JALAL UDDIN RUMI

The evening before the first annual meeting of members,
lawyers from the Bank of America asked for a meeting, saying they had something they wished to discuss that must be held
in complete confidence until it could be made public. I was
speechless at what they had to say. The bank had been in secret
discussions with American Express for months, developing a
plan for the two companies to jointly create, own, and control a
credit card authorization system. The plan would be announced
within days. At the time, American Express was, by a huge margin, the largest multipurpose credit card issuer in the world.
Bank of America was, by a similar margin, the largest bank credit
card issuer. Other credit card issuers would be invited to

become participants in the new system, each paying a substantial sum at the time of commitment, which would provide most of the capital for development of the authorization system.

It was contrary to the spirit of the effort to form NBI and could materially affect its success. The joint venture, from my perspective, was nothing but an attempt by the two credit card giants to make tenant farmers of the remainder of the industry. In fairness, their effort may have been under way before it was certain NBI could be brought into being. It may also have been initiated by a department of the bank not familiar with the organizational effort. I could say nothing without breaching their confidence.

I felt completely betrayed. Throughout the effort to form NBI, all participants, including those from Bank of America, had agreed one of the principal reasons for its formation was to create an effective means of authorizing credit card transactions. There was nothing to do but swallow my feelings and move ahead, trusting that the new NBI concept was weak, indeed, if it could not survive storms of opposition.

The announcement was made with great fanfare. The two organizations swept the country with salesmen. They found no more than a handful of takers. Nearly all NBI members found the new concept of organization compelling enough to wait to see what it could achieve. Within months, the joint venture died a quiet death—well, almost.

During the years that NBI had been in process of formation, the American Bankers' Association had organized an effort to examine growing problems of the paper check-clearing system. A nationwide Money and Payment System (MAPS) committee of bank executives had been formed, along with a plethora of subcommittees. Its charge was to examine in depth the problems of the check-clearing system, which was owned and operated by the Federal Reserve banks. By law, only commercial banks had access to the clearing system. Prevailing wisdom at the time was that the check-clearing system must be converted from paper to electronics. However, competitive electronic authorization and check-clearing systems for financial transactions were not considered economically feasible. It was common belief that any such system should be a natural monopoly of the Federal Reserve system.

The MAPS committee was in the final phases of its work when NBI came into being. I was asked to participate. On occasion, I shared my conviction that the real message of electronic technology was not gadgets, but radical social and institutional change. Some listened politely, but few were interested. The MAPS committee concluded that the Federal Reserve paper check-clearing system was likely to collapse within ten years if it were not fully converted to electronics. That should be done by the Federal Reserve system. Preaching institutional change in this venue was like preaching Protestant theology in a medieval Catholic church. The committee report, which predicted disaster ahead if "something" was not done, was widely distributed, discussed, filed, and forgotten.

In the process, the Bank of America–American Express joint venture was resurrected in a more ominous form. A committee was formed composed of representatives from the two companies, other large bank card issuers, travel and entertainment card issuers, and major retail merchants. NBI and Interbank were invited to participate. The intent was to investigate the possibility of forming a single electronic authorization system as a joint venture of all credit card issuers.

Neither the institutional nor technical thinking made sense. It had always seemed to me that one of the principal tricks of evolution was to preserve the substance of the past by clothing it in the forms of the future. Creating a single, monopolistic electronic payment system seemed precisely the opposite. It was an attempt to warp the substance of the future in order to perpetuate past forms. It was another attempt to centralize power and control. It was contrary to all my beliefs about the nature of organizations and the possibilities inherent in electronic communications. Exchanging authorization information and monetary value in the form of electronic particles not only might become, but *ought to be* a highly decentralized, competitive business. Trying to design and impose a single, monolithic system on such an essential flow of information seemed absurd.

> **MiniMaxims**
>
> *Substance is enduring, form ephemeral. Preserve substance; modify form; know the difference.*

Old Monkey Mind and I had spent countless hours trying to understand information and its relevance to organizations, asking our endless questions. What is the significance of the "in form" part of the word *information?* What is the nature of that which is received from external sources and "forms us" within? What is the nature of that which forms within us which we then feel compelled to transmit, and how does it form others when it is received? What allows formation of information, permits it to endure unaltered, yet be available at any time for transformation in infinite ways? Why and from where came the universal, perpetual urge to receive and transmit in*form*ation—the incessant desire to communicate? Is it an urge at all, or is it an unavoidable necessity—an integral component essential to life? Indeed, is it the essence of life itself? Or is it a principle beyond life itself? Could it be the *fundamental, formative essence* that gives shape and distinction to all things—part of an inseparably whole universe?

It helps to think what information is not. Certainly, it is not just another "thing"; one more finite, physical entity. Certainly, information is far more than digits and data. They may be components of it—the shape it sometimes takes. They may be of it, but they are not it. In a rare insight, Gregory Bateson proposed that "information is a difference that makes a difference." If something is received that cannot be differentiated or, if once differentiated, makes no difference, he asserts it is just noise.

Bateson's perspective is fascinating but limited, for it implies only mind-to-mind communication. If you are hiking alone in the wilderness and a rock comes bounding down the mountain, breaking your leg, that is certainly a difference that makes an enormous difference. The same can be said of running barefoot through the house and breaking a toe on a chair leg. Is that information? Both are certainly a difference that makes a difference. Both certainly convey meaning. If your broken leg and crushed toe are a difference that makes a difference, then, by Bateson's definition, condensed, inanimate matter and gravitational force clearly have the ability to communicate. Locked in our box of self-awareness, we think of it as one-way communication—rock to leg, or chair leg to toe, but we truly have no way of knowing what information, if any, flows the opposite way.

Unlike finite physical resources, information multiplies by transfer and is not depleted by use. Information transferred is not lost to the source, yet is a gain to the recipient. Information can be utilized by everyone without loss to anyone. As far as we know, the supply of information is infinite; therefore, it does not obey any of our concepts or laws of scarcity. It obeys only concepts and principles of infinite abundance, infinite utilization, infinite recombination. We have only dim perceptions of what those principles might be, or if they exist at all.

Projecting onto information our old notions of property, thus turning it into a method by which one person can extract wealth from another, neither reveals nor changes the extraordinary nature of information. It reveals only the limited nature of man and his reluctance to change internal models of reality or external behavior.

Information is a miser of energy. It can endlessly replicate, move ubiquitously at the speed of light, and massively condense in minute space, all at minuscule expense of energy, in other words, cost. In countless ways, it is becoming a replacement for our present enormously wasteful use of matter. To the extent that we increase the value of the mental content of the composition of goods and services, we can reduce the value of the physical content. We can make them lighter, more durable, more recyclable, more versatile, and more transportable.

Information breeds. When one bit of information is combined with another, the result is new information. Information is boundaryless. It cannot be contained. No matter what constraints we try to put on information, it will become the slave and property of no one. Efforts to make information conform to archaic notions of scarcity, ownership, and finite physical quantity—concepts that grew out of the agricultural and industrialized age—merely lock humankind into old, mental boxes of constraint and exploitation.

Information is ethically neutral. Its immense power is as applicable to destructive, inequitable, violent ends as it is to constructive, equitable, peaceful ends. The history of modern science has been an effort to divorce the ethical dimensions of life from the physical; to divorce subjective values from objective observations; to divorce spirituality from rationality. The effect has been deification of the rational, physical, objective perspective as ultimate truth, and demonization of the subjective, ethical, and spiritual perspective as superstition, delusion, and ignorance.

Products, services, and organizations in which the value of the mental content begins to dwarf the value of the physical content require wise people of deep understanding. To endlessly add to the quantity of mechanistic information, knowledge, and technology without similar evolution of values and wisdom is not only foolish, it is dangerous. To massively develop means and act in accordance with what those means permit without careful consideration of ends in the context of values is equally idiotic.

Thinking about a society based on information and one based on physicality requires radically different perspective and consciousness. However, we prefer too often to ignore the fundamental differences and carry over into the Chaordic Age of managing information, ideas and values, concepts, and assumptions that proved useful in the mechanized, Industrial Age of machine crafting, the age of managing things; concepts such as ownership, finite supply, obsolescence, loss by conveyance, containment, scarcity, separability, quantifiable measurement, statistical economics, mathematical monetarism, hierarchal structuralism, and command-and-control management.

The birth of the Chaordic Age calls into question virtually every concept of societal organization, management, and conduct on which we have come to rely. Clinging too rigorously to old concepts, dismissing new concepts too lightly, protecting old forms that resulted from those concepts too fiercely, imposing those forms on a changing society too resolutely, are a certain path to failure. As Sir Francis Bacon put it precisely centuries ago, in admonishing those who opposed the mechanistic concepts of Newton and Descartes: "They that reverence too much the old times are but a scorn to the new."

The new concepts Bacon so ably defended with that assertion are excruciatingly old today. They are concepts that we now reverence too much.

We were not going to revere too much the old times at NBI. We would pay them due respect and try to preserve their substance, but we would challenge their forms at every opportunity.

We began quietly to collect data and explore the feasibility of building our own proprietary electronic system. If we could build an efficient, cost-effective, proprietary system, it would shatter conventional wisdom and the natural oligopoly argument forever. We had little experience building such systems. We had few employees with the requisite skills.

Years of iconoclastic management—of watching ordinary people consistently do extraordinary things when their spirit was challenged and their ingenuity released—had given me confidence in the infinite capacity of every individual. One need not know and be able to prove in advance what could be accomplished. One need not have a precise plan about how to get there. In a complex, rapidly changing world, a clear sense of direction, a compelling purpose, and powerful beliefs about conduct in pursuit of it, seemed to me infinitely more sensible and robust than mechanical plans, detailed objectives, and predetermined outcomes. Yet my confidence was scarred by years of conflict and rejection.

> **MiniMaxims**
>
> *A clear sense of direction and compelling principles about conduct in pursuit of it are far more effective than long-term plans and detailed objectives.*

The unanswered questions were legion. What degree of innovation could members and the board accept? How much risk and uncertainty could such a new organization tolerate? Could extraordinary results be delivered by ordinary people on a large scale? Could an innovative, unorthodox organization survive and prosper embodied in an extremely conservative industry? Much of what we ought to do seemed impossible. Yet I had a strong belief that what is possible cannot be determined by opinions, but only by attempt. And we were determined to make the attempt.

The NBI board was composed of senior bank officers, many of whom had participated in the miracle of the formation of NBI and its early accomplishments. Pleased with the swift success of the organization and the benefits it had brought to their troubled card programs, they had become less apprehensive about iconoclastic thinking.

The board meeting at which the decision was made was unforgettable. We proposed that NBI break with the industry, withdraw from the joint effort, and announce intent to build a proprietary, competitive system for electronic authorization of sales and clearance of transactions and payments. There followed intense discussion among twenty-two powerful directors with diverse opinions strongly held. It was a far more important decision than any we had yet made. Failure meant risking the reputation of the new company, its ability to attract new members, its opportunity to undertake major ventures, and its financial stability. Near the end, when there was little left to say, one of the more dubious directors asked bluntly, "Precisely how will you proceed, and what if you fail?"

There was only one honest answer. "We have no precise plan, only a clear sense of direction. If we make an all-out attempt and fail, that will teach us what to do next. However, failure is not really an option. If you approve the attempt, we will get it done, whatever that requires."

There was a momentary silence as he pondered my answer, heaved a sigh, and said, "I move that we approve the effort. How many of you want to join me and vote for this shot in the dark?"

They did, every last one of them, bless their souls. The next day we shocked the industry with an announcement that NBI was withdrawing from the industrywide effort and would build its own competitive, proprietary system. We were off the high dive. There was no way back. The only question was how we would hit the water.

It was a horrendous belly flop. Fail is exactly what we did. With very little experience among the staff, we had agreed it would be prudent to hire a systems development expert from outside the company. Within days, our expert persuaded us to follow tradition, write a request for proposal, and put it out to bid with leading development companies. It seemed sensible enough. As the weeks went by, I became a little nervous. The "expert" leading the effort continually assured me all was well, but seemed reluctant to share much information, claiming he wanted to be certain of his facts before making a final recommendation. Well, trust is not negotiable. One either trusts or one does not, and I prefer trust.

Eventually, the day came. The best bid from a responsible vendor was several times the anticipated amount approved by the board. The system would take twice as long as expected to build. No vendor was willing to warrant the performance of the system that might result. It was no problem in the mind of the expert or the leading vendors. We should go back to the board and ask for more money and time. It was customary in the computer industry. Well, it was not going to become a custom at NBI. Some lessons must be learned over and over again before they sink to the bone. Emerson said it best. "Trust thyself. Every heart vibrates to that iron string."

The people involved in the effort were brought together, everyone, inside and outside the company, at every level. There was little that needed to be said. "We're told the system can't be built within the time and with the money we expected, some of which we have already wasted. If it can, it's clearly up to us. There is no answer 'out there.' If there is an answer, it's in here, in us. We can go back to the board for more money and time, or we can accept that there is more intelligence, ability, and ingenuity in this room than the job requires. If there are enough of us with sufficient desire and trust in one another, we can meet tomorrow, close the door, and not come out until we have decided how to meet our commitment within the time and with the money remaining."

Intense, innovative discussion erupted. There were more than enough excited, committed people, but the "expert" was not among them. Two or three exceptional people from vendors leaped at the challenge and joined the company. We shut ourselves in a room and didn't come out until we had an approach to which we were totally committed. We called it Bank Authorization System Experimental (BASE 1).

The following months were among the most exciting in the history of the company. We were determined the needs of our members and cardholders would be served, not the needs of technology or vendors. That required internal responsibility. We decided to become our own prime contractor, farming out selected tasks to a variety of software developers, then coordinating and implementing results. Conventional wisdom held it to be one of the worst possible ways to build computerized communications systems.

We rented cheap space in a suburban building and dispensed with leasehold improvements in favor of medical curtains on rolling frames for the limited spacial separation required. IBM, then the infallible behemoth of the computer industry, was the supplier of computers to 80 percent of our members. Early in the process, as we had prepared the proposal to the board, IBM had promised a quarter million dollars of support in connecting members to the system. Now they waffled, saying only that they would see what they could do when the time arrived. We threw them out, telling them not a single piece of IBM equipment would come through our doors in the future, not even a typewriter. We selected a relatively new, then innovative company, Digital Equipment Corp., which we believed would be more responsive to the spirit of our people, to provide our computers.

Swiftly, self-organization emerged. An entire wall became a pinboard with every remaining day calendared across the top. Someone grabbed an unwashed coffee cup and suspended it on a long piece of string pinned to the current date. Every element of work to be done was listed on scraps of paper with the required completion date and name of the person who had accepted the work. Anyone could revise the elements, adding tasks or revising dates, providing they coordinated with others affected. Everyone, at any time, could see the picture emerge and evolve. They could see how the whole depended on their work, and how their work was connected to every other part of the effort. Groups constantly assembled in front of the board as need and inclination arose, discussing and deciding in continuous flow; then dissolving as needs were met. As each task was completed, its scrap of paper would be removed. Each day, the cup and string moved inexorably ahead.

Every day, every scrap of paper that fell behind the grimy string would find an eager group of volunteers to undertake the work required to remove it. To be able to get one's own work done and help another became a sought-after privilege. Nor did anyone feel beggared by accepting help. Such Herculean effort meant that at any time, anyone's task could fall behind and emerge on the wrong side of the string.

Leaders spontaneously emerged and reemerged, none in control, but all in order. Ingenuity exploded. Individuality and diversity flourished. People astonished themselves at what they could accomplish and were amazed at the suppressed talents that emerged in others.

Position became meaningless. Power over others became meaningless. Time became meaningless. Excitement about doing the impossible increased, and a community based on purpose, principle, and people arose. Individuality, self-worth, ingenuity, and creativity flourished; and as they did, so did the sense of belonging to something larger than self, something beyond immediate gain and monetary gratification.

No one ever forgot the joy of bringing to work the wholeness of mind, body, and spirit; discovering in the process that such wholeness is impossible without inseparable connection with others in the larger purpose of community effort. Money was a small part of what happened. The effort was fueled by a spontaneous expansion of the nonmonetary exchange of value—things done for one another without measurement or prescribed return—the heart and soul of all community. People discovered that any receiving worthy of the name is an inexorable product of giving. They gave of themselves without expectation and received in ways beyond calculation. A few who could not adjust to the diversity, complexity, and uncertainty wandered away. Dozens volunteered to take their place. No one articulated what was happening. No one recorded it. No one measured it. But everyone felt it, understood it, and loved it.

No one replaced the dirty string and no one washed the cup. "The Dirty Coffee Cup System" became legendary—a metaphor for the company for years to come. The BASE-1 system came up on time, under budget, and exceeded all operating objectives. Out of initial failure grew a magnificent success. It forced the industry to abandon notions of natural monopoly, to innovate and create other systems. It was a foundation of commitment and practice from which the global VISA communication system evolved.

Long before, during, and after the BASE-1 year, Old Monkey and I continued to explore the significance of information in the form of arranged particles of energy, trying to get at the essence of its ultimate meaning. By then, peeling such a mental onion by asking hundreds of layered questions was not only habit, it was recreation. In time, a new perception gradually emerged, based upon trying to understand the history and effect of a single, fascinating capacity: *the Capacity to Receive, Utilize, Store, Transform, and Transmit Information (CRUSTTI)*. Not information from the common misperception of alphanumeric data, but from Gregory Bateson's perspective that "information is a difference that makes a difference." If something perceived cannot be distinguished from its surroundings in a relevant way, it's just noise. If it can be differentiated and truly makes a difference, then it becomes in-*form*-ation. It is capable of in-forming us, forming us within, and allowing us to formulate differences that can make a difference to others.

In a very real sense, one can think of new information as boundary acid. It dissolves old boundaries and creates the conditions for new patterns of relationships to emerge. To understand CRUSTTI, it is essential to begin at the beginning.

If one is to examine early examples of single-celled life, it is apparent they possess the capacity to receive, store, utilize, transform, and transmit information. In fact, this capacity precedes even such simple life forms, for it is the very essence of DNA. It even precedes DNA, for when physicists attempt to examine the smallest known particles, the particles change their behavior. And when they do, the physicists change their behavior in response. Particle and physicist find themselves in a fascinating, quantum, cosmic dance. Clearly each is perceiving a "difference that makes a difference." They are exchanging information.

In ways we don't begin to understand, information escapes particles, transcends them, and binds them together into more complex systems in which all particles constantly exchange information. It seems a principle of evolution, perhaps *the fundamental principle*, that the greater the capacity to receive, store, utilize, transform, and transmit information, the more diverse and complex the entity. It holds true from neutrino, to nucleus, to atom, to amino acids, to proteins, to molecules, to cells, to organs, to organisms. From bacteria, to bees, to bats, to birds, to buffalo, right on through to baseball players.

> **MiniMaxims**
>
> *The greater the capacity to receive, store, utilize, transform, and transmit information, the more diverse and complex the entity.*

CRUSTTI didn't stop there. In time, information transcended the boundaries of organisms and led to communication between them. Whether the dance of the bees, the pheromone of ants, the sonar of bats, the song of birds, or the language of people, once that capacity transcended organisms, there was immediate evolution of complex *communities* of organisms—hives, flocks, packs, colonies, herds, and tribes.

Let's follow that capacity with respect to our species. Throughout history, many of our finest minds have argued that the two characteristics that most distinguish the human species are memory and language. Memory, but the ability to store and recall images. Language, but the means to share those images. Over the centuries, we have ascended a ladder of diversity and complexity. With language, information escaped the boundaries of a single mind and experience became shared. Immediately, there was a corresponding leap in societal diversity and complexity. With written language came expansion to that which could be manually recorded and personally transported. Another leap in capacity, another leap in societal diversity and complexity.

Leap followed leap, each exponentially greater and more frequent. With mathematics came expansion to that which could be commonly understood by means of a global language. With the printing press came expansion to that which could be mechanically recorded and transported. A library, after all, is nothing more than the collective memory of the species. With the telegraph came electronic alphanumeric capacity. With the telephone came phonic capacity. With television came visual capacity, followed by multimedia capacity. Leap followed leap, each exponentially greater and more frequent. Each was immediately followed by an even greater leap in societal diversity and complexity.

One could paraphrase Einstein's most famous equation and say that where I equals the capacity to receive, store, utilize, transform, and transmit information, D equals societal diversity, and C equals societal complexity, the equation is:

$$I = DC^2$$

The capacity to receive, store, utilize, transform, and transmit information equals societal diversity times societal complexity squared.

Then it happened! Suddenly, with the revolution in microelectronic technology, in less than twenty short years, we have on the order of a thousand times better algorithms, five hundred thousand times more computing capacity per individual, and five hundred million times more mobility of information. All known and recorded information, the entire collective memory of the species, will soon be no more than a few keystokes away. Software to navigate that immensity of information is rapidly emerging. We don't begin to understand the significance of all this, let alone the societal change unleashed, or the institutional change it demands.

But that is nothing compared to what lies ahead. Around the corner are other revolutions of enormously greater significance, such as nano- and biotechnology. Simply stated, nanotechnology is the engineering of self-replicating assemblers and computers so tiny they can manipulate atoms, the basic building blocks of nature, as though they were bricks. The necessary science has already been discovered. What remains to be done is the engineering of tools at the atomic scale. In his book *Engines of Creation*, K. Eric Drexler, a pioneer in the field, writes: "When biochemists need complex molecular machines, they have to borrow them from cells . . . advanced molecular technology will eventually let them build nanocircuits and nanomachines as easily as engineers now build microcircuits or washing machines."

In answer to the question, "What could we build with these atom-stacking mechanisms?" Marvin Minsky, professor of science at MIT, writes: "We could manufacture assembly machines much smaller even than living cells . . . make materials stronger and lighter than any available today, hence, better spacecraft, hence, tiny devices that can travel along capillaries to enter and repair living cells."

The possibilities are profound. Efficient solar collectors durable enough to repave highways and parking lots or to surface buildings. The ability to create large structures on site swiftly at little cost from material as common as dirt and air by arranging atoms into a desired object. Even more important, the deconstruction into atoms of garbage, industrial waste, and atmospheric pollutants, thus turning them into abundant, cheap, raw material.

There is nothing new in all this. It is the fundamental technique that nature has used to create everything since the beginning of time, whether trees, monkeys to climb in them, or people who cut them down. Information in the form of DNA is endlessly replicated at no cost and distributed in seeds. A process of replication driven by the power of the sun begins. Molecules and cells assemble on the spot into known patterns from atoms of surrounding air, soil, and water. In the case of animals, it happens not only on the spot, but on the move. When such creations are no longer viable, nature breaks them down into atoms once again for re-creation into something new and useful—a never-ending, effective, nonpolluting chain of events of ever-evolving diversity and complexity. No factories, no waste, no despoiled resources, no pollution, no mechanistic organization, and no command and control. Nature does it all with chaordic organization—a complex, diverse flow of information that chaordically mobilizes physical materials into both animate and inanimate forms.

How soon and how likely are such things? One need only remember that a few decades ago the atomic bomb was scarcely a theory, travel to the moon a fantasy, television the dream of a few odd engineers, a plastic card for the global exchange of value unthinkable, and genetic engineering securely locked up in the secrets of DNA. Yet none had a better theoretical or scientific foundation then than do nanotechnology or biotechnology today, and none were being driven by the incredible forces of change now common throughout the world. As microtechnology builds down and nanotechnology and molecular biology build up, they will come together. Within two or three decades, for better or worse, we will be constructing products and services from the atom up and the capacity to receive, store, utilize, transform, and transmit information will be at the heart of it. The message is simple.

Fasten your seat belts, the turbulence has scarcely begun. Unless evolution has radically changed its ways, we are facing an explosion of societal diversity and complexity hundreds of times greater than we now experience or can yet imagine. If we think to perpetuate the old ways, we should try to recall the last time evolution rang our number and asked consent.

And we're going to manage such a society with the same old, seventeenth-century mechanistic concepts of organization and management? Not the chance of a snowball in that proverbial hot place. Within a few decades, we will look on our present methods of manufacturing, transportation, finance, and organization as quaint relics of an archaic Industrial Age.

In the words of T. S. Elliot, we will "come full circle to the place from which we set out and see it for the first time."

CHAPTER THIRTEEN

The Victim of Success

*There is nothing more difficult to take in hand,
more perilous to conduct or more uncertain in its
success, than to take the lead in the introduction
of a new order of things.*
— NICCOLÒ DI BERNARDO MACHIAVELLI

*The moving finger writes; and having writ
Moves on; nor all your piety and wit
Shall lure it back to cancel half a line,
Nor all your tears wash out a word of it.*
— OMAR KHAYYAM

Judged by orthodox methods of objective measurement—
growth, size, profit, market share, and volume—VISA has
been a phenomenal success. It would be a lie to deny a strong
sense of privilege and substantial pride in presiding at its birth
and guiding it to maturity.

But there are other methods of evaluation that transcend
measurement and objectivity. By the standards of what VISA
might have become, and what it ought to be, it would be a lie to
deny a strong sense of failure. Strangely, it is from some of the
things that appeared to be a part of VISA's success that the
strongest sense of failure has emerged. The issue of duality was
the greatest example. On no issue were we more right. On none
did we fail more ignominiously. On none did our failure have a

greater effect on the future of payment systems, or a greater outward appearance of success.

Having come from a relatively poor family, I knew that the economic power of ordinary people arises from freedom of choice and sufficient resources to pursue them. It led me to strong belief that they would be best served by many competing card systems and many competing card issuers within each system. I was deeply convinced that there could and should be many card systems within the consumer banking industry, and that there was ample opportunity for others to emerge among retail, travel, communications, and other industries.

I was equally convinced that complete freedom of banks to become owner-members of both Mastercharge and BankAmericard would inevitably lead to all banks becoming owner-members of the two systems, interlocking them, foreclosing the emergence of new systems, and severely limiting consumer choice.

There were compelling arguments on both sides of the issue. Banks wishing to become owner-members of the two systems argued that an NBI prohibition of dual owner-membership would infringe on their freedom to offer any products they wished to consumers and merchants, thus restraining bank-to-bank competition. No one denied that prohibition of duality would place some constraint on bank behavior. But was that a necessary restraint in order to preserve and foster even greater competition? I, along with many others, thought that it was.

Banks would not band together, incur the expense, and take the risk of forming a new system if their competitors were free to join and reap the benefits the moment the new system became effective. And what group of institutions in any other industry would take such a pointless risk? I was equally convinced that interlocking ownership of Mastercharge and

BankAmericard would inevitably result in diminishment of competitive vigor between the two, eventual dominance of one or the other, and possible merger of the two, in substance if not in fact.

Was prohibiting institutions from becoming owner-members in competing systems an essential restraint to foster the emergence of many systems and ensure maximum competition between them, as well as between banks? I thought that it was. Would unlimited dual owner-membership in competing systems allow rapidly consolidating giant banks to dominate all systems? I thought that it might. Would unlimited duality lead owner-members to close ownership to new participants, thus restricting system deliberations, decisions, and power to a self-selected group? I thought that it could.

At its inception, NBI inherited a two-tiered system created by the Bank of America licensing program. Banks were divided into two classes, A and B. The A class was composed of two hundred card-issuing, merchant-servicing banks that became full owner-members of NBI. The remainder were class B members—participants sponsored by A members. They enrolled merchants, bought merchant transactions, entered them into the system, and assisted A members in developing cardholders. Naturally, the B class wanted to be dual in order to offer merchants a single point of deposit for card transactions from both systems. This, in turn, placed pressure on A members to also become dual in order to offer merchants the same services. A few had already done so before NBI was formed. NBI placed a moratorium on duality until the board could thoroughly look into the matter and try to determine what was likely to produce maximum competition.

The NBI board was divided. So was management. If we decided on a complete prohibition and no new systems developed, evidence might someday emerge that competition had suffered. The possibility of class-action lawsuits alleging violation of antitrust laws with treble damage liabilities could not be discounted. If we took no action at all, the same anticompetitive consequences might emerge, but the chance of damages would be minimal, for it would be the acts of countless banks that led to the eventual result, not the act of the NBI board. If the Department of Justice took no action to prevent duality, the NBI board could hardly be blamed for not acting to do so.

There were signs that the same division of opinion existed within the Department of Justice. At the time, the antitrust division was headed by a knowledgeable lawyer, Donald Baker, who had a good grasp of the issues and deep interest in them. It was without question the most complex, difficult issue we faced and the subject of intense investigation and debate. The system was growing rapidly. Pressures were mounting and a decision could not be delayed.

In the midst of our efforts to find our way through the legal, operating, and competitive complexities of dual ownership, one of our smaller class A members, the Worthen Bank of Little Rock, Arkansas, which had also become a member of Mastercharge, threatened to sue NBI if it adopted a proposed bylaw prohibiting duality. I flew to Little Rock to meet with the president and other senior officers of the Worthen Bank in an effort to persuade them that the issue was larger than a single bank and obtain their support. I was greeted with the graciousness, charm, and hospitality for which the South is justly famous, and discovered the steely, stubborn determination so often attributed to it. There was conviction on both sides. We could not agree.

Near the end of 1971, the VISA board adopted a bylaw prohibiting duality in competing systems by class A members, but allowing class B members to continue to accept both BankAmericard and Mastercharge sales drafts from merchants. The Worthen Bank promptly filed a lawsuit alleging violation of the antitrust laws and asking for an injunction to prevent enforcement of the bylaw. We were served with the usual interrogatories, part of pretrial discovery allowed by law. The plaintiff demanded we produce copies of every possible record which could have any bearing on the issues at hand and make available for extensive depositions all people who might have had anything to do with the decision.

We were a small staff with limited resources in the midst of incredible industry problems and insatiable demands on our time. Since the beginning of the company, I had insisted that the nature of the company and its beliefs required that we do nothing we would be reluctant to see on the front page of any newspaper. The need to deserve the respect and trust of all participants demanded no less.

The burden of searching our files was punitive for such a small staff. We swiftly decided on a course of action without precedent. We filed a petition with the court stating we had neither time nor resources to produce the requested documents, offering instead to provide office space, copy facilities, and other amenities to the plaintiff's lawyers. *All records* of the corporation and *all employees* would be available for examination by them. For weeks on end and lawyers on end—and I mean lawyers literally on end—they bent over file drawers, combing our records in vain for evidence of a conspiracy to violate the antitrust laws.

Depositions were long and wearing. To a sheep never before involved in a lawsuit, the plaintiff's lawyers seemed unduly antagonistic, sarcastic, abusive, and not above lawyerly tactics to try to induce testimony that might appear contradictory. In the midst of such pressure came another of those dark periods of the soul, which are so much a part of attempting anything new.

In the mail delivered to our home one morning was an envelope containing a sheet of paper on which an anonymous message was pasted composed of words, letters, and partial sentences cut from newspapers and magazines. It was extremely abusive and warned of dire things to come. It appeared to be from a deeply disturbed person.

The former FBI agent who headed our security and fraud department agreed to look into the matter and advised me to try to put it from mind. That became impossible when I entered my office two weeks later to discover a huge cross slashed on the back of my chair. Nothing appeared missing, and no message was left. Questions flooded my mind. Had the cross been there some time unnoticed? Not likely, or at least, not for more than a few days. Were the two incidents connected, or were they pure coincidence? One would be foolish to assume the latter. If connected, it meant this was not the act of some unknown crank, but the deliberate act of someone who not only knew me, but had access to my office. Meanwhile, the incredible demands of the burgeoning system, disruption of our offices by plaintiff's lawyers, and the pressure of personal depositions ground on.

Within the week, concern became deep distress. A package arrived at my home. Carefully prepared to conceal its origins, it contained an unusual, out-of-print, small volume of *Gracian's Maxims,* unmistakably stolen from my library. Driven through the book from cover to cover was a huge screw. Another cut-and-paste message warned of catastrophe ahead. It was not uncommon to move my books between home and office libraries. The questions became frantic and incessant. Had the book been stolen from my home or from my office? Did the person responsible have access to one or both? Was it someone intending only to terrify, or someone with serious intent to harm? Why was this happening now? Every day, I had to rise and deal with countless problems, for the business went on and responsibilities could not be shoved aside. I began to slide into depression, the dark, dismal swamp that robs one of ability to think or function normally.

We consulted local police, the FBI, and other law enforcement agencies. They would do nothing without specific death or bomb threats. Ferol and I discussed the matter and could think of nothing to be done. She is much braver than I— more inclined to deal with problems if they occur, rather than invite them by excess

> **MiniMaxims**
>
> *Fear is an internal narcotic that paralyzes mind, body, and spirit. The power of things we fear lies solely in our opinion of them.*

worry. Yet, she was concerned that I might not be able to bear up under the strain. It was not my courage which brought us through, it was hers. She reminded me of all the difficulties in our past, and the comfort we had taken in the parental homily, "This, too, shall pass." She insisted we must go about our affairs in accordance with our beliefs, taking what precautions we could, but not allowing circumstances to dictate our lives, trusting in The Essence That Is to set things right.

Throughout the affair, nothing was said to anyone but NBI security people, counsel, and law enforcement officials. We did not want to disturb others, cause rumors to emerge, or give any indication to the person responsible that their efforts had an effect. Twenty years making and collecting loans had taught me that anger, blame, condemnation, and all other negative emotions are fueled by like response. They are least able to be sustained when met with calm indifference. It has always been my natural inclination to quietly suffer through adversity while attempting to find a constructive solution. It was slim comfort now.

During dark times, long walks in the woods have always sustained me. I broke the law to do it. The closest open space was the San Francisco watershed—miles of forested hills bordering Crystal Springs Reservoir near where we lived. It was posted everywhere with No Trespassing signs. I would walk along the bordering road until there was no sign visible in either direction, pretend they did not exist, excuse myself on the basis of dire need, slip through the fence, and lose myself deep in the woods. There, I would climb wooded hills for hours, licking my wounds in the hope a solution would appear. A sense that in the great picture of things my trials and tribulations were of no consequence would slowly seep into my bones and allow me to face the next week.

When and how the answer appeared I did not know then and do not know now. Somewhere, somehow, at a level beyond conscious thought, I knew who had done the deed, and why. I knew that it was something they had never done before. I knew they were capable of worse, but also capable of reversing course and taking their dirty little secret quietly to the grave. How to give them that opportunity was the question. If the threats continued, we would have no alternative but to identify beyond question those involved and prosecute them, which we preferred not to do, hoping the situation would end without damage to anyone. That message was selectively conveyed to others in ways we were confident would get back to the source of the problem. The threats and intrusions vanished as mysteriously as they appeared. Whether the threats were indirectly connected with the lawsuit can never be known. It was many months before the depression gradually faded, and years before the memory became less painful.

Turmoil, stress, and depression notwithstanding, Old Monkey Mind and I could not free ourselves of obsession with information and its effect on institutions. We began to puzzle over words and concepts thrown about interchangeably with little thought of their relationship or meaning when the subjects of cognition and learning arise: knowledge, data, wisdom, information, understanding. We began to examine the essential nature and distinguishing characteristics of each and relate them in order of quantity and quality, knowing that such distinction, while useful, can never extinguish the essential wholeness of that which they compose. All such words are directly involved with *the capacity to receive, utilize, store, transform, and transmit information.*

Noise, in its broadest sense, is any undifferentiated thing which assaults the senses. It is pervasive and ubiquitous, whether auditory, visual, or textural. The supply of noise is infinite. Noise becomes data when it transcends the purely sensual and has cognitive pattern; when it can be discerned and differentiated by the mind. Data, in turn, becomes information when it is assembled into a coherent whole which can be related to other information in a way that adds meaning. (Bateson's "difference that makes a difference.") Information becomes knowledge when it is integrated with other information in a form useful for deciding, acting, or composing new knowledge. Knowledge becomes understanding when related to other knowledge in a manner useful in conceiving, anticipating, evaluating, and judging. Understanding becomes wisdom when informed by purpose, ethics, principle, memory of the past, and projection into the future.

The fundamental characteristics of the opposite ends of this spectrum are very different. Data, on one end of the spectrum, is separable, objective, linear, mechanistic, and abundant. Wisdom, on the other end of the spectrum, is holistic, subjective, spiritual, conceptual, creative, and scarce.

Science has traditionally operated in the provinces of data, information, and knowledge, where measurement, particularity, specialization, and rationality are particularly useful. It has largely ignored the provinces of understanding and wisdom. Theology, philosophy, literature, and art have traditionally operated in the provinces of understanding and wisdom, where subjectivity, spirituality, and values are particularly useful. That is, when it has not succumbed to envy of the hard sciences and tried to emulate their hubris, particularity, and certitude.

When there is an explosion in the capacity to receive, utilize, store, transform, and transmit information, it first creates an immensity of new data, thus transforming the ratio of higher cognitive forms to the lower, drowning wisdom and understanding in a flood of data and information.

In time, the data may gradually become information, the information knowledge, the knowledge understanding, and with enough time and good fortune, the understanding may become wisdom. We are now at a point in time when the ability to receive, utilize, store, transform,

> **MiniMaxims**
>
> *When we fish for absolutes in the seas of uncertainty, all we catch are doubts.*

and transmit data—the lowest cognitive form—has expanded literally beyond comprehension. Understanding and wisdom are largely forgotten as we struggle under the avalanche of data and information. In the ever accelerating assault of data and information on cognitive capacity, understanding and wisdom may be declining in absolute as well as relative terms.

We are drowning in a raging flood of new data and information, and the raft of wisdom to which we desperately cling is breaking up beneath us. The destructive capacities of the flood of technology it has brought about have led to great despair and cynicism, the worst of all possible tools with which to deal with the situation, and it's rapidly getting worse. What the emergence of nanotechnology and biotechnology will do to these ratios is impossible to know, but the direction is not. If we fish for absolutes in seas of uncertainty, all we will catch are doubts.

Native societies which endured for centuries with little increase in the capacity to receive, store, utilize, transform, and transmit information had time to develop a very high ratio of understanding and wisdom to data and information. They may not have *known* a great deal by today's standards, but they *understood* a very great deal about what they knew. They were enormously wise in relation to the extent to which they were informed, and their information was conditioned by an extremely high ratio of social, economic, and spiritual value.

In contrast, our society understands very little about what it knows. It has ever less wisdom in relation to the information it commands. The immensity of data and information that assaults our cognitive capacity is also conditioned by a very small ratio of social, economic, and spiritual value. The result is vast technological power unleashed with inadequate understanding of its systemic propensity for destruction, or sufficient wisdom to guide its evolution in holistic, creative, constructive ways.

It leaves us locked within our separatist, linear, mechanistic institutions, confined within our ever more isolated specialties, constricted by ever narrowing perspectives, while in millions of rational, insular, isolated acts we pour billions of tons of seventy thousand man-made chemicals into the biosphere that it cannot recycle—allow them to accumulate

> **MiniMaxims**
>
> *If life on earth depends on wolf or man, take the wolf every time.*

with little perception of how they are systemically combining to affect all living things—punch holes in the ozone layer of the atmosphere—dissipate and alter genetic material and destroy species by the tens of thousands. It leaves us denuding the land of tens of millions of acres of trees and plants essential to maintenance of the chemical balance of the atmosphere—destroying topsoil at thousands of times the rate at which it can be replaced—creating countless tons of virulent poisons, some with a half-life of twenty-four thousand years, and committing thousands of other isolated acts with little understanding or concern that they are cumulative atrocities and even less of how they are combining to affect the planet, our health, and the lives of future generations.

Each hour alone, we destroy forever 210 species, decimate 6,700 acres of virgin forest, destroy 3 million tons of topsoil, and starve 1,200 babies to death. Who could have imagined that such an explosion of mechanistic, separatist science, education, governance, and rationality could have resulted in collective madness, but so it has.

Meanwhile, the problem of dual ownership grew more acute as the Worthen lawsuit dragged through the labyrinths of the judicial system. It was not until February 1974 that the appeals process was exhausted, the injunction denied, and we were free to enforce the bylaw. Duality had spread rapidly among class B banks, and gradually among class A owner-members. Creative sponsoring contracts between class A and class B banks blurred the operational distinction between the two. It no longer seemed feasible to try to enforce a prohibition among one class and not the other.

The only alternative appeared to be a complete prohibition of dual membership at all levels. A bylaw to that effect was adopted. However, it would not be enforced until after asking the Department of Justice for a "railroad letter." That was a term used for a process whereby the Department of Justice would neither approve nor disapprove the proposed policy, but would give assurance they would take no immediate action, retaining their freedom to act when and how they chose when the effects were known. We assumed that the issues and pressures were well understood by the antitrust division of the Department of Justice and a prompt reply could be expected. We were wrong.

The department put themselves above reproach and announced they would launch a full-scale investigation, putting staff in the field to interview all parties and investigate all issues in depth. And they did—the most junior and inexperienced staff they had with neither experience nor capacity to understand the full complexity of the issues. Bank after bank assured the investigators they would never become dual issuers because of duplicate cost and lack of consumer demand. Senior people in the department appeared to share some of our concerns about the possible anticompetitive effects of unlimited duality, but they were obviously influenced by consistent denial by banks that they would ever become dual issuers.

The investigation by the Department of Justice crept along month after month for a year, then into a second year. Pressure for a decision continued to build. At the critical stage, in one of those political brouhahas that periodically sweep Washington, it was suddenly announced that Donald Baker was stepping down as head of the antitrust division to be replaced by an academic lawyer from a Midwest university. The investigation slowed to a crawl. It was the better part of two years after our request for a railroad letter before we were informed that a decision was imminent. We asked for an opportunity to plead our case before the head of the antitrust division and full panel of investigators. It was granted. Our corporate counsel, antitrust counsel from our outside law firm, and I flew to Washington.

The staff of the department sat as solemn as a flock of crows on one side of the room, we on the other. They said little as we passionately argued our convictions. The senior investigator informed us that a large preponderance of banks had assured them they would never go dual. He reminded us that

Mastercharge, our principal competitor, then larger than NBI, had publicly announced that they did not share our views and had no intention of adopting a similar prohibition. What evidence did we have for our conclusions?

"Look," I argued, "there is never a way to prove a prospective situation. It's not a matter of evidence, it is a matter of judgment. I've spent the last seven years intensely involved in this business, working at the heart of how banks act and react. If we withdraw or fail to enforce a prohibition against duality, within two years you will find it difficult to discover a half-dozen banks which are not dual owner-members of both systems. They will be aggressively issuing both cards and, within a year or two more, questioning why they should support two systems and urging management of both to coordinate their activities. If you refuse us the letter, it is unlikely we can sustain enough support from our board and membership to enforce the prohibition. We can't fight the Department of Justice and intense pressure from many of our own members at the same time, no matter how strong our convictions." They sat, impassive, listening intently but hearing nothing. I plunged on.

"If you take a neutral position and issue the letter, we have a decent chance to roll back duality. If we're successful, we'll see the emergence of a third and fourth, perhaps fifth and sixth bank card system, for no bank in a given market will then want to share products with another. There will be real economic benefit to them in the formation of a separate system. If that happens, retailers and others with ample ability and resources will form their own systems, for they will have no justification to demand entry and owner-member participation in bank systems."

They continued to sit impassive, unresponsive, as I continued. "If we do not prevent duality now, there will never be more than two bank card systems and pressure to diminish their competitive vigor, perhaps even to merge, will never end. The precedent will roll over into cards used for direct access to bank accounts (debit cards) and other payment systems. It's not a matter of proof, it's a matter of common sense." There was no response but polite thanks. They were lawyers. Disbelief was in every pair of eyes.

On the way out our antitrust counsel was hopeful. "I think we got our point across. I think we may get the letter."

My heart was in my shoes as I replied, "You're the expert, but if I were on trial for a capital crime and that was the jury, I'd be thinking about my last meal."

The labyrinthine Department of Justice, like all mechanistic, Newtonian, Industrial Age organizations, was fat on data and information and starved for understanding and wisdom. The letter was denied. If we attempted to enforce the bylaw, we could expect to be sued. Strong convictions notwithstanding, subjecting the new organization and its members to treble damage antitrust penalties in the face of such a divided industry and in defiance of the Department of Justice seemed impossible. I gave up. After four years of extraordinary expense, effort, and trauma, I recommended to the board that we accept our destiny, withdraw our prohibition on duality, and turn our attention to everything we could do to enhance bank-to-bank competition and minimize erosion of competition between the systems.

What I told the hanging jury at the Department of Justice was wrong. The banks didn't take two years to go dual. They did it in six months. Today there is no third, fourth, or fifth bank card system. Diners Club and Carte Blanche are wholly owned subsidiaries of Citicorp. Sears made a mighty effort to interlock their Discover Card by becoming a VISA issuer. The Eurocard system has emerged in Central Europe, but is interlocked with Mastercharge. The JCB card system emerged in Japan. JCB and

Eurocard have achieved limited regional acceptance, but neither has prospects of becoming a global presence. VISA and
Mastercharge are swiftly emerging as dominant debit card systems. Although there is now some effort to prohibit banks from
issuing competing debit card brands, it may prove more form
than substance.

VISA has 60 percent of the global bank card business and
continues its exponential growth. Within VISA, card issuance is
rapidly consolidating in the hands of giant card issuers. Processing
of merchant transactions is rapidly consolidating in the hands of
a few banks and joint stock companies. It is conceivable that two,
at most three payment system behemoths may straddle the earth
and that a handful of financial institutions will control boards and
management of all three. If it is to be so, better they be distributive behemoths such as VISA than single stock companies, or an
extension of some government entity, but not by much. It need
not have been so in the past. It should not be so now. It might be
worse in the future. *It ought not to be so, ever.*

To this day I regret I did not screw my courage to the sticking point and fight on; go down then and there, unbowed and
unrepentant. To this day I wonder if the implied death treats
affected my courage and judgment. Whether recommending
removal of the prohibition on duality was a prudent act or failure of conviction and courage, I shall never know. What the
eventual end of it will be I shall never see. Robert Frost, in one
of his most loved poems, immortalized such choices:

> I shall be telling this with a sigh
> somewhere ages and ages hence:
> Two roads diverged in a wood, and I—
> took the one less traveled by,
> and that has made all the difference.

CHAPTER FOURTEEN

The Golden Links

What was the scenery of this beautiful universe which we inhabit; what were our consolations on this side of the grave—and what were our aspirations beyond it, if poetry did not ascend to bring light and fire from those eternal regions where the owl-winged faculty of calculation dare not ever soar.
— PERCY BYSSHE SHELLEY

As NBI struggled with duality, communications systems, marketing, security, and other major efforts required to turn the BankAmericard system around in the United States, the Bank of America Service Corporation continued to license banks in the remainder of the world. Each license was different, leading to a morass of different marketing, computer systems, operations, and names. The blue, white, and gold card known as BankAmericard in the United States was known as Sumitomo Card in Japan, Barclaycard in the United Kingdom, Chargex in Canada, Bancomer in Mexico, and by a multitude of names in other countries. The situation quickly led to even greater and more complex problems throughout the world than those experienced earlier in the United States, due partially to the diversity of language, currency, culture, and legal systems.

Influenced by the formation of NBI, international licensees formed a committee and made an effort to create a similar international organization. The effort failed. Late in 1972, the international committee requested that the management of NBI undertake the formation of a worldwide organization. We were not averse to the idea, although it raised complex issues. How could NBI take the lead without extending the perceptions and experience of one culture into many others? That would be anathema to the remainder of the world, and properly so. Could we reconcile our clear obligation to act in the best interests of NBI members with an obligation to act in the best interests of banks outside the United States? Could we afford to divert time and energy from the many difficult problems in the United States? On the other hand, could we afford not to, since our success was irrevocably intertwined with the success of the program overseas? How could our ultimate dream of a global device for the exchange of value be realized without an effective global organization?

The effort would be immensely more complex than NBI. A global organization would need to transcend diverse languages, cultures, currencies, customs, legal systems, political traditions, and technologies. It would involve thousands of banks scattered around the world, as well as national consortiums of banks in France, Canada, Scandinavia, Japan, the United States, and other countries. It must anticipate that tens of thousands of diverse financial institutions in more than two hundred countries and territories might wish to participate. It could easily take two years of effort with no assurance of success. Yet, such an organization, if it could be created, would be a huge advantage in the domestic market. Clearly, the experience gained and trust developed in the formation of NBI would be invaluable. It was time for NBI to be a good global citizen.

I approached the U.S. board in the spirit of Maxwell Carlson, pointing out that the management of NBI could not undertake the effort unless released from obligation to represent the interests of NBI. Nor could the effort succeed if we were without position, income, or ability to continue to lead NBI. Many of the NBI directors, including the chairman, Sam Stewart, had been on the NBI executive officers' organizing committee. They understood how important my independence from the National Bank of Commerce had been to the success of that effort. They knew how fiercely I had defended that independence, and the right of the organizers to act openly and in the best interests of all.

By board resolution, they authorized the management of NBI to act as organizing agent with freedom and obligation to act in the best interests of all parties worldwide. We were released from any obligation to act in the express interests of NBI in connection with the international organizing effort. The executive committee of the NBI board was charged with representing NBI in the event of conflict of interest. It was an extraordinary act on the part of the NBI directors. Thus began two years of simultaneous service as the president and chief executive officer of NBI, and as independent organizing agent on behalf of the international licensees. It was fascinating beyond description, filled with euphoria, betrayal, support, and surprises beyond anything I could have imagined.

It was once again necessary to organize regional committees with representatives from every licensee—in Europe-Mideast-Africa, Asia-Pacific, Latin America, and North America. Each multinational regional committee was, to some degree, composed of subcommittees within countries or areas of common interest, such as Scandinavia. Each regional committee contained representatives from countries with long histories of bitter commercial, ethnic, and cultural conflict, including open warfare and periodic subjugation of one another.

Language, cultural, religious, ethical, and economic differ-

> **MiniMaxims**
>
> *Language, invented to reveal meaning, is more often used to confound or conceal it.*

ences made communication difficult and possibility of misunderstanding infinitely greater. After hours of intense discussion, one or another of the participants would inevitably draw me to one side for a bit of private persuasion or complaint.

Patterns emerged. Rarely was a person referred to by name. The language suggested object or thing, not person. There was classification of individuals by nationality, race, or religious origin, and generalizations about each class. There was reluctance to deal with others as human beings. There was even greater reluctance to be revealed as one—with all attendant weaknesses, hopes, and dreams. There was the usual, penguin-like business dress and the stiff behavioral dance by which people demonstrated mastery of the role of "a sensible, practical businessman."

Casually, bit by bit, without suggesting that anything was amiss, I disciplined myself to respond by using the name of the person complained about, while gently questioning the characterization. Imperceptibly, meeting by meeting, the tenor of the language changed. Minds began to open, mine foremost among them. Trying to understand others is a reflective mirror. It teaches far more about self than about others. I could not bring about the change without becoming the change I wanted to bring about. It was unwelcome, often unpleasant, always difficult. No matter how constant my effort, I could never fully get beyond that which I *was* and become that which I *ought to be*.

Nine months into the effort, progress slowed considerably. Something not readily apparent was awry. Actions by some of the international committee members between meetings were inconsistent with what they professed during the meetings. I began to watch patterns of behavior much more closely and make discreet inquiries that might illuminate whether we were merely frustrated by lack of progress or had a correct intuition that things were not as professed. The more I observed and reflected, the greater my concern.

At a meeting of the international organizing committee in Mexico City, things came to a head in a way no one expected. The two of us from NBI were convinced that some members of the committee, for reasons unknown, had decided to circumvent the formation of an international organization. But who, and why? Did it reflect the views of their institutions or was it self-interest? Was it sincere conviction that the present system was superior to anything that might be proposed? Was it misunderstanding? Was it fear of change? Was it due to weakness in our performance as organizing agent?

Even if we knew identities and reasons, confrontation would bring denial, polarize the situation, and make agreement impossible. It was a perplexing problem that I thought about long into the night before the last day of the meeting, trying to understand what might lie beneath the surface of so many contradictory words and acts.

During the sixteen years of conflict with Industrial Age command-and-control organizations and the extraordinary experiences forming NBI, Old Monkey and I had constantly encountered unusual, often bizarre behavior that radical change often incites. Nor were we strangers to the fact that innovative change is never accompanied by sufficient information and knowledge; it often requires acting wisely and prudently on the basis of minimum data, facts, and information.

Making good judgments and acting wisely when one has complete data, facts, and knowledge is not leadership. It's not even management. It's bookkeeping. Leadership is the ability to make wise decisions, and act responsibly upon them when one has little more than a clear sense of direction and proper values; that is, a perception of how things ought to be, understanding of how they are, and some indication of the prevalent forces driving change.

> **MiniMaxims**
>
> *Making good judgments when one has complete data, facts, and knowledge is not leadership—it's bookkeeping.*

Old Monkey Mind and I spent many years trying to understand why, in the midst of an abundance of information, we find it so difficult to act with wisdom, foresight, or compassion. One way to understand the situation is to examine the means by which we create understanding and wisdom. Every individual is embedded in an increasingly complex, diverse number of communities—customers, competitors, suppliers, cities, states, nations, governments, churches, corporations, schools, and countless other institutions and entities, to say nothing of the natural world. At the superficial, sensory level, we continually act, experience the results of those acts, learn from the experience, make decisions based on that learning, and act again.

This does not happen in linear, singular manner, but in a continuous, integrated flow of countless events, second by second, minute by minute, and hour by hour. Nor can this flow of acting, experiencing, learning, and deciding be either completely voluntary or controlled. Countless other people and organizations are doing the same. We are affected by their acts, experiences, and judgments, and must respond. Myriad living entities and physical things composing the natural world are continually acting and reacting as well and we must respond to them. All our acts, experience, learning, and decisions are an inseparable flow of larger wholes. They are equally an inseparable flow of smaller wholes of which each individual is composed. No one is without some autonomy, yet no one is separably autonomous.

At a deeper, partially subliminal level, we assimilate experience, relate it to other experience, attempt to understand the relevance, and make projections about the future based on that understanding. It is those predictions, immediate and long-term, which largely determine the decisions we make, the acts we take, and the results we experience.

At a much deeper level, usually without awareness, we inevitably construct a concept of reality, a worldview of perceived reality, against which we compare current experience in order to create meaning. It is here we make sense of the external world, our place in it, ourselves, and our actions. It is, or at least ought to be, the home of understanding and wisdom.

When there is an explosion in the capacity to receive, store, utilize, transform, and transmit information, the external world changes at a rate enormously greater than the rate at which our internal model evolves. Nothing behaves as we think it should. Nothing makes sense. The world appears to be staging a madhouse. It is not a madhouse. It is merely the great tide of evolution in temporary flood, moving this way and that, piling up against that which obstructs its flow, trying to break loose and sweep away that which opposes it. At such times, we experience extreme dissonance and stress.

At the heart of that dissonance and stress is paradox. The more powerful and entrenched our internal model of reality, the more difficult it is to perceive and understand the fundamental nature of the changing externalities we experience. Yet without such perception, it is extremely difficult to understand and change our internal model.

This is precisely where we are today, and it is rapidly getting worse. Deep in most of us, below our awareness, indelibly implanted there by three centuries of the Industrial Age, is the mechanistic, separatist, cause-and-effect, command-and-control machine model of reality.

People are more than machines. The universe is more than a clock. Nature is more than a sequence of cogs and wheels. Nor is it a collection of bits and bytes. Numbers are not values. Numbers are not the measure of all things. Words and syllables are not reality. And science is not God. All knowledge is an approximation.

When our internal model of reality is in conflict with rapidly changing external realities, there are three fundamental ways to respond.

First: we can cling to our old internal model and attempt to impose it on external conditions in a futile attempt to make them conform to our expectations. That is usually what our institutions compel us to attempt and what we continually dissipate our ingenuity and ability to achieve.

Second: we can engage in denial. We can refuse to accept the new external reality. We can pretend that external changes are not as profound as they really are, or deny that we have an internal model, or that it bears examination. When the world about us appears to be irrational, erratic, and irresponsible, it is all too easy to blame others for the unpleasant, destructive things we experience, abandon meaning, and engage in fantasy and erratic behavior. The world is filling with such people.

Third: we can attempt to understand and change our internal model of reality. That is the least common alternative, and for good reason. Changing an internal model of reality is extremely difficult, terrifying, and complex. It requires a meticulous, painful examination of beliefs. It requires a fundamental understanding of consciousness and how it must change. It destroys our sense of time and place. It calls into question our very identity. We can never be sure of our place or our value in a new order of

> **MiniMaxims**
>
> *Change is the thief of identity. We can never be sure of our place or value in a new order of things.*

things. We may lose sight of who and what we are. It requires an enormous act of faith, for new internal concepts of reality require time to develop, and we require time to grow into them.

Those with the greatest power and wealth and the most prominent place in the old order of things have the most to lose. It is, therefore, understandable that so many of them close their minds to different possibilities and cling tenaciously to the old order of things. It is understandable that they engage in cosmetic change to palliate their discomfort and placate critics. It is understandable that they seek one another and merge the institutions they control to amass more and more power and wealth in order to perpetuate that to which they cling. It is understandable that they blind themselves to the fact that they are attempting to preserve the form of things long after form no longer serves function, a certain formula for failure, since the closest thing to a law of nature in the organizational world is that form has an affinity for expense, while function has an affinity for income.

Those in positions of power, wealth, and prestige who tenaciously cling to the present order of things deserve understanding, not condemnation, for they intuitively sense what Machiavelli discovered five centuries ago when he wrote: "Nothing is more difficult to take in hand, more perilous to conduct, or more uncertain of success, than to take the lead in the introduction of a new order of things." No one should be condemned for failure to welcome change. It is a pervasive problem plaguing us all.

Dostoyevsky put it into perspective in the last century when he wrote: "Taking a new step, uttering a new word is what people fear most."

The undeniable fact is that we have created the greatest explosion of capacity to receive, store, utilize, transform, and transmit information in history. There is no way to turn back. Whether we recognize it or not, whether we will it or not, whether we welcome it or not, whether it is constructive or not, we are caught up together, all of us and the earth as well, in the most sudden, the most profound, the most diverse and complex change in the history of civilization. Perhaps in the history of the earth itself.

And what if those with the greatest power, wealth, and position were to open their minds to new possibilities, loosen their tenacious grasp on the old order of things, abandon the palliative of cosmetic change, open their eyes to new forms of organization, seriously question their internal model of reality? *What if they were to cage the Four Beasts that devour their keeper—Ego, Envy, Avarice, and Ambition—and take the lead in a new order of things? What if they were to go before and show the way?* Ah, there's a challenge worthy of both the best in them and the best among them. I know that they can. And I believe that they might.

As the two of us from NBI talked long into the night in Mexico City, we could find no way to be certain of who was involved in the effort to subvert formation of a new international organization. It was not really important. The struggle to form the organization on the basis of complete openness and trust had been breached.

> ### MiniMaxims
> *A bit of carbon in iron makes powerful metal; a bit of truth in a lie makes powerful deceit.*

The meeting of international licensee banks was but six weeks away. Licensees would want to know the prospects for formation of the new, international organization. It was another of those circumstances when one must act on conviction and principle, openly and nonjudgmentally, trusting that constructive events will emerge.

The next morning I announced that the management of NBI could no longer act as organizing agent. We were willing to be part of the committee but would no longer lead the effort. There was immediate consternation. Those honestly supporting the effort demanded to know the reason for our sudden withdrawal. Our explanation was simple:

"We're convinced that the process is not as open and honest as it ought to be. Our conviction may be in error, but we're compelled to step aside as organizing agent, since we no longer sense the commitment or trust that the process requires." There were immediate demands for a detailed explanation. We refused. "We're not here to accuse or condemn. We're here to help create an equitable, transnational organization if conditions are such that it is possible. At the moment, they are not."

There was intense discussion about what should be reported to the annual meeting. We maintained the committee ought to report the facts—we were withdrawing as organizing agent because we no longer felt everyone was acting in good faith. Under the circumstances, we did not feel the organizing effort was something that we could continue to lead. It was as simple as that.

The meeting adjourned at noon, all agreeing nothing further could be done until after the annual meeting of all licensees in Spain a few weeks hence. Upon our return to San Francisco, we immediately wrote to all parties involved conveying our decision to withdraw. The board of NBI was supportive. Telephones were soon ringing off the desks. We adamantly refused to say more.

The meeting was planned and conducted by the Bank of America Service Corporation in concert with the chairman of the international committee. Attendees had but one thing on their minds: What had happened to the effort to reconceive the international program? There was considerable surprise when the meeting began as though nothing had happened. One could feel the tension in the room mount as the meeting droned on with presentations about plans to seek more licensees and make adjustments to some of the operating regulations. Three hours into the morning, an agenda for the remainder of the three days was proposed. It contained nothing about the failed effort at reorganization other than a brief report at the end of the final day. An annoyed murmur swept the room. A member rose and angrily complained.

"We didn't travel halfway around the world to spend three days on this agenda. We came to find out what happened to the effort to reconceive the system and create an equitable, international organization. I, for one, have no intention of waiting until the end of the last day to find out." A chorus of "Hear, hear," "Absolutely," "Right on," immediately arose. An officer of the Bank of America Service Corporation tried to paper over the difficulty with generalities. The hum of discontent grew louder. The chairman of the international committee rose to offer his version of the situation and induce the members to accept the proposed agenda, as did another member of the committee. No one admitted that they were opposed to the effort. But it was obvious who wanted to discuss the organizational derailment in depth and who didn't. We sat quietly and said nothing. The murmur of discontent grew louder. Another member rose.

"We came expecting to hear from the organizing agent. Why are they not on the program? What is going on here?" Another crescendo of "Yes," "Hear, hear," "Absolutely." All eyes were now looking at us, leaving nothing for the meeting chairman to do but ask if we had anything to say. I rose to speak briefly.

"We're here to participate as one licensee among many. We believe deeply in the effort to create an equitable, international structure. Some may honestly feel that the present system is preferable. That would be understandable and welcome; however, we believe that some are not acting openly in that regard. No equitable organization can arise under such conditions. It is not constructive to say more, for our belief may be in error. If you wish to know more, it must come from other sources."

Efforts to continue the proposed agenda collapsed, as members demanded time to meet privately with one another and discuss the situation with their representatives on the organizing committee.

Ken Larkin, the most senior representative of the Bank of America and a member of the NBI board, immediately sought me out. Although we did not always agree, mutual respect and trust had grown steadily. He was deeply concerned. "Dee, what's going on here? This is not at all what I expected, based on what I've been told."

"Ken, some of your people may not yet understand Bank of America's commitment to the international effort. That's not for me to say. It's not my affair. You know the depth of our commitment to these concepts. You know that withdrawing as organizing agent is not a decision we came to lightly. To say more would not be productive."

"What can be done to get things back on track?"

"I don't know. It may already be happening. Ken, we've worked through some difficult times together. If you were to assure the group of your personal commitment to the effort and the commitment of the Bank of America, I would certainly accept it and expect the others would as well. Perhaps you should give everyone space to meet and talk as they like. Perhaps the licensees themselves will lead us where we ought to go."

In the afternoon, Ken rose to express his personal concern and assure everyone of his commitment and the commitment of the Bank of America. He asked if they would like time to discuss the situation with others and contact their institutions, if required, to determine if they wished to abandon the effort or continue and, if so, how they wished to proceed. They were confused but delighted, assembling and disassembling for short meetings and private discussions far into the night.

We participated in none. No accusations were ever made. But most licensees were digging to learn all that they could and form their own conclusions. The agenda was resumed the second day, but few paid any attention. Self-organizing discussions continued. By the end of the second day, several people had gracefully withdrawn from the committee with profuse thanks for their hard work. Others had been appointed. The chairman had withdrawn to allow others an opportunity to serve.

In the late afternoon of the third day, the newly constituted committee met, firmly pledged themselves to a renewed effort, and asked if we would resume our efforts as organizing agent. We agreed, providing only that henceforth all differences should be open, honest, and constructive. All agreed that was as it should be, and from then on, with minor exceptions, so it was. By the end of the meeting, no one

> **MiniMaxims**
>
> *It is enough that error be corrected. It is excessive to insist it be admitted.*

had lost face, all those who had served were honored for their efforts, no more was said of the past, and everyone's energy turned to the future. There were extraordinary problems ahead and times when it appeared the new international organization would never come to be, but that future was not to be denied.

The most treasured memory came at the end of the effort. After two years of constant struggle we had resolved an incredible number of differences, but three powerful disagreements remained. The conflicting positions had been adopted at the highest level of each licensee bank as a condition of their participation in the new organization. The differences seemed impossible to reconcile. The committee had agreed to a final day-and-a-half meeting, after which the effort would be abandoned if positions had not changed. In conversations leading to the meeting, it became apparent that positions, rather than softening, had hardened. As organizing agent, we were desperate to think of a way to break the impasse. We could think of no compromise that had a chance of being accepted.

I had a lifelong habit of backing away from difficult situations and approaching them in a playful, unorthodox way. I gave up efforts to find a compromise and began to reflect on the exceptional effort of the past two years and the progress that had been made. I began to peel the mental onion, to get at the essential nature of that which had lifted such a complex, diverse group over seemingly insurmountable obstacles. It was hard to get at, but simple when it emerged. At critical moments, all participants had felt compelled to succeed. And at those same moments, all had been willing to compromise. They had not thought of winning or losing but of a larger sense of purpose and concept of community that could transcend and enfold them all.

Several members of the staff joined in and within the hour, we had a plan. We reduced our thoughts to the simplest possible expression: *the will to succeed, the grace to compromise.* Conveying those principles in the living language of any member of the group was sure to give offense to others. It must be in a dead language. A linguist was asked for a translation into Latin, which he rendered as "Studium ad prosperandum, voluntas in conveniendum." To this day I do not know the accuracy of his translation, nor does it matter, for it has taken on a meaning larger than the language itself. We contacted a local fine jeweler and asked that a die be created from which to cast sets of golden cuff links. On one would be a half-round of the earth with continents in relief; circling it in raised letters, "Studium ad prosperandum." On the other cuff link would be the other half of the earth and its continents, circled with "Voluntas in conveniendum." We had a set made for every member of the committee. We said nothing to anyone about what we had done.

The meeting convened on a splendid, warm day in San Francisco. It was polarized and cantankerous. The four large banks which composed Chargex in Canada were adamant. Unless others around the world came to their position, they would not participate. In desperation, I looked around the group and asked, "Well, it is obvious Canada cannot accept the position of others on this issue. Is it the sense of the group that you wish to proceed to form the new organization without our friends from Canada?" Nods all around. "Well, then, it appears Chargex representatives will no longer be part of the process. Would it be appropriate to have them remain as observers with the understanding they will not disrupt remaining discussions?" Again, nods all around. The Canadians were shocked, but did not leave.

Things got no better. There was adamant disagreement on the remaining issues. As the day ended, gloom deepened. I suggested we adjourn the meeting, since agreement appeared impossible. We could meet in the morning to discuss how to disband the effort. Meanwhile, in recognition of an extraordinary effort, NBI wanted them to experience the finest that San Francisco had to offer. We boarded a private boat at Fisherman's Wharf for a trip across the bay to a fine French restaurant, Le Vivoire, in Sausalito. It was within a block of where Sam, Jack, Fred, and I met four years before to ask the impossible question, "If anything imaginable was possible, if there were no constraints whatsoever, what would be the nature of an ideal organization to create the world's premier system for the exchange of value?" It seemed fitting to bury that idea where it had been born.

Mother Nature could not have been more generous. As the boat departed from Fisherman's Wharf, a magnificent sun was sinking behind the Golden Gate Bridge, painting huge cumulus clouds overhead spectacular shades of pink and purple—turning the colossal bridge to its famous, flaming, golden color—bringing out the marvelous pastel hues of the city and swathing the deep blue of the bay with a path of sparkling light from the boat to the horizon. It was shirt-sleeve weather as the boat circled the fortress-like buildings of the former federal prison on Alcatraz Island, then slid past the lush green of Angel Island to dock among the quaint houseboats lining the shores of Sausalito.

After a short walk to the restaurant, a few bottles of fine wine, and a splendid dinner, it was a mellow group of people who faced me when I asked to say a few words before the evening ended. After reminiscing for a few moments about the many experiences we had shared, the obstacles overcome, and the exceptional effort expended, as the small gift was placed before them, I concluded.

"It is no failure to fall short of realizing such a dream. From the beginning, it was apparent that forming such a complex, global organization was unlikely. We now know it is impossible, notwithstanding two years of exceptional effort. Not knowing with certainty how today's meeting might end, as organizing agent we felt compelled to do something which would be appropriate no matter what happened. Would you please open the small gift on the table before you?" As they opened a small, beautifully wrapped box and began to examine the contents, I quietly continued.

"We wanted to give you something that you could keep for the remainder of your life as a reminder of this day. On one cuff link is half of the world surrounded with the Latin phrase 'Studium ad prosperandum'—the will to succeed. On the second cuff link is the other half of the world surrounded with 'Voluntas in conveniendum'—the grace to compromise. We meet tomorrow for the final time to disband the effort after an arduous two years. There is no possibility of agreement. As organizing agent, we have one last request. Will you please wear your cuff links to the meeting in the morning? When we part, each of us will take them with us as a reminder for the remainder of our lives that the world can never be united through us because we lack *the will to succeed and the grace to compromise.* But if, by some miracle, our differences dissolve before morning, this gift will remind us to the day we die that the world was united because we had *the will to succeed and the grace to compromise.*

> **MiniMaxims**
>
> *With the will to succeed and the grace to compromise, all things become possible.*

There was a half-minute of absolute silence as they examined their gift. The silence was shattered by one of my more exuberant Canadian friends, God rest his soul, who exploded, "You miserable b———!" The room dissolved in laughter.

The next morning, every arm was adorned with cuff links. Many had been up much of the night calling officials of their bank or members of their constituency, demanding authority to reach agreement. The chairman was greeted by silence as he opened the meeting with a quiet question, "Is there anyone who wishes to speak of disbanding the effort?" The Canadians immediately ceded their previous position in deference to the others and announced that they were to be part of the new organization. Within the hour, as individuals quietly touched one or the other of their cuff links, agreement was reached on every issue.

When the international organization, now VISA International, came into being a few months later, *the will to succeed, the grace to compromise* became the corporate motto. As far as I know, to this day, every new director receives a set of the golden cuff links and a parchment relating the story. Money could never compensate me for mine.

CHAPTER FIFTEEN

What's in a Name?

*Either the stars are great geometers or the eternal
geometer has arranged the stars.*
— VOLTAIRE

*It was perfect—perfect in its beauty—and perfect
because, from the sun in the heavens to the fly
with burnished wings on the hot rock, there was
nothing out of harmony.*
— MARK RUTHERFORD

In 1973, it became apparent that continuing proliferation of names for the card could hinder growth of the system. At the time, the only common worldwide identity was the blue-white-gold bands design. The product had a different name in every country and in some countries, several names. In the United States, the common name was BankAmericard. In Canada, Chargex. In the remainder of the world, it was usually known by the name of the issuer, such as Sumitomo Card in Japan or Barclaycard in the United Kingdom. Once the card had been introduced in the name of one bank, others were reluctant to join. The multitude of names was confusing to merchants, seriously undermining card acceptance. Ability to conduct international marketing and ensure acceptability of cards was severely limited.

Merchant windows and counters were plastered with the name of the bank that contracted with the merchant for acceptance of cards. "Barclaycard Welcome Here." "Sumitomo Card Welcome Here." Merchants resented bank commercialization of their premises. Cardholders were often confused, thinking only cards of the named bank were acceptable, a misunderstanding some of the banks were not unhappy to perpetuate. As the system grew, so did the problem. In the United States, the name BankAmericard was limiting, as other banks were not happy promoting the Bank of America's identity. Savings and loan companies and credit unions gained legal authority to enter the business. They did not like the "Bank" connotation of the name. The "American" connotation of the card was not appreciated in other countries. "Card" was out of keeping with possible new products such as travelers checks and money orders. Each year that passed made solution of the problem more difficult. With the formation in June 1974 of Ibanco—the name chosen for the fledgling international organization—the whole of the enterprise finally had a governance mechanism capable of approaching such vast, complex problems.

At the formation of Ibanco, another extraordinary event occurred. As the international committee turned its attention to management of the new corporation, many members began to explore how the trust and effective relationships between NBI and Ibanco and the members of both might be sustained. Could there be common management between two such organizations? At first, it seemed impossible. They were two entirely different legal entities: National BankAmericard, composed of U.S. banks, and Ibanco, composed of several national consortiums, such as NBI, Chargex, and Carte Bleue, and hundreds of individual banks throughout the world. The best interests of NBI would often be opposed to those of Ibanco. Conflicts of interest would be inevitable, yet such conflicts were exactly the case during the two years we acted as organizing agent to create Ibanco. We agreed to look into the matter.

An unusual agreement was devised. Ibanco and NBI would enter into a management agreement in which the same staff and officers would serve both organizations. Any officer could be terminated by either board, but it would take both to appoint them. Thus, management would be promoted and rewarded by joint agreement but could be discharged or demoted by unilateral decision of either. In the event of a conflict of interest, management would be obliged to declare it and announce which party they intended to represent. The other party would be represented by its board. This arrangement would require extraordinary trust and credibility, along with exceptional standards of fairness and candor. It would mean constant scrutiny, suspicion, and criticism. What person of sound mind and body would want to work under such conditions? In ways, no one, but I had been doing it for six years, and with too much success to back away from another challenge.

Conventional management wisdom held that common management reporting to such diverse, autonomous parties with divergent interests could never function effectively, but it did, surprisingly well, as the problem of diverse names so amply demonstrated.

We approached the boards of both NBI and Ibanco for authority to investigate adoption of a common, worldwide name. It was an awesome task for a new organization. Every card in the world would have to be reissued. Every merchant decal on every window and at every point-of-sale counter would have to be replaced. Every electronic sign would have to come down, twenty thousand in Japan alone. Every form, every bit of stationery, and every sign in every bank would require replacement.

All advertising would have to be changed. It would involve dozens of languages, cultures, and legal systems. No single center of authority or management group could ever hope to know, let alone understand, the full extent of the diversity and complexity involved.

Not only would such immense change have to occur, it could not be done in lockstep. It would have to be done by an incredibly diverse complex of thousands of independent institutions, each of which would need autonomy in making their part of the conversion. Each would need freedom to explain and market the change in competition with all others. Yet, it must happen swiftly and cooperatively, with equity and fairness. It must seamlessly blend cooperation and competition.

The situation was further complicated. Although Ibanco had obtained an exclusive license from the Bank of America for the blue-white-gold bands design and the name BankAmericard, both were still owned by that bank. Fortunately, at the time of formation of Ibanco, we had negotiated an agreement compensating the Bank of America for surrender of ownership of the international part of the system. The agreement provided that should a new name be adopted acceptable to 80 percent of the system, ownership of the bands design would be transferred to Ibanco without additional compensation. Use of the name BankAmericard would be discontinued by all banks and revert to the Bank of America for their exclusive use. Conversion to a new name under such circumstances was another of those problems for which there was no pattern and little experience.

We'd had enough of outside experts during our initial efforts to create electronic systems. I had great confidence in the ingenuity and ability of our modest staff. When their creativity was challenged and they had latitude to use it, their accomplishments had been extraordinary. If such a monumental change was to happen, they must be the ones to do it. We again turned to our growing habit of looking for underlying purpose and principle as the point of beginning. The purpose part was quite simple—to create a common, worldwide name for the organization and all its products to complement the common blue-white-gold bands design, with ownership of both cooperatively vested in the totality.

With no thought to what the new name might be, we began to create principles that it must embrace. One by one they emerged. The new name must be short, graphic, and capable of instant recognition. It must be easily pronounceable in any language. It must have no adverse connotations in any language or culture. It must be capable of worldwide trademark protection for the exchange of value and all related activities. It must have no restrictive connotations, whether related to geography, institution, service, or form, such as *Ameri, Euro, bank, charge, credit,* or *card.* It must have implications of mobility, acceptance, and travel. Before we were done, the list contained more than fifteen principles to which any new name must conform. It was daunting. We decided to simply release human ingenuity and see what happened.

We called the entire staff together, from the newest mail handler to management. If they wished, anyone was free to participate in any way they found interesting and challenging, whether individually or in self-organized groups. A representative group would form to consider all suggestions and help formulate the best possible answer. There would

> **MiniMaxims**
>
> *Money motivates neither the best people nor the best in people. It can move the body and influence the mind, but it cannot touch the heart or move the spirit.*

be no consultants or outside experts. The employees were the experts, one and all. The person who came up with the answer would receive a munificent $50 check. Should it be a team effort that produced the result, each member of the team would have a check. The payment was purely symbolic. A large amount would produce a tendency to hoard ideas and information. Desire to have the check as a framed memento, in addition to the pleasure of open participation, was compelling enough.

There was an explosion of ingenuity. The effort swiftly self-organized. Those technically inclined wrote software programs to fabricate names from letters of the alphabet. Family and friends were engaged. Dictionaries of roots and meaning in numerous languages were sifted and combed. Meetings and groups evolved and dissolved. I doubt anyone involved read, saw, or experienced anything in their daily lives without wondering if it might contain a clue to the answer. Great excitement arose each time someone thought they had solved the puzzle, only to be met with good-natured skepticism and challenge by others. Marketing people felt compelled to find the answer before someone in the mail room beat them to it. People throughout the company felt challenged to demonstrate they were as creative as anyone in marketing, which many proved to be.

Lists of possibilities emerged, were combined in various ways, suggestions appearing and disappearing as the winnowing process continued. Hundreds of ideas emerged, failed to meet the test of purpose and principles, and were abandoned. Within months, no more than a handful remained. One, which had been discounted on the assumption it was so common it could never meet the test of trademark protection, continually reappeared and often rose to the top. *Visa.* Was it possible such a common name, used for centuries to denote an entry document to a foreign country, might be capable of trademark protection worldwide? Maybe, just maybe, it was so old and common that no one had thought of using it for financial services.

A worldwide trademark search was quietly undertaken to determine if it had ever been used in the field of financial services. One by one, the reports came in. There was a Visa car. There were Visa golf clubs. There were Visa fabrics. We held our breath. There were Visa pens. There were Visa appliances, there were Visa products of many kinds, but we could find no use of Visa for financial services, publications, or related activities of any significance. We filed worldwide trademark registrations in every possible jurisdiction for the use of the name for financial and related services.

Whether or not we could gain worldwide acceptance for the change among our members was unlikely, but at least we had a beginning, a name to propose. But who was to get the $50 check? There were dozens of different recollections of where and how the name first appeared. No matter how hard we tried, none among us could unravel the puzzle. The name had appeared as an integral part of a self-organizing process. In a staff meeting to celebrate our success and untangle the puzzle someone wisecracked, "Maybe it suggested itself. Make the check payable to 'everyone.' It belongs to us all." Amid much laughter, the matter was settled.

How the largest, most complicated trademark conversion in commercial history was agreed upon, then completed in a third the time anticipated, would require a book of its own. However, memories of a few critical moments remain strong. One came near the end of the approval process. After nearly two years of intense effort, most members had slowly become convinced of the need for the change. However, a few were strongly opposed. We were reluctant to proceed if the decision had to be imposed on anyone.

The Sumitomo Bank in Japan was very concerned. They had, at great expense, installed thousands of electronic signs at merchant locations with "Sumitomo Card Welcome Here" emblazoned in the middle of the blue-white-gold bands design. The cost of changing the signs and the thought of removing their identity from merchant premises and substituting a generic blue-white-gold VISA was a bitter pill to swallow. On the other hand, sense of belonging to a greater whole and accepting sacrifices for the common good was a powerful tradition in Japanese culture.

It was not so in other cultures, such as Britain and France. Our only member in Britain was Barclays Bank, one of the oldest, proudest, and largest financial institutions in Europe. With a substantial presence in countries throughout the world, they were by no means free of imperialist notions or the sense of manifest destiny. In France our member, Carte Bleue, was a consortium of large French banks. Carte Bleue, quite rightly from their perspective, felt entitled to more consideration than any single bank. The leader of that group felt that there was insufficient consideration given to the difficulties of maintaining cohesion and cooperation among diverse French banks.

It was the kind of situation to which one had to adjust in such a chaordic organization. Rarely was there clear right and wrong at VISA. There were only differing perspectives and perceptions. There was rarely a best at VISA. There was only better. Interests were diverse and positions often diametrically opposed. Each was legitimate, powerfully held, and ably defended. Each, from the perspective of a given culture, custom, or law, was undeniably constructive, fair, and right, yet from the aggregate perspective, each could be destructive, selfish, and wrong.

It was at an international member meeting in Hawaii that the final decision would be taken. I was frantic to know how to bring everyone to the table in constructive agreement. The night before the meeting, as Ferol and I wandered alone along a path bordering the ocean, we noticed an enticing promontory and walked out to sit on a bench. Another couple appeared, and asked if they might enjoy the sunset with us, to which we warmly agreed. We fell into pleasant conversation about the beauty of the spot and the spectacular show Mother Nature was providing as the sunlight faded and stars emerged.

The next day, as the meeting began, I discovered my acquaintance of the evening before, John Clinton, was a managing director of Barclays Bank, concerned enough to travel halfway around the world to persuade others that the name change was a wrongheaded notion. Discussions were intense, differences strong, and nothing resolved as the day progressed. In accordance with our custom, the meeting was adjourned early in the afternoon so that people could mingle, privately share views, and enjoy the company of one another. John asked for a private word with me. We agreed to meet on the beach in an hour.

As we lay prone on two lounges he explained with great clarity and depth why Barclays Bank simply could not accept the change. I listened carefully, trying to put myself into his skin and see things through his eyes. Clearly, from his perspective, he was right. Were anyone in a similar situation, they would feel the same. There was no point in argument. On the other hand, had he put himself in the skin of others? Could he see with their eyes? Were other perspectives equally relevant to the interests of Barclays Bank?

I asked if he had time to listen to the perspectives of others, which I would try to convey. He readily agreed. I smoothed out a section of wet sand and began to sketch merchant decals and card layouts, illustrating the difficulties experienced worldwide and the opportunities presented by a common name. From one corner of my eye I could see a member of the NBI staff, signaling an urgent need to speak to me. I waved him away, since John was swiftly absorbing dimensions of the problem that had escaped his attention and I did not want to break the flow of conversation. My back was beginning to burn. I choked back a grin as the inevitable parental homily popped into mind: "It's no skin off my back." This may well be skin off mine. It was a small price to pay.

Within the hour, John said, "We may not have fully understood the issues. I want to think about this overnight and speak with others from Barclays. We may be able to support the name change." I thanked him and left.

The staff had bad news. Bernard Sue, head of Carte Bleue, had been roughly handled by some of the proponents of the name change. He had angrily announced he was returning to France on the next flight, would no longer participate in the meeting, and stormed away. It could easily disrupt the consensus that had been building.

"Where is Bernard?" I asked. "Has he left yet?" Someone extended his arm, pointing to the ocean. I could see nothing. As the swells rose, Bernard appeared, far out in the ocean. My heart sank. A dinner meeting at which I must preside was but an hour and a half away. I was determined Bernard should be there. In his youth, Bernard had been an Olympic-class swimmer. I was a country kid, reasonably at home in ponds and canals, but the ocean was another matter. Duty calls in strange ways. There was nothing for it but to plunge in and slowly work my way out. Fortunately, Bernard was on his way in.

We met a hundred yards offshore, treading water as we spoke. It was a stroke of good fortune, for he was relaxed and in his element. We talked for more than half an hour; rather, he spoke and I gasped. Whether it was pity for an awkward creature in distress, or the calming effect of the great mother ocean is hard to say, but he was receptive and kind, agreeing that the importance of Carte Bleue to the system was too great to be jeopardized by unintended offense, no matter how egregious. He would set the matter aside and remain.

Good and bad fortune, like bananas, often comes in bunches. At dinner that evening, I sat next to the representative from Japan. We fell into a deep discussion about bonsai, a hobby I was then clumsily pursuing. He was an expert in the field and gently told me of a bonsai tree handed down through five generations of his family. It was now in his custody. It gave him a profound sense of the continuity of life, the importance of honoring ancestors, and the obligation to respect the needs of generations yet to be. When he traveled, he had concern about remaining too long, for he felt great personal responsibility for the tree. It must be passed to the next generation, healthy and enhanced. I shared with him my deep conviction that life is not a possession. Nor is it merely a contract between the living and dead. Life is a sacred contract between the dead, the living, and the unborn.

Without intention on either part, the conversation drifted to Ibanco, the extraordinary relationships on which it was based, the sacrifices that had been required to bring it into being, and whether it too was a living thing that should be passed from generation to generation enhanced. We lapsed into silence, realizing a profound sense of shared responsibility. Not a word was said about our differences regarding the name change. Not a question was asked or answered. Yet in the beautiful, subliminal way that comes so easily in Eastern cultures, I had the feeling that we were becoming as one on the work to be done.

When it came time to make a few remarks to end the dinner, I asked his permission, then quietly shared the story he had told me about his family bonsai and concern for its welfare. I reminded the group that the Sumitomo family had originated as Samurai warriors four hundred years earlier, migrating into the mining of copper, eventually into banking and a great many other businesses, adding: "We should think carefully before we drag out our discussion tomorrow, put in jeopardy the life of such a tree, or arouse the Samurai spirit of one who is responsible for its life." He was smiling gently as I finished.

One can never understand why things happen as they do. Perhaps it was no more than imagination, but discussions the next day seemed to have a different quality. They were no less intense and penetrating, yet with a subliminal feel of desire for commonality rather than difference; a feel of something beyond self, nation, culture, or institution tugging at one's sleeve. A unanimous decision emerged at that meeting to change the corporate name Ibanco to Visa International Services Association. The acronym, of course, was VISA. National BankAmericard became VISA USA. At the same time, a decision was taken to change all products to the name VISA. Thus, the corporate names and product names became one. Those decisions caused many individuals great trouble as they returned to explain to others within their institutions what had happened. It may have been detrimental to some of their careers, yet they made the decision and never turned back.

> **MiniMaxims**
>
> *People must come to things in their own time, in their own way, for their own reasons, or they never truly come at all.*

Within weeks, plans were made for a four-year phase-in of the conversion to allow time for the complex work to be done. General objectives were established that allowed every institution complete freedom to make the conversion in any way they chose. There were no commandments, threats, or penalties. No member was told how to do anything. Instead, dates were agreed on by which they would be expected to reach certain objectives. Cardholders and merchants responded with enthusiasm, the conversion self-organized, and a year and a half later there were few old cards, decals, or forms to be found. It was done in a third the time anticipated. Within another three years, VISA had surpassed all its rivals by a substantial margin.

Whether we were in the middle of trauma or triumph (there seemed little else in those early years), Old Monkey Mind and I could not stop playing with the future.

We are emerging from a society based upon industrial production for more than a century, dominated by the separatist, mechanistic concepts of corporation and nation-state, into an extraordinarily complex, diverse, global technocracy, wherein it is increasingly possible to produce at any point on the globe a unique product or service for a single individual located at any other point.

The very foundation of such a society is the intricately webbed, global data communication systems now rapidly emerging. Just as the human body is organized around biological neural systems so complex as to defy description, so too are increasingly complex electronic neural networks evolving and interconnecting, around which the world's political, social, and commercial bodies will be forced to reconceive themselves, and wholly new and different ones will be formed.

The production of goods and services has progressed from the age of handcrafting, through the Industrial Age, more accurately thought of as the age of machinecrafting; into the so-called information age, which can best be understood as the age of mindcrafting, since information is nothing but the raw material of that incredible processor we call mind and the pseudomind we call computer. Software, the tool with which we shape information, can be best understood as "thoughtware" since it is clearly a product of the mind. The Industrial Age (the age of machinecrafting) was primarily an extension of muscle power. The information age (the age of mindcrafting) is primarily an extension of mental power. Whether it will also lead to yet another age characterized by an extension of ethical and spiritual power is a much more compelling question.

In the age of handcrafting, the dominant forms of organization were the all-powerful churches, kingdoms, and handcraftsmen guilds. Just as the age of machinecrafting led to the emergence of today's organizations, ending the dominance of guilds, kingdoms, and churches, so too will the Chaordic Age give rise to new concepts of organization that will end the dominance of today's organizational structures.

Changes in existing organizations and the evolution of wholly new ones will have many characteristics in common. Just as the human body is not a vertical hierarchy with each part superior to another in ascending, linear order, organizations of the future will not be so structured. Great pyramids of superiors and subordinates will yield to affiliations of semi-independent equals, whether they be individuals within an organization or organizations within a larger whole. This is not to say that all present industrial organizations are doomed. Evolution is rarely so cruel, for it is patient, though inexorable. Most organizations will evolve, however slowly and painfully, into a form in which power, wealth, and information are more widely diffused and commonly shared.

The concept of organizations composed of semiautonomous equals affiliated for common purpose, such as the VISA organization, has intensified the endless debate as to whether competition or cooperation should rule the day. Each has passionate messiahs to preach its virtue.

Competition and cooperation are not contraries. They have no opposite meaning. They are complementary. In every aspect of life, we do both. Schools are highly cooperative endeavors within which scholars vigorously compete. The Olympic Games combine immense cooperation in structure and rules with intense competition in events. As the runners leap from the blocks, competition and cooperation are occurring in a single, indistinguishable blur. One simply cannot exist without the other.

No societal, commercial, or governmental endeavor has ever existed without combining the two. Human history has always been a race without a victor between combat and compromise; between concepts of power and concepts of service. Cooperation gone mad results in the mindless pursuit of equality, then uniformity, use of centralized force to achieve it, ever increasing coercion, and eventual slavery. Competition gone mad results in the mindless pursuit of self-interest, abuse of others, retaliation, accelerating anarchy, and eventual chaos. Only in a harmonious, oscillating dance of both competition and cooperation can the extremes of control and chaos be avoided and peaceful, permanent order found.

In the Chaordic Age, it will be much more important to have a clear sense of purpose and sound principles within which many specific, short-term objectives can be quickly achieved, than a long-range plan with fixed objectives. Such plans often lead to futile attempts to control events in order to make them fit the plan, rather than understanding events so as to advance by all means in the desired direction. In time of rapid, radical change, long-term plans are often so generally stated as to require endless interpretation, in which case they are no plan at all, or they become so rigid that they diminish thought, obscure vision, and muffle advocacy of opposing views.

In the Chaordic Age, the centuries-old effort to eliminate judgment and intuition—art, if you will—from the conduct of institutions will change. Organizations have too long aped the traditional mechanistic, military model wherein obedience to orders is paramount and individual behavior or independent thinking frowned upon, if not altogether forbidden.

> **MiniMaxims**
>
> *Judgment is a muscle of the mind, developed by exercise. There is nothing to lose by trusting it.*

In chaordic organizations of the future, it will be necessary at every level to have people capable of discernment, of making fine judgments and acting sensibly upon them. The Industrial Age trend toward stultifying, degrading rote work that gradually reduces people to the compliant, subordinate behavior one expects from a well-trained horse will not continue.

It extends far beyond a factory worker on an assembly line. Vast white-collar bureaucracies exist everywhere, with mountains of procedures manuals depressing minds, avalanches of directives burying judgment, forests of reports obscuring perception, floods of studies inundating initiative, oceans of committees submerging responsibility and drowning decisions. You know what I mean. You have endlessly suffered through it and, worse yet, are probably inflicting it on others.

It has created a society of people alienated from their work and from the organizations in which they are enmeshed. Far too much ingenuity, effort, and intelligence go into circumventing the mindless, sticky web of rules and regulations by which people are needlessly bound.

In the Chaordic Age, success will depend less on rote and more on reason; less on the authority of the few and more on the judgment of many; less on compulsion and more on motivation; less on external control of people and more on internal discipline.

The global name change to VISA was only the beginning. In time, we reached a point where management thought it possible to reduce the size of the VISA name and logo from the face of the entire card to a much smaller logo in the center of the card, opening up space for greater bank identification and cobranding with nonmember bank customers. It was the same old story. The customary had become sacred. Reasons why it should not be done came fast and furious. "Bank identification will dwarf and degrade the name and marks"—"Merchant clerks won't recognize the reduced logo"—"Consumers will see the product as inferior and turn to competitive cards with more powerful identification"—"It's foolish to diminish a dominant brand." There was a hue and cry for exhaustive market research and ample documentation. Powerful directors from some of the largest card-issuing banks were opposed. We reluctantly agreed to design a research program that would answer all questions in a compelling way.

As a management group, we were not persuaded of the efficacy of reliance on statistical, supposedly objective research, for it seemed to result in catastrophic mistakes as often as success. Nor, after constant pioneering in incredibly short time frames, were we inclined to drawn-out processes. We enjoyed approaching problems in a playful, innovative way with raucous laughter, freewheeling discussions, and nothing off-limits or too unusual to be heard. Yet the discussions were serious, for decisions had to be made, the consequences were huge, and an incredible complex of members must be induced to agree.

We returned to our old habit of peeling a complex mental onion with constant questions. What is the ultimate test of the acceptability of a card? What is the most difficult, most risky card to present and have accepted? Who does it? How is

> **MiniMaxims**
>
> *Wool should be grown on the hide, not in the head.*

it done? An idea emerged that was compelling. The most difficult card to create, market, and have accepted was a counterfeit card. Our wallets and purses emerged as we examined the cards we carried. There were at least two or three issued by each of the most reluctant banks. What if we were to design a card with a reduced logo identical to what we were proposing, emboss them with the bank identification and card numbers of each of our own cards, and simply present them in the normal way, at normal times, without comment, recording transaction-by-transaction what we experienced and what the merchant said and did? *What if we counterfeited our own cards?* Now that was a fiendishly intriguing idea.

It had a major flaw. Our experience would be suspect, for we were recommending the change. What if we enlisted the employees of our accounting and law firms, asking them to allow us to counterfeit their cards as well and to help design an impeccable process to tabulate and verify the results? Within a day, we had all the elements figured out and individuals designated to conduct confidential discussions with card suppliers, accountants, and lawyers.

We could say nothing to members or directors without compromising the validity of the counterfeiting test. It was beautiful. Not a procedure to change, not a customer to disturb, not a questionnaire to create, not an expert to hire. Just a simple booklet in which everyone would record exactly what happened when they presented their counterfeit card to merchants. We were the only ones to be discomfited if our cards were questioned, and could carry a properly issued card in our wallets for backup in the event that happened.

It was with considerable trepidation that I pulled into a gas station and, for the first time, removed the counterfeit card from my wallet and nonchalantly hung it out the window while the attendant pumped the gas. He looked at the card, did a double-take, and asked, "Is that a new VISA card?"

"I don't know," I replied. "I just got it."

"Wow, I bet it cost a lot to get one of those" was all he said as he took the card without hesitation.

In the weeks that followed, the booklets began to fill. Not a card was rejected because of the new design. There were no significant negative reactions. Most cards were accepted without comment. Many responses were positive, usually from merchant employees wondering when they would get their "new VISA card." It was as though the public had come to expect innovation from VISA. They assumed that the new model was somehow superior to the old. The results of our counterfeiting exceeded all expectation.

On the eve of the board meeting I decided on the ultimate test, inviting Ken Larkin, senior vice president of the Bank of America, and three other directors who opposed the change to dinner at the Bankers' Club, a private luncheon club during the day and fancy restaurant open to the public at night. They had a fascinating discussion about all the problems that were certain to occur if we were to adopt a new design. I said as little as possible in order to avoid biasing the discussion.

In time, I signaled for the bill, which the waiter brought on the usual tray. I produced my counterfeit card, and laid it on top of the bill in full view of everyone. No one noticed as the discussion continued. The waiter approached, picked up the tray, and walked away, returning shortly with a sales draft for signature. With the card in full view, I looked the draft over and signed it. The waiter picked it up and walked away without a word. No one noticed. I left the card on the table, casually edging it toward the center as talk about the problems we would encounter with the new design continued. No one noticed. I picked up the card and began to fiddle with it in full view. No one noticed. The suspense was excruciating. The card was practically in front of Ken Larkin's nose. A huge man and a former college football lineman, he was not unacquainted with locker-room language when excited. Finally, it came.

"What the hell is that!?" With what I am certain must have been a devilish grin I softly replied, "I think it's the new VISA card from Bank of America."

"The hell it is!" He scrutinized the numbers. He had everyone's attention, including people at surrounding tables. *"That's embossed with our bank identification number, where did you get this?"*

The other directors were grabbing at the card as I chuckled in delight, "Well, Ken, to be honest, it's counterfeit, but I certainly hope that after tomorrow's meeting you'll send me a legitimate one."

At the board meeting we confessed our sins and revealed the results of our "market research." We asked each director if they would like a counterfeit card of their own to validate the data. They didn't. The decision was taken and the results are history. At times, it was great fun to "work" at VISA.

CHAPTER SIXTEEN

The Process Opens

*The true strength of rulers and empires lies not in
armies and navies, but in the belief of men that
they are inflexibly open and truthful and legal. As
soon as government departs from that standard, it
ceases to be anything more than "the gang in possession," and its days are numbered.*
— H. G. WELLS

*They that reverence too much the old times are but
a scorn to the new.*
— SIR FRANCIS BACON

When VISA International came into being, its behavior was
neither traditional nor merely innovative. It was chaordic
and open to surprise. It was, for example, impractical to convene
a board composed of people from a dozen countries more than
quarterly. Each meeting was held in a different country to familiarize directors with other cultures. One of the four meetings was
held in conjunction with the annual meeting of members,
attended by hundreds of people from dozens of countries.
Meetings required simultaneous translation in four languages. In
the beginning, the annual meeting followed a typical pattern:
business meetings for representatives and a separate program for
spouses and guests. In an effort to broaden the perspective of
members, we began inviting world-class speakers and

entertainers from a variety of cultures to stretch imagination beyond the limited, traditional world of banking payment systems.

Accustomed to the openness of VISA staff meetings and our policy of inviting families to all management retreats, several spouses approached me at one of the annual meetings to ask why they were invited to attend tours and other such events when they thought the business meetings might be much more interesting. "Would it be possible for us to attend?" they asked. It had not occurred to me that they would have more interest in activities of the organization than in programs arranged for their entertainment. There was no plausible reason why they should be excluded. An invitation was issued. The attendance was overwhelming and interest high, swiftly putting an end to separate programs. Thereafter, member events and sessions were open to everyone, whether representatives, spouses, or guests.

At the end of one such meeting, I was again approached by a half-dozen spouses who knew me well, some of them wives of directors. They were quick to the point. For years, they had listened to stories of board meetings and how decisions were made. They were fascinated by what they had experienced at the annual business meeting of members. Was there any possibility they could be invited to a board meeting? Whoa, Nellie! This was a horse of a different color. I bit off an emphatic "no," thinking to engage them in some clever dissuasion. It was an error in judgment.

"There is an immense amount of work at each meeting which could not possibly be done if there were audience participation," I argued. *Of course, but why did I think they would not honor that need and remain silent? All they wanted was to observe and be informed.*

"There are confidential matters to be discussed which must not be carried from the room." *Yes, but why did I think they would be any less conscious of that or any less responsible than a director or a member of the staff?*

"It would make the directors ill at ease and self-conscious." *Yes, but isn't that just the result of custom? Would they not become accustomed to an open meeting?*

"It would require a large room with circular seating in order for all to observe and hear." *Yes, but facilities for that are available at hotels able to accommodate the annual meeting. Why couldn't locations be selected with that in mind?*

"We could not invite spouses and leave out other guests." *Of course not, why should we?*

Pride at being a powerful persuader began to take a terrible beating, but I pressed on: "It just isn't done in the business community." *Well, why not?*

"The board would never accept such an arrangement." *Perhaps, but how could I know that without making the attempt? Isn't innovation what VISA is all about?*

Desperate, I called on Sir Isaac Newton for a little command and control. "There is no way it can be done! The answer is no!" Withering looks. *That's not a reason. That's just another version of "because I said so." It just means you refuse to consider it.*

I limped off in defeat with a lame, "Well, if that's the way you want to put it." A group of people I genuinely loved and respected walked away, denied and disappointed.

It gnawed at me for months. Old Monkey and I replayed past board meetings as though they had been conducted in front of members and spouses. I could recall nothing that had been said or done that would be a compelling reason against making the attempt. There was the risk of premature disclosure of confidential matters, but we were not a shareholder company where that could have effect on the price of stock. And why was secrecy such a fetish in our institutions anyway? Might it be doing more harm than good? Might observing their elected board in action not reassure members about the extent of discussion and intense effort made to act for the good of the whole? Had I not argued since the beginning that the true capital of VISA was credibility, not money? Would such a step increase or decrease our credibility?

Three months before the next annual meeting of members, I screwed my courage to the sticking point and asked the board for permission to conduct each board meeting contiguous to the annual meeting of members in open forum, with the board surrounded by the people they were elected to serve. You shall be spared details of that discussion. There are some things best left to the silence of the past. Yet, they agreed to try.

Three months later, in just such a setting, I rose to welcome an audience of four hundred, asking only that they respect the process and refrain from audible response to what occurred— no comments, cheering, jeering, or applauding, please! They were superb. So were the directors. Within half an hour, we were so involved in discussion that few were even conscious of the audience. I could detect no lack of intensity, candor, or involvement by directors. There were, however, a few slight differences. I pointed them out to the audience as the meeting ended and I thanked them for their interest and courtesy. "Never have we been more to the point, more gracious to one another, or more willing to understand a different point of view. For that, we thank you most kindly." After the meeting, my former interrogators crowded around. "Fascinating." "Better than any play I ever attended." "Now I understand what board meetings are all about." "Will we be able to come again next year?" And, of course, they did, year after year.

During the seventeen years forming and leading the VISA family, there were many customs that saw us through difficult times. From the beginning, we were determined that we would neither seek nor offer favor of any kind. During those years, we never parted with a penny to a politician, to any regulatory body for approval, or to anyone for entry into a country. It was a price we would not pay for success, regardless of the sum. We never gave or accepted gifts of any kind, except for small tokens in cultures where to arrive without one would give offense. Nor were we interested in the entertainment syndrome. During all those years, I assiduously declined all invitations to rocket launchings, Super Bowls, golf tournaments, and other extravaganzas. Even complementary copies of magazines in which we bought substantial advertising were returned with a gracious declination. In retrospect, it seems almost absurd, but then as now, to do otherwise to me seemed demeaning.

For more than a decade, until I left in 1984, I worked in the midst of such increasing complexity, testing its strengths and weaknesses, learning from both joyous and bitter experience the demands of leading such systemic diversity, discovering the richness of diffusion of power and wealth, exploring the limits of individual capacity for change, and studying how to increase it. It was nothing but learning, learning, learning as we walked the knife's edge between order and chaos, between cooperation and competition, between compelled and induced behavior; struggling to escape the mechanistic, separatist, linear mindset that insists we bifurcate everything into quantifiable, combative opposites. At the end, I was reporting to more than a hundred directors from dozens of countries composing six boards meeting on nearly every continent as the sales volume rocketed past one hundred billion dollars, with virtual certainty it would increase eightfold each decade well into the next century. But such success was only part of the story.

ℒ♥

In spite of its successes, VISA was badly flawed. So was its leader. It is painful to think and write about failure and weakness, but it is an essential part of the story. As an archetype of chaordic organization, we never got VISA more than a third right. As an archetype of leaders of the future, I would be delighted to think I came anywhere near that level. But that is all right, for the important question is not whether either institutions or individuals reach their ultimate potential, but whether they are constantly rising in the scale. I have never been able to clearly distinguish between success and failure, so they shall appear as they were, irrevocably interconnected.

Many of my present beliefs were only then emerging. They were often difficult to formulate. Devotion to them was difficult to sustain. The methods and beliefs of mechanistic command and control I had been taught, had been too thoughtlessly accepted, and more skillfully practiced than I then realized or even now care to admit. It would take someone of much greater character, clearer perception, and more generous disposition than mine to be immersed in a world in which such concepts are dominant and remain free of the taint. Round up a dozen CEOs, belly us up to the bar of power, open a few bottles of "Old Dominator," and there's a reasonable chance I'll drink most of them under the table. Power may be the ultimate addiction.

One of the first failures came with permanent NBI quarters. It was in the heyday of gigantic corporate headquarters with palatial executive offices and scaled-down warrens of compartments and cubicles for the lesser folks. Something about such corporate "show-and-tell" quarters offended me, probably because I was normally excluded from them, or rarely had good experiences in them. Nonetheless, I learned to crave them, for were they not a primary symbol of success?

Something about confinement in private quarters had always annoyed me. To a lover of woods and fields, restraint in a building for the better part of every day was depressing, smacking of the prisons of school and church. Yet, in the world of institutions, physical separation from others is the mark of success, power, and prestige.

I convinced myself that banks, government officials, suppliers, and prospective employees would never accept NBI as a substantive organization if it were located in inexpensive, modest quarters. At the time, that judgment may have been right. What is now clear is that I lacked perception, ability, and courage to lead in the direction of natural inclination, rather than acquired behavior.

Our first permanent office was a compromise. We leased a half-floor high in the Bank of America building in San Francisco. Around the core of the building, containing elevators and mechanical systems, we built a series of private conference rooms similar to those at the National Bank of Commerce.

> **MiniMaxims**
>
> *Leadership is to go before and show the way.*

In the outer projecting corners, we built guest sitting rooms with round tables and comfortable chairs. Otherwise, the office was completely open, with huge bay windows framing immense vistas of the city, bay, bridges, ocean, and mountains, spreading for more than thirty miles in every direction.

Employees were at amply spaced desks with enough plants to differentiate space. That is, all employees but one, for with a constant stream of visitors, I spent far too much time in the outer conference room, which became, de facto, "my office." It was the purest form of leadership. I "went before and showed the way." But it was absolutely the wrong way. There was constant pressure from other senior people for offices, something to which they had been accustomed at other companies. Instead of demolishing the outer room and disciplining myself to behave in accordance with my better instincts, I succumbed to the pressure, and bit by bit, the magnificent space was cut into offices. However, I insisted on one principle: there would never be an employee cut off from full view of the outside. Interior walls of all offices would be floor-to-ceiling glass so that every employee could see through to the outside. And so it was in every VISA office for the fourteen years until I left. Slim consolation. Today, so I hear, VISA has more blind cubicles than the popular cartoon characters Dilbert could count or Dogbert could mark.

Perhaps the greatest mistake was to completely underestimate the degree of individual cultural change such an organization required, both in self and others. Nor did I anticipate how pervasively and persistently old concepts would reassert themselves, or the covert, tenacious resistance new methods would evoke. The organization was so new, success so immediate, growth so explosive, and resources so short it was necessary to hire most management from outside the company. Each person came full of the techniques, culture, and habits of the world from which they emerged. Many took the openness and liberty of VISA as applicable to them in relation to those to whom they reported, but not in relation to those over whom they had authority. As the company grew, time after time I would discover departments within the company where people were subjected to intolerable rules and regulations, as those who promulgated them discovered when I insisted they must submit to them as well if they were to be continued. Without deep cultural change, they would naturally see my efforts to restrain their conduct as command and control, and so it was.

I used command-and-control techniques to prevent command and control. Plain stupid!

At critical points of difficulty and stress, my impatience would rise, the old ways would overpower inclination, and I would seize control of a project, always with the excuse of dire necessity and, later, with much regret. Each such act put the lie to what I believed and tried to persuade others to accept. All too often, I was simply unable to be the change I wanted to see.

Members of the board brought to the table all the old assumptions about good management. The success of the organization created considerable tolerance of new and different management techniques. On the whole, however, each new approach was on sufferance. Each failure brought pressure to conform to the old ways. Since the board was deliberately structured so that management could not control its composition, and to ensure 10 or 15 percent annual turnover as well, there were always new directors with a full load of old management baggage who had little or no idea of the concepts that had led to the success the organization now enjoyed.

No matter how much success we had, they were convinced it could be much greater if done in the manner to which they were accustomed. No matter what the failure, they were persuaded it could have been prevented had it been handled in the traditional way. Occasionally, there was some truth in what they said. Always, there was no way to refute it. The pressure to revert and conform, both from within and without the organization, was intense and unceasing. On the whole, we had poor methods and techniques and far too little of them to bring about the cultural change that a chaordic organization requires, nor did we have a leader who was fully alert to the need for it.

In the beginning, there were no titles at NBI. When recruiting new people accustomed to the old ways, the question of titles would inevitably come up. In my desk was a long typed list. With a serious expression, I would explain it was our custom to have each employee select their own title, which they could change from time to time if it failed to meet their needs. On the list was a rich selection: Grand Duke, Lord, Lady, Prince, Queen, Princess, King, Duchess, Ayatollah, Bishop, Samurai, and so on. If they wished to add a descriptive addition, that would be all right. They could be the Ayatollah of Advertising or the Grand Duke of Accounting. The only requirement was that the title must be used on all occasions.

Using the same logic, we had no job descriptions. I was often asked, "How will people know what I do?"

"If what you do is not readily apparent to everyone by your words, conduct, and acts, that becomes a very interesting question," I would reply. It was great fun while it lasted. Unfortunately, we were embedded in one of the most title-conscious industries that ever existed; one with a long tradition of rewarding people with labels rather than income. In time, we bent to the pressure and accepted the need for "manager of" or "director of." Bit by bit, the old patterns reasserted themselves until a host of "vices" arose, all bred from the simple fact that I was not farsighted enough to embed in the original bylaws something other than "president," thus becoming the first virus to infect the lot.

In time, there were some promises we could not keep, although they were few and far between. One was immense. After a number of early successes in building an electronic system for authorization, BASE 1, and another for clearing transactions, BASE 2, we were approached by several members who professed to have common needs (mistake one, they did not), asking if we would undertake the creation of cardholder and merchant-processing software for the banks to use, BASE 3. By pooling money and effort, it was thought much more sophisticated software could be developed at reduced cost. The members having immediate need would underwrite the development of the product. It would then be available to all other members who would, if they elected to use it, pay a proportionate share of the development cost, to be distributed to the initial funders.

A group of VISA people interested in the project assembled, along with representatives of interested banks. A decision was reached to purchase previously developed software that could be adapted (mistake two, it could not) to build the new system. The mistakes pyramided, and I was instrumental in every one. Costs soared above the original estimate and we went

> ### MiniMaxims
> *Failure is not to be feared. It is from failure that most growth comes; provided that one can recognize it, admit it, learn from it, rise above it, and try again.*

to the board for more money (mistake three). A vendor with marginal worth underbid a major part of the job and we were blinded by price (mistake four). Members could not agree on specifications. The scope of the project expanded without careful analysis of time or resources required.

The people handling the project were blinded by desire to succeed and determination not to let the company down. We made another trip to the well for more money and time, thinking it would surely see the project to even greater success than originally planned. It did not. The lesson finally sank in. We had never gone back to our purpose and principles to ask what card-processing software for bank use had to do with "creating the world's premier system for the exchange of value." It had nothing to do with our purpose, or our belief about decentralization of function in pursuit of it.

It was not a mistake of the people, it was a mistake of leadership. We were extremely good at some things, we were very good at many things, but we were not good at everything, and at some things we were pathetic. It is one of the principal arts of leadership to make that distinction, and I did not.

> **MiniMaxims**
>
> *Mistakes are toothless little things if you recognize and correct them. If you ignore or defend them, they grow fangs and bite.*

I called each director to take full responsibility for the failure and advised them that unless they had compelling reasons to the contrary (they did not), we would immediately cancel the project, return all money paid by the participant banks, and assist them in any way possible to pursue other alternatives. We would announce publicly the failure of the project and absorb a $3 million loss from the general revenues of the company. It was a bitter pill to swallow, for the third attempt may well have been successful. But that was precisely the problem. Such a success would lead us further and further from our purpose and principles.

During the formation of NBI and Ibanco, wrack my brain and twist Old Monkey's tail as I might, I could devise no way to include cardholders and merchants as owner-members of the system. They should have been, for they are certainly relevant and affected parties. The slightest hint of the subject in 1969 and those involved in the reconception of the BankAmericard system went into shock. Such thoughts had to be set aside, since everyone was already pushed to the limits of their ability to accept change by that which was being proposed.

At the time NBI was formed, Bank of America cardholders produced more than a third of the volume of the system. It was neither possible nor equitable to induce the bank to surrender ownership of the system, give up the quarter percent of the sales volume they extracted from all other banks under the licensing agreement, and accept the obligation to pay a third of the service fees of the new system as well. It was agreed they would pay at the same rate as all other banks, but with a prescribed maximum. It was my belief that, as sales volume became more evenly distributed, the maximum would be eliminated.

Quite the opposite occurred. As the success of the system pushed the volume of other members near the maximum, they banded together to assert that the success was due to their superior efforts and insist that they were also entitled to pay at the lower rate. No amount of persuasion could open their minds to another view. The board, over my opposition, decided that the maximum should apply to all banks whose volumes reached the prescribed level *no matter what percentage* of system volume they enjoyed. In my mind, the inequity of larger members paying at a lower rate than the smaller members was apparent, but it made no difference. The cap remained as a sort of divine right of kings; the right of those with the largest incomes and most power to pay the lowest taxes.

We did not foresee the intense pressures that would be exerted both within the staff and by members for the recentralization of power and wealth. At the time, I did not understand the depth that mechanistic, dominator concepts held on the minds and hearts of people, including my own, nor how tenaciously and powerfully they would reassert themselves. It was not then apparent how difficult it was to sustain new beliefs and concepts or how long it would take for them to sink to the bone and become habitual conduct. Although VISA arose from thinking about organizations as living, biological systems, I missed completely the need for an institutional immune system to thwart the viruses of old ways.

From the beginning, I thought, believed, and worked for a complete transition from the concept of credit card to the concept of transaction device. It was my hope that issuers would evolve from marketing the card primarily as an instrument for debt to marketing it as an instrument for the exchange of value. It was my hope that revenues of issuers would evolve from reliance on interest on cardholder debt, and discount from merchants, to reliance on transaction pricing for services provided. It was my hope that this would equitably distribute cost between the most affluent and least affluent customers. Twenty-nine years later, that has not happened, and interest on debt of those who need to pay monthly supports free service to the affluent.

In spite of my pride in all that VISA demonstrated about the power of chaordic concept of organization and all the things it has accomplished, I do not believe that VISA is a model to emulate. It is no more than an archetype to study, learn from, and improve upon.

In the chapters to come, we will leave bank cards and move into the beginning of an odyssey incomparably more interesting and important than VISA. Before we do, there is one more memory I must share.

How could you treat people who performed a miracle of communications with a piece of string and a dirty coffee cup as though they were no more than "Human Resources"? You couldn't and we didn't. The greatest delight from all those days were open staff meetings, from which we never wavered. Within a day after every board meeting, open meetings were held to include every employee of the company, at every level including the newest. They were conducted by the most senior person present. At the meeting, every decision of the board was fully disclosed. Every employee was free to ask any question about the decisions, or anything else of concern to them. They were answered fully. "That's confidential" was not considered an answer. "I don't know but I'll find out and tell you at the next meeting" was permissible, but only if the promise was faithfully kept.

All that I ever said of a cautionary nature was, "You realize that some things you will learn could be detrimental to our community if they were bandied about publicly or prematurely leaked to the press. However, until we are consistently proved wrong, we will do our best to behave in accordance with belief that mutual respect and trust is the strongest bond among people, and can be relied upon."

The promise of open meetings and candor was often put to the test by skeptical employees. Near the end of one meeting, after reminding the people that nothing was off-limits and asking if there were more questions, a secretary rose, fixed her eyes on mine, and said, "Yes, I would like to know what you are paid, all the other perks you enjoy, and why you think they're justified." There was absolute, ominous silence as I stood before three hundred intent faces, collected my wits, consulted conviction, and answered, fully and in detail.

On another occasion, a new employee with a rather abrasive manner rose to say, "No company tells the truth to its employees and I don't believe that this one is different. There is no way you tell us everything." In your teeth, Mr. President, you're a liar, was the unspoken message. Her comment did not rise from desire to create trouble, but from conviction she was being lied to and resentment at that perception. What could I say that would not result in confrontation, yet reassure her that we did our very best to live up to our beliefs?

It was taken out of my hands. Rising with an accusatory finger pointing like a dagger at the questioner, a woman half-shouted in a voice shaking with outrage, "You don't know what you're talking about! I've typed the board minutes for ten years and you're told everything. Everything!"

There was no need to do more than to say, "When we act from our deepest convictions it is impossible to reach perfection. The question was sincere. So was the reply. And so is our effort to live in accordance with our beliefs about an open company. If we can all accept that, there is nothing more to be said." And nothing more was.

In time, a custom emerged that I dearly loved. When the people had their questions answered and the meeting was nearing an end, it would be my turn. "What is the latest rumor about the company circulating the halls and circling the water cooler?" With great laughter, they would be obliged to respond. It was marvelous fun to speculate where the rumors may have originated, admit how much truth there was in them, and wonder whether that which was false originated from fear, suspicion, or anxiety, or from plain old human love of stories to tell. I have always suspected that the more creative people concocted outrageous rumors for the fun of having them revealed at the meetings. I may have planted one or two myself, but if I did, no one will ever know.

> **MiniMaxims**
> *You can't tickle yourself. It's a social act.*

In the darkest times, and there were many, I could never look out at so many wonderful people and engage with them in laughter and give-and-take without walking from the room filled with wonder at the human spirit. They could do anything! Anything! And so can everyone, everywhere, if our minds are open enough, our hearts warm enough, and our spirits strong enough to conceive of institutions that enable us to do so.

CHAPTER SEVENTEEN

The Jeweled Bearing

I cannot praise a fugitive and cloistered virtue,
unexercised and unbreathed, that never sallies out
and sees her adversary, but slinks out of the race,
where that immortal garland is to be run for, not
without dust and heat. Assuredly we bring not
innocence into the world, we bring impurity much
rather; that which purifies us is trial, and trial is
by what is contrary.

—JOHN MILTON

Early in 1984, the curtain came down on my performance as CEO of VISA. The business costume went into the closet and I went directly from the commercial theater to life on two hundred acres of remote, ravaged land. It was shockingly difficult; an aching void emptied of things once craved—money, power, prestige, position—all achieved and now abandoned. The lifelong dream of pioneering a new concept of organization had been realized. There was pride and gratification in knowing what it had been, what it now was, and what it might become, but there was a deep sense of failure about what it ought to be. The world was marveling at its success, but to me the flaws were all too apparent. There was also a sense that courage had failed. I had quit. Given up. Must I always feel like a sheared sheep? Well, so be it. Life flows on. Bishop Butler had the right idea.

"Things are as they are and will be as they will be, why choose to be deceived?"

One by one, I picked up the frayed ends of brighter, more beautiful threads, and slowly rewove them deeply into the fabric of becoming—nature, literature, grandchildren, art, contemplation, and humility. Gradually the void filled, pain eased, and ten drastically different but wonderful years emerged.

It was in 1993, the ninth year of that decade of seclusion, when Thee Ancient One, Old Monkey Mind, and I had our glorious day together ending with a splendid storm, Mitchell Waldrup's book, *Complexity*, sauna, and bed. In the middle of the night, as the lamp was damped and the soft blanket of lightless night muffled the buzzing hive of consciousness, the book dropped from my hand.

> **MiniMaxims**
>
> *Fame is fool's gold of the ego; as soon threadbare and out of fashion as a suit of clothes.*

Morning brought a clear sky, cool air, a world dripping from rainfall and filled with sparkling sunlight in the aftermath of the storm. At the breakfast table, as I shared with Ferol my amazement that concepts now emerging in science were surprisingly similar to organizational concepts that I had been working with for decades, she laughingly remarked, "You haven't been this excited since you had those crazy notions about a global device for the exchange of value twenty-five years ago. Come down off the ceiling, call the people at the Institute, and find out what's going on."

"No way," I replied. "It's okay to think about, but it was hard enough to put all that aside once. I'm not going to get involved again."

I whistle up Baron, our German Shepherd, and set out on a walk through the woods. This day belongs to Baron, Old Monkey, and me, to reflect and reconnect with reality and nature as it is, not as the scientists in the labs claim it to be. Their claims lie in the rational corner of the mind, that small place where the trickster Measurement creates mechanistic, particulate thought. In that world, we can never be more than "thing." Well, I'm not feeling like "thing" this morning. I feel more like "becoming."

Baron has no adjustment to make. In his German Shepherd mind, he is always whole and at one with the world. Overjoyed at sight of the walking stick, he leaps straight up, expressing in every way, "Yeah! Let's live a little." His nose is high, straight into the wind, as he roves from side to side, perceiving what lies in the dense woods ahead. From time to time, he lowers it to grass and ground, examining each creature that passed in the night. His ears are twitching with sounds beyond my ken. The mental map he creates of the morning is one I can never know. What an adventure it would be to borrow his nose for a day and connect with the world in his way. It's beyond imagining. How many ways of knowing are there which escape human perception?

We are stopped in our tracks by a cacophony in the mouth of the canyon a quarter mile ahead. It takes a few seconds to realize it is a pack of coyotes in conversation about something we can't discern. Their vocal range is extraordinary. In the dark of night, I have mistaken them for a screaming child, a moaning cow, an injured dog. What images they are communicating to one another and to Baron's German Shepherd mind, I can't imagine.

Baron races ahead, and returns, barking and whining to urge me on. We circle the pond, climb to the summit of the ridge, and sit for an hour, enjoying the immense panorama of forested hills, village, valleys, farms, and ocean. I pick up a stick and begin scratching at the forest debris beneath my feet.

Billions upon billions of self-organizing interactions are occurring second by second in the square yard of soil, each interconnecting, relating, creating, and shaping self and others. Every particle is inseparably interacting and relating to others, and they to still others, unto the remote reaches of the universe and beyond—beyond knowing—but *not beyond awareness, respect, and love.* The mystery of it all is overwhelmingly beautiful. Were it fully explained, what would be the point of life? Could there even be life? I am lost in the wonder of it all.

One thought returns continually, each time more compelling, each time more universal. The sheep's first law of the universe: *Everything is its opposite.* In Western, mechanistic minds, the head and tail of a coin are separate things, yet one defines the other. It is impossible to conceive of the tail of the coin without the concept of *the other side* as the head. If the coin were sliced, separating the "head" and "tail" side as we know them, the concept of two sides of each half would remain. One could go on slicing and reconfiguring the coin forever, and the concept of "sides" would remain, one defining the other.

This separatist, mechanistic concept is a powerful way of viewing the world, a useful way of perceiving some aspects of reality and a practical aid in day-to-day activities. Difficulty begins when it is held forth as *the best way* of perceiving reality. Destruction begins when it is held forth as *the only way.* It is only one perspective; only one way of perceiving reality. And it is the best way only for narrow, limited, quantifiable purposes.

A deeper manifestation of mechanistic, separatist thought is perception that things are either separable or inseparable, either distinguishable or indistinguishable. In truth, *any thing both is and is not; is both same and opposite, depending on the perspective with which we choose to think of it.* To worship one perception and deny another, no matter which we worship or deny, is the curse of modernity.

When we behave as though the linear, mechanistic, separatist, cause-and-effect perspective is the only way to understand, we mentally disconnect from the beautiful, magnificent flow of life and retreat into ever smaller compartments of specialized denial.

> **MiniMaxims**
>
> *All distinctions are useful, but none are truth or reality.*

We no longer affirm the mystery of endless connectivity and wholeness—awareness that we, the quark and the universe, are both one and many, both infinite and finite, both particulate and whole. We begin to shrivel our life into the whining, puerile, pitiful little concepts of *me* and *mine, get* and *keep, win* and *lose.* Life is emptied of content. Self-interest and greed become worthy of emulation. Winning is all that matters. Wealth, fame, and power become deities to worship. It is a desperately sick society that does so; a society that turns its back on life and moves toward destruction and death. It is just such a society we are creating.

It is an equally sick society that denies separability, individuality, and difference. Such a society loses the creative force of conflict, the formative tension of opposing forces, the vitality of change, the creativity of difference, and the beauty of distinction. It sinks into uniformity, conformity, and indifference. It would be a great mistake to sink into such a gray miasma in an effort to correct present ills.

Baron has had enough sitting. We rise and work our way down the ridge for a bit of lunch. At the house, on the message machine I hear the sound of an unfamiliar voice. "This is Steve Millard." The voice claims we met once years before, gives a telephone number, and requests a call. I can't remember a meeting. After ten years of isolation and an unlisted telephone number, calls from strangers are rare. Probably another hustling salesman. I reach for the erase button, then pause. Something in the voice has aroused my curiosity. I dial the number and am soon connected.

"You may not remember," he explains, "but we met once for lunch five years ago when I tried to persuade you to do some consulting. For some reason, you popped into my mind this morning and I decided to call. We're forming another company and your experience could be helpful. Could we discuss it?" A vague recollection of the meeting comes to mind. I am annoyed, anxious to end the call and less than gracious.

"Nothing has changed. I severed all connections with business nine years ago. There is no chance whatever that I would do any consulting."

He laughs and replies. "You made that clear at our last meeting. I thought perhaps you had changed your mind. I don't want to intrude, but somehow I felt compelled to call." Memory sharpens as Steve reminds me that during the lunch, we had discovered a mutual love of literature. We had happily talked away half the afternoon about things we were reading.

"Have you read anything lately that has caught your interest?" Steve asks.

"I just finished a book called *Complexity*. It's about a handful of scientists speculating about the nature of complex, adaptive systems. It's extraordinary, for whole paragraphs and sentences of the book echo what I have been thinking and arguing about with respect to organizations for—" He cuts me off midsentence.

"I don't believe it! This is extraordinary! You must be talking about the Santa Fe Institute. I've been there many times. The chairman, Jim Pelkey, is a friend of mine. He lives in Atherton, not ten miles from your place." The hair begins to rise on my arms and the back of my neck as he continues, "You simply have to meet him. I'll arrange lunch." And he did just that. One can never know when one will step on one of the tiny, jeweled bearings on which a life can turn. Within the week, Jim Pelkey, a venture capitalist, and I are at lunch, spewing over each other like two small, erupting volcanoes, as we share his experience with the Institute and mine with VISA. He is insistent that I must visit the Institute and become involved. One thing is plain. There should be no misunderstanding.

"Jim, there is something which you should know. I have nothing to give the Institute. My entire net worth is no more than a few hours' interest on Bill Gates's petty cash account." He is a bit taken aback, expressing amazement that one could spend the better part of their life struggling to create and bring to maturity a trillion dollar company without any possibility of equity or wealth. Nor can he understand why, at the peak of success, one would simply walk away from the security, power, and position that such success provides. It is too complicated to explain, and I do not try. He assures me my lack of money does not matter. I can make a contribution to the organization in other ways, perhaps in helping to raise money.

"Jim, I have never asked anyone for money in my life. I have no talent for it and no connections that would lend themselves to doing so." Whether he believes me or not is hard to say, but he pushes on, pointing out the error of making judgments without first visiting the Institute. I thank him for the invitation and agree to think about it.

In the week that follows, it is as though the early days formulating patterns of thought about a global device for the exchange of value are repeating themselves. My mind is leaping into the future. Could such an institute be reconceived in order to self-organize into hundreds, then thousands of fractals worldwide? Could such an organization develop social and organizational concepts more in harmony with science, the human spirit, and the ecosphere? It is not so much the science they profess to study that intrigues me, but the Institute itself. What is the nature of the organization—its structure, its governance, its conceptual beliefs? Do its nature, anatomy, and behavior reflect the emergent science it studies?

Nothing in the next week resolves the turmoil, nor can the extraordinary synchronicity of events be put from my mind. An inner voice experienced at pivotal points in my life will not be silent. "Something is trying to happen. It is filled with potential and fraught with peril. It wants to use you. Set foot on the path, and there is no turning back. The choice is yours—refuse or be used." I cannot put to rest a vague sense that the something which is trying to happen may be what my life is about. Sharp in mind is the lifelong sense of not belonging, of everything experienced as only preparatory. Recollection of inability to identify myself with the president of VISA returns, stronger than ever, as does the only explanation I could offer when leaving VISA: "I simply want to open my life to new possibilities." The humor does not escape me. If these are the "new possibilities," they were infernally slow coming.

Ferol and I agree that nothing is to be lost by an open mind and trip to the Institute. Let things evolve as they will. If it comes to nothing, well, nothing is where it began. I call Jim to say that we will go, explaining that it is the structural aspects of the Institute that interest me most. If he will provide copies of organizational documents, the history of the Institute, and make arrangements for me to speak with founders about their concept of the organization and its purpose, I will be happy to go, providing we agree there are no commitments, one way or the other. He seems pleased.

The drive up the valley from the airport to the Institute is somberly beautiful. Mountains to the east, barren, dry land in the valley, the vast bowl of the sky, and towering cumulus clouds on fire from the afternoon sun remind us powerfully of our childhood mountain home.

Meetings over the next few days are disappointing. The structural concept of the Institute is seventeenth century. It seems little different than a thousand other institutes, with the exception that it promises to be multidisciplinarian, rather than a single academic silo. I have no desire to engage in academic study and publish obtuse papers about complexity theory in the midst of crumbling societies, a disintegrating biosphere, mass violence, and starving people. I want to do something about them. Whether the smallest discernible bit of matter is a wave or a particle seems akin to old religious arguments about how many angels can dance on the point of a pin, and in the midst of critical social problems, just about as useful. Thought of becoming enmeshed in such a situation seems increasingly wrong. Yet the ideas which have dominated my life have been aroused and feelings that they might find acceptance are unsettling.

At a break in a meeting at the Institute, a thin, intense young man appears, introducing himself as Joel Getzendanner, vice president of the Joyce Foundation, saying he had been told to look me up. Joel wants to discuss how VISA came into being and the chaordic concepts on which it is based. He keeps me up far into the night, asking countless questions, challenging my beliefs and assertions. Whether he is deeply interested or merely argumentive is impossible to know. He probes ever deeper into the past, then into the future, as he searches for understanding about chaordic concepts and how they might be applied to other organizations. "I agree we are in the midst of a global epidemic of institutional failure," Joel says, "but I'm not clear about where you think it will lead."

"Joel, in my view, institutional failure will continue to escalate. There will be enormous social carnage. People will demand order in the streets. There will be regression to even more dictatorial institutions, both political and commercial, which could well last for fifty or a hundred years. Such repression cannot endure. Those institutions, in turn, will collapse, leading to even greater social carnage. Maybe then, changed consciousness throughout society and different conditions may allow chaordic concepts of organization to become universally understood and accepted. The problem is, there may not be much left to emerge from."

"But, that's just not acceptable," Joel vehemently replies.

I tease him with a smile. "You must have a marvelous telephone, Joel. Evolution has never rung anyone I know to ask consent."

He grins. "Fair enough. But if chaordic organizations like VISA and the Internet could emerge, surely equally substantial change could occur elsewhere. Surely, institutional failure doesn't have to be catastrophic before change is possible."

"Joel, the question is not whether something is theoretically possible, but whether or not it will happen. Social evolution has always been filled with institutional collapse and reconstruction. New concepts and ideas can certainly change the world. In fact, they may be the only thing that ever has. But that doesn't happen until masses of people are prepared to act on them. It will take massive failure, regression, and failure again, before the old concepts are entirely discredited." Joel will not accept my argument.

"We have to do better. No matter how much money the Joyce Foundation and other philanthropic organizations give to foster constructive social change, it doesn't seem to be working. I've never before met anyone who consciously set out to create such an organization, let alone succeeded. These ideas are important. You can't just sit in the woods and think. You ought to do something!" We argue into the night and part without agreement.

Over the next few months, Joel continued to pester me. He couldn't get chaordic concepts out of his mind, or the thought that they might have broad application. He was intrigued by the notion that four ordinary vice presidents of modest banks challenged themselves with a simple question: If anything imaginable was possible, if there were no constraints whatever, what would be the nature of an ideal organization to create the world's premier system for the exchange of value? He was fascinated at how it led to a sort of institutional genetic code—simple principles that allowed the VISA system to self-organize.

Joel wouldn't give up. He traveled to the ranch to dig ever deeper into the concepts. In the end, he threw my own words back in my face. "You did it once. Why not try again? Why not ask yourself, if anything imaginable was possible, if there were no constraints whatever, what would it take to create massive chaordic institutional change throughout society?" It was an irresistible question. It plagued me and Old Monkey Mind week after week. We prowled my library, bought more books, pored over hundreds of pages of past notes. Joel wouldn't leave it alone. He called several times urging us on. In time, it came down to four things.

EXAMPLES

At least a dozen extremely successful, new examples of chaordic organization, similar to VISA and the Internet, would have to evolve. They must emerge in such different fields as education, government, social services, commerce, and the environment, as well as in all nations and cultures, so that no one could argue the concepts were not universally applicable. They must transgress all existing organizational boundaries, linking people and institutions in diverse fields. Opportunities to create such organizations must be discovered. Methods and resources must be brought to bear to bring them about. Existing chaordic organizations must be analyzed, understood, and documented. People simply will not accept new concepts of organization or methods of management until they see a substantial number of such organizations obtaining superior results in correcting the vast systemic problems that plague society.

MODELS

Four-dimensional physical models of such structures would need to be created, so that people have something tangible to examine, relate to their existing organizations, play with, and enhance. Chaordic organizations cannot be portrayed in two dimensions on a traditional organization chart. They are more akin to the organization of neurons in a brain. Yet even the three dimensions of complex physicality are not enough. The fourth dimension must be the spiritual and ethical dimension—something we have largely lost sight of in existing organizations. How to physically embody and portray that dimension will be one of the great challenges.

In addition to the physical models, computer models would need to be created, collapsing time and graphically demonstrating in thirty minutes how, based on clarity of shared purpose and principles, chaordic organizations self-organize and evolve, creating and governing diversity and complexity beyond any possibility of central design, engineering, or control. People must see the thirty-year evolution of VISA, the Internet, and other such organizations in thirty minutes. The models must demonstrate how such organizations contain similarity of self-organizing patterns that would allow spontaneous interconnection into an equitable, enduring, twenty-first century society in harmony with the human spirit and the biosphere.

INTELLECTUAL FOUNDATION

The examples must be supported with an impeccable intellectual foundation. Whether we like it or not, whether it is a good thing or not, science is the religion of the twenty-first century, and academia is its church. The economic, scientific, political, historical, theological, technological, and philosophical rationale for such organizations would have to be documented and synthesized. Much of the work has already been done; however, it is not yet complete, exists in insular specialties, and lacks coherence and clarity. Far more important, neither the language nor metaphors necessary for massive dissemination and understanding have yet evolved.

ORGANIZATION

A global organization would have to emerge, linking in a vast complex of shared theoretical and experiential learning, people and institutions of every persuasion concerned about institutional failure and committed to doing something about it. It must self-organize in accordance with the principles it espouses and, itself, be one of the successful examples of chaordic organization. The sole (one might even risk saying soul) purpose of the organization should be the development, dissemination, and implementation of new, chaordic concepts of organization. Were the global organization properly conceived, it would organically dissolve into the fruits of its labor.

I told Joel of the four conditions and my conviction that if all were to be set in motion simultaneously, supported by a substantial, eclectic group of credible people, and be well under way by the turn of the century, no institution, political, commercial, or social, could ignore the movement. They might ridicule it. They might fight it. They might support it. But they could not ignore it. There was a good chance that such a movement would capture the imagination of the world and catalyze the massive institutional change that a liveable future demands. And I told Joel that there was absolutely no possibility of any of the four emerging in the foreseeable future, let alone all of them at once. I thought Joel would go away, but he didn't. Joel sticks like a burr.

Old Monkey Mind and I had long played with thoughts about the causes of institutional failure. We had concluded it had little to do with money, modern economic theory, or business cycles. When organizations lose shared purpose and principles—their sense of community—they are already in process of decay and dissolution, even though they may linger with outward appearance of success for some time. Businesses, as well as races, tribes, and nations, do not disappear when they are conquered or repressed, but when they become despondent and lose excitement and hope about the future. When institutions reach that stage, people withdraw relevance from them and from those who purport to manage them. They turn away. They stop listening. When people no longer believe in existing institutions and societal norms, they often turn to destructive behavior in the name of self-interest. What people no longer believe in building up, they will inevitable tear down.

We have lost our local, communal stories and destroyed the places for their telling. Nor do we yet have a new compelling global story or communal places for its telling. The stories now endlessly drummed into us are not our stories. They are the sto- ries those with escalating power and wealth tell to one another. Stories they incessantly pour into us through commercializa- tion of media and every other

> **MiniMaxims**
>
> *The surest way to satisfy the greed of the few is to arouse it in the many.*

aspect of life. They are stories designed to arouse greed in the many to satisfy it in the few. They are stories that appeal to the worst, not the best in us. They are false stories. Deep inside, we no longer believe them. Neither do those who tell them, if the truth be known.

If the story of a truly different and better society could be told, no matter how remote, no matter how difficult to realize, or even the story of a path to that end, it would capture the imagi- nation of the world. It would submerge the urge to isolation and destructive behavior in excitement and new hope for the future. People would then see the wisdom of preserving the substance of the past, while enhancing and clothing it in the forms of the future. They would see the wisdom of sustaining the old order of things, even as they assist in its transformation. For the first time in history, we might engage in global evolutionary social and insti- tutional change without an appalling cycle of destruction and reconstruction.

Joel returned to argue on. How could anyone be certain that the objectives were impossible? Perhaps the world had shifted in my decade of isolation. Hadn't my thinking about chaordic concepts evolved in the past ten years? What if thousands of people brought their abilities to bear on the concepts? If soci- etal perceptions had altered, if the concepts had evolved, if concern had increased, if science was shifting, perhaps there was some possibility that the four objectives could be realized.

Joel made an absurd proposal. If the Joyce Foundation would make its first unconditional grant to an individual to cover expenses, would I contribute my time to investigate as freely and broadly as I liked whether or not the four objectives were indeed impossible, and if I should change my mind, what might be required to set them in motion?

"Joel, it's ridiculous. An asthmatic, hard of hearing, sixty-six-year-old man who has lived in isolation and anonymity for nine years is not going to accomplish anything. It would be a complete waste of money and time. This has been an interesting exercise, but it makes no sense to go on."

"You can't be sure of that. People have lost faith in existing institutions. They're growing desperate for new ideas. If you're wrong, and the four conditions could be set in motion, the payoff could be enormous."

"Joel, the need is obvious, but you don't know how incredibly difficult it is to gain acceptance of new concepts that call into question the old. I don't agree that society has shifted that much. I've done my bit. This has been interesting, but nothing can come of it. The answer is no!" As Joel left disappointed, neither of us knew it was not the last word on the subject.

A week later, as Ferol and I happily prepare to welcome the family for a holiday at the ranch, a lynx appears, concentrating on a freshly dug gopher mound in the green grass of the undulating hillside below the study window. The binoculars bring it within a few feet. It is a poem of coordination and concentration. Each paw is sequentially raised in imperceptible, liquid motion, moved forward, and inserted toes-first into the grass, then angled to rest silently on the earth. In slow motion the lynx flows forward, six-inch tail motionless, eyes unblinking. It slowly shifts weight onto its haunches in a half-crouch, muscles in back and forequarters rippling under the sleek coat. If there is a more perfect manifestation of The Essence That Is, I've never seen it. Too quick for the human eye, it leaps. A gopher, kicking dirt as it backs from the burrow, is impaled on curved claws. Lunch is served.

Old Monkey Mind is fascinated and can't leave it alone. Lynx happens but cannot be done. The essence of lynx is beyond measurement, design, engineering, or knowing. It is not chaotic. It is not controlled. It is orderly pattern at the edge of chaos. It is chaordic. Lynx is not a thing of the rational mind. It is in the realm of spirit, intuition, feeling, and wisdom. If we knew everything about every atom of its structure, and about every particle of every atom, we would know nothing about lynx. Lynx is an inseparable, interacting relationship between earth, grass, light, air, gravity, rodent, heat, man, and countless other things. Each thing, in turn, is another interacting relationship between countless others, unto infinity. Lynx is atoms formed and re-formed in countless ways throughout eternity. Lynx is time and time is lynx. Lynx is universe and universe is lynx. Man is atoms formed and re-formed in countless ways throughout eternity. Man is lynx and lynx is man, formed of one another. Who can know the composition of the next minute? Certainly neither lynx nor man.

The next morning, sitting once again in the study as seven grandchildren play happily in the grass and flowers where yesterday lynx dined on gopher, I can't put Joel's proposal from mind. If we can't conceive of institutions as more than machines; if they can't be brought into harmony with the spirit of grandchildren, lynx, and land, then accelerating institutional failure and social and ecological carnage are certain. If the epidemic gets out of hand, it could happen within the next two or three decades. My grandchildren and their children will be caught up in the carnage. I could still be alive. They might find out their grandfather was asked to try to do something and refused.

"Why didn't you do it?" they would be certain to ask. What would I say? Too old? Not enough time? Too difficult? No money? No power? There could be no answer, only excuses. It's a conversation I do not care to contemplate or dare to risk. The image that has appeared to me at every low and high point in my life returns, more vivid than ever. Someone raises their arms to the heavens crying, "Why me, God?" The bemused reply is ever the same, "Why not?"

Joel answers on the first ring. "Joel, if you can arrange a meeting with your board of trustees so that I can make certain they understand the odds of success are too small to calculate, and if they then want to cover the costs, I'll do it."

A week or so later, in 1994, I am at dinner in Chicago with Joel, Deborah Leff, president, and the board of trustees of the Joyce Foundation. They have listened with interest and asked a great many questions, some with considerable skepticism. Whether it is a subconscious wish to be relieved of the responsibility or desire to make certain they understand the full extent of the risk is not clear, but I finish by saying, "Were I a trustee of the Joyce Foundation, I could not, in good conscience, approve such a grant, for the chances that anything can come of it are too small to calculate. However, the decision is yours. If you wish to make the grant, I'll make the effort."

The long flight home is filled with misgiving. Joel calls the next morning. "Pack your bags, it wasn't unanimous, but they said yes."

The Odyssey

This is the true joy of life, the being used for a purpose recognized by yourself as a mighty one; the being throughly worn out before you are thrown on the scrap heap; the being a force of Nature instead of a feverish, selfish little clod of ailments and grievances complaining that the world will not devote itself to making you happy. . . . The only real tragedy in life is being used by personally minded men for purposes that you recognize to be base.
—GEORGE BERNARD SHAW

God will not ask me why I was not Moses. He will ask me why I was not Susya.
—RABBI SUSYA

In April 1994, I set out on an odyssey more improbable than VISA, and incomparably more important, searching out people concerned about pervasive social and ecological problems and committed to doing something about them. I asked the same questions over and over again of everyone I met. "Is there some pervasive cause we're not getting at underlying so many intractable societal problems? Is there an epidemic of institutional failure? What is the connection between the two? Are the dominant organizational metaphors and concepts any longer relevant? Do you think there is critical need for massive institutional reconception? If there is such a need, are the four objectives the right objectives? Do you think there is any chance they can be set in motion within five years?"

If the response was positive, I would add, "If an effort were undertaken by responsible people to realize those objectives, would you care enough to help bring them about?" Before parting I would ask, "Who do you think I should talk to that I have not met? What do you think I should read that I have not read?"

The odyssey led to shelves of books and articles. It led to hundreds of extraordinary people, inner-city leaders, scientists, corporate CEOs, Native American leaders, authors, software and communications experts, educators, entrepreneurs, environmentalists, politicians of every persuasion, economists, and theologians. It also led to a great many less specialized souls of exceptional understanding and wisdom.

Some were negative, indifferent, or bewildered. Most were deeply interested. Some were excited and anxious to begin. Invitations to speak began to arrive from diverse groups—the Life Insurance Marketing Association, the Arabian Gulf Business Awards Convention in Bahrain, Rabbobank executives in the Netherlands, environmental organizations, universities, school systems, trade associations, futures institutes.

Audience response was unlike anything I had previously experienced. Most would settle into deep silence as they struggled to absorb and understand the VISA story and the concepts. At the end, questions were usually intense and prolonged. Later, people would crowd around asking endless questions. Had I written a book? Where could they learn more? How could they help? When would an effort to set the objectives in motion begin? How can chaordic organizations be created? Can existing organizations transform themselves or must they be replaced? How can someone begin such work within a command-and-control organization? Where is this way of thinking taught? There seemed an insatiable hunger for new concepts—for renewed hope and a more creative, constructive path to the future.

It was difficult to accept the reaction. Thirty years of often bitter experience during which I had encountered an abundance of flattery, opposition, and deception had left me inclined to be cynical and cautious. But would so many strangers engage in deception by telling me what they thought I wanted to hear? What motive could they have for concealing their real thoughts? There was nothing I could do to help or to harm any of them. Why would they waste their time? To what purpose? My conviction that the four objectives were impossible to achieve began to waver. Maybe Joel was right. Maybe society had shifted in the past ten years.

Fascinating patterns began to emerge. Most women seemed to understand the concepts quickly, deeply, and intuitively. People raised in Eastern cultures and religions were also swift to understand. Native peoples had no trouble at all. Exceptions to the patterns were numerous, and pronounced, but the patterns were unmistakably there. Those who had the most difficulty with the concepts were often Caucasian men from Western societies in positions of power. People like me!

We were the ones who had created the old concepts. We were the ones who fought to sustain them. We were the obstacles to be overcome. It was our internal models that would require the most rigorous transformation. No wonder it had been a difficult lifelong struggle for me, and it was far from over. Not happy thoughts at all.

Within a year and a half after the odyssey began, it was devouring my life. It was beginning to seem like 1969 all over again, only multiplied a hundredfold. The concepts and ideas did not belong to me. They belonged to evolution—to all people.

They had a life of their own. The "I" that *is not* me had taken over and inexorably revealed its eternal nature; a "we" of such diversity and complexity that it is beyond knowing or even imagining, let alone controlling. But not beyond understanding.

In time, one thing became apparent. I had been wrong. There was a chance the four objectives could be realized. There was a possibility they were the right objectives. And if they could be set in motion, there was a chance they might attract enough attention to catalyze the massive cultural and institutional change that a liveable future demands.

I became convinced that with an intensive effort by a few hundred deeply committed people and institutions and $2 or $3 million a year for research, travel, and professional support, it all might happen. So what if I didn't have a small fraction of the cash required, a staff to make the attempt, or facilities from which to operate? Money is not the measure of man.

> **MiniMaxims**
>
> *Money is not the measure of man.*

Old Monkey Mind jumped on it. Okay, so now what, old man? Do we write to the Joyce Foundation and say we were wrong, it could happen, and wish them well? Do we write to those people whose interest has been aroused and say thanks a bunch for your time, for showing us we were wrong, and good luck to you? Do we call those who are willing to make an attempt to reconceive themselves as a chaordic organization and tell them it's been interesting, but you're on your own? Do we stop answering the telephone and ignore the mail? Those grandkids aren't going away. What are seven grandchildren worth anyway? And their children; and their children's children? What are a few billion grandchildren worth? Old Monkey and I finally got the message. We're pretty slow. It only took sixty-six years.

Realization of what I must do came in the form of questions to which there can be no answers, only insatiable desire to find out. Is this why I was so badly bloodied fighting my battles with institutions? Is this why I knew I had to endure the years with VISA, but could never identify "self" with "president?" Is this why I walked away for reasons I never fully understood? Is this why I've already had my "retirement"—ten wonderful years of bliss with nature and family? Was everything merely preparatory? *Is this what my life is all about?*

There it was, as simple and plain as that. An overwhelming sense that something extraordinary was trying to happen. It wanted to use me. I could say yes or no. That's what free will is all about. If I said no, life would be pleasant and comfortable, but I would be in denial of my becoming. *A life can't be made of denial. A life must be made of affirmation.* I knew without doubt that saying yes meant night-and-day labor, stress, criticism, deception, and frequent failure. But how else can one know growth, joy, and happiness? *Everything is its opposite.*

> **MiniMaxims**
>
> *A life can't be made of denial.*
> *A life is made of affirmation.*

There was no reason to hold back. I had already enjoyed more than my share of good things. *Life is a gift, bearing a gift, which is the art of giving.* It was time to make return. I would continue to earn an occasional speaking fee, as I had done in years past to supplement my pension. But I would restrict the speaking engagements to no more than 10 percent of my waking hours. I would reserve another 15 percent for family and self-indulgent pursuits. The remainder, at least seventy hours a week, and a portion of my income, I would devote to an effort to realize the four objectives. That work would be a labor of love for which I would take no compensation. It would be my legacy to my grandchildren, and to all grandchildren, everywhere.

Finally, at the age of sixty-six, four years before the millennium, I understood what my life was about. This was the direction I must go. This was the unknown I must explore. Wherever it led. Whoever my companions. No matter what the obstacles. For as long as I could endure. And a joyous decision it was.

> **MiniMaxims**
>
> *The eternal, internal light casts no shadow.*

𝒵♥

The extraordinary events that have happened since would require a book of their own, which you can begin to explore in the Epilogue. Nothing describes that which happened better than a paragraph from *The Scottish Himalayan Expedition,* by W. N. Murray. The last two lines are often attributed to Goethe, the German poet, philosopher, and scientist, one of the greatest spirits of the past few centuries.

Until one is committed there is always hesitancy, the chance to draw back, always ineffectiveness. Concerning all acts of initiative and creation there is one elementary truth the ignorance of which kills countless ideas and splendid plans. The moment one commits oneself, then providence moves too. Multitudes of things occur to help that which otherwise could never occur. A stream of events issues from the decision, raising to one's favor all manner of unforeseen accidents, meetings, and material assistance which no one could have dreamed would come their way:

"Whatever you can do or dream you can, begin it. Boldness has genius, power, and magic in it."

And so I began, and so this tale must end with a few final thoughts.

Aristotle argued that for a community to function properly all citizens should be within the sound of a single voice. He could not have dreamed that modern communication would make of the world but a single village composed of countless villages at hundreds of scales—from communities of four or five to a community of billions—and even beyond that to a community of trillions of life forms, all within the sound of a single voice.

Just as we are citizens of a city, province, or nation by right of birth, so too are we citizens of the world, for we were most certainly born there also. We are no less citizens of corporations, churches, and countless other organizations by right of choice. If we do not develop new and better concepts of organization and leadership wherein persuasion prevails over power, reason over emotion, trust over suspicion, hope over fear, cooperation over coercion, and liberty over tyranny, we shall never harness science or technology in the service of humanity, let alone in the service of all other creatures and the living earth on which we depend.

Instead, with the great levers of science and technology, we shall socially, economically, politically, and physically continue to tear this world apart. While that would bring bitter pain to us and shame to our ancestors, to our grandchildren, their children, and their children's children, it would be a legacy of agony and evil beyond comprehension. To the universe, it would be an event scarcely discernible, let alone worthy of note.

The American writer Norman Cousins put our dilemma succinctly two decades ago when he wrote, "A great technological ascent has taken place without any corresponding elevation of ideas. We have raised our station without raising our sights. We roam the heavens with the engines of hell—whatever mankind's success in intermediate organization, he has failed to make an organization of the whole. His finest energies have gone into interim projects. He has made a geographical entity of his world without a philosophy for ennobling it, a plan for conserving it, or an organization for sustaining it."

In his book *Celebrations of Life,* René Dubos, the world-renowned scientist and philosopher, wrote, "It is fortunate that practical necessities will compel local solutions to global problems. . . . The ideal for our planet would seem to be not a world government, but a world order in which social units maintain their identity while interplaying with each other through rich communications networks."

In his book *The Third Wave*, futurist Alvin Toffler suggests that ahead lies "a matrix of organizations with common interests, densely interrelated like the neurons in a brain."

How are we to discover these new ideas of community, these new concepts of organization? One can find no better answer than the words of Camus. "Great ideas," he wrote, "come into the world as quietly as doves. Perhaps then, if we listen attentively we shall hear, among the uproar of empires and nations, the faint fluttering of wings, the gentle stirrings of life and hope. Some will say this hope lies in a nation; others in a man. I believe rather that it is awakened, revived, nourished by millions of solitary individuals whose deeds and works every day negate frontiers and the crudest implications of history. Each and every one, on the foundations of their own suffering and joy, builds for all."

We are at that very point in time when a four-hundred-year-old age is rattling in its deathbed and another is struggling to be born. A shifting of culture, science, society, and institutions enormously greater and swifter than the world has ever experienced. Ahead, lies the *possibility* of regeneration of individuality, liberty, community, and ethics such as the world has never known, and a harmony with nature, with one another, and with the divine intelligence such as the world has always dreamed.

Chaordic we are, chaordic we will remain, chaordic the world is, and chaordic our institutions must become. It is the path to a liveable future in the centuries ahead, as society evolves into ever increasing diversity and complexity. Unfortunately, ahead lies equal possibility of massive institutional collapse, enormous social carnage, and regression to that ultimate manifestation of Newtonian, mechanistic concepts of organization—dictatorship—which, in turn, would have to collapse with even more carnage before chaordic institutions could emerge. It matters not a whit whether such regression is in the hands of governmental, corporate, or religious organizations.

Or have we, have we at long, long last, evolved to the point of sufficient wisdom, spirit, and will to discover the concepts and conditions by which chaordic institutions can find their way into being? Institutions that have inherent capacity for their own continual learning, order, and adaptation; institutions in harmony with the human spirit; institutions with capacity to co-evolve harmoniously with one another, with all people, with all other living things and with the earth itself to the highest potential of each and all.

I simply do not know the answer to that question, but as I said in the beginning, this much I do know—it is far too late and things are far too bad for pessimism. In such times as these, it is no failure to fall short of realizing all that we might dream; the failure is to fall short of dreaming all that we might realize.

We must try!

Then Providence Moved Too

If you read the last three chapters of the book, you realize that providence was moving even before I decided to commit the remainder of my days to realization of the four objectives. With commitment, it became a flood. "A multitude of things occurred to help that which could otherwise not occur. A stream of events issued from the decision, raising to my favor all manner of unforeseen accidents, meetings, and material assistance which I could not have dreamed would come my way." The tale of a single event shall stand for hundreds.

In the midst of the odyssey, even before I was persuaded the four objectives might be possible, Deborah Leff, president of the Joyce Foundation, called to say she had been discussing social problems with an old friend, Ralph Nader, who had challenged his Harvard Law School class to do more than hold reunions. He pointed out that most of them were now among the more fortunate members of society. They should do something about pressing societal problems. The challenge was taken up. Thirty came together to form the Appleseed Foundation, with the idea of organizing lawyers nationwide to donate time, resources, and skill to work for systemic societal change. Debbie had told Ralph about the grant the foundation had made to me, a bit about chaordic concepts, and urged him to meet with me. He was not enthused, but had not refused. Would I call Ralph and arrange a meeting?

"Debbie, are you mad? Nader is a radical liberal. I'm a conservative businessman. We wouldn't have two civil sentences to say to one another. It sounds like a meeting from hell." She was not to be put off.

"Look, I know you both. Call him. Arrange a meeting. You might both be surprised."

Two of my calls are not returned. Aha! Just as I thought! Well, I promised Debbie, so I'll make one last attempt. The person who answers brusquely claims "Mr. Nader is not available." The persistent part of me comes to the fore.

"Look, I'm going to be in Washington next week. If you have Mr. Nader's calendar, please see what hours are open and write in my name. He can scratch it out if he wants. No harm done."

She warms a little. When will I arrive? Will I hold for a moment? Suddenly, Nader is on the line, curtly explaining, "Hearings on the trade bill are scheduled next week and my calendar is filled."

I answer in kind. "Sorry to have troubled you. Debbie Leff seemed to think we should meet. I can't imagine why." There is a moment of silence.

"Her judgment is very good," he quietly replies. We agree to meet at 6:30 the night of my arrival, a week hence. On the plane to Washington I read material about the fledgling Appleseed Foundation. It has been in existence for a short time, has limited funding, and seems more idea than substance.

It is growing dark as I apprehensively walk five blocks from the hotel to Nader's office, along eerily empty sidewalks with sirens wailing and cars rushing by. I arrive at a shabbily pretentious old building, ascend wide stairs to a landing, and repeatedly ring a bell near a massive, weathered door. Eventually, someone arrives to usher me along a narrow hall and up an ancient wide, circular, marble staircase into a three-story, dimly lit, unheated rotunda. Three or four straight-backed chairs sit in the gloom at one side.

"Make yourself comfortable," my guide somberly declares. "Mr. Nader will be with you shortly." He disappears into the dark recesses, his footsteps echoing long after he has vanished. The silence of the tomb descends. This is real Phantom of the Opera stuff. I smile at a random thought. Will a masked Nader suddenly swing down from the shadows to the sound of organ music?

More echoing footsteps approach and a thin, ordinary-looking man walks out of the gloom, with a wry smile, holding out his hand. "I'm Ralph Nader." I compliment him on the impressive reception area. He explains that it is the rarely used rotunda of a building owned by a major foundation, in which he occasionally meets guests, since his adjacent offices are often jammed with people preparing for congressional hearings.

He immediately probes deeply into my activities and shares his hopes for the Appleseed Foundation. His interest rises swiftly, as does mine. I instinctively like the man. We use similar language and share many concerns. He is direct, unpretentious, with deep intelligence, quick perception, and a brusque, intense manner. Within the hour, he insists we have much to talk about. Can I find more time before I leave town? Of course.

I walk back to the hotel through streets empty of people, anxiety hovering over my shoulder. In the heart of the nation's capital, crowds of people vanish with the twilight. It's really two cities. During the day, it belongs to the affluent and powerful. At night, it belongs to the dispossessed, poor, and criminal. What more needs saying about present institutions?

Two days later, I meet with Ralph and Linda Singer, deputy director of the Appleseed Foundation, a lawyer in her late twenties, articulate, direct, and with a ready smile. Ralph seems to have an intense interest in chaordic concepts. They do not seem offended when I express doubt about Appleseed's organizational concept.

"Ralph, if you continue to structure Appleseed as a centralized foundation with a self-selected board which licenses and controls subordinate foundations, the more successful it becomes, the more it will behave exactly like the systems you try to change. There is no way to change mechanistic, dominator behavior by creating more mechanistic, dominator organizations, regardless of how many truckloads of good intentions you mix into the concrete. Centralization of power is centralization of power. It will inevitably corrupt and be corrupted."

Linda is blunt. "Will you help us reconceive the Appleseed Foundation? Could we be one of the new examples of chaordic organization you refer to in the first of your four objectives?"

Old Monkey Mind chatters in my ear. "Hold on here! Let's back up a minute! When did *the* four objectives become *our* objectives? We're just beginning to explore whether there is any possibility they might be brought into being. We don't yet believe they can, or that we want to be involved even if they are." I hedge.

"If you're serious and prepared to undertake a year or more of the most difficult work you are ever likely to do, and if you think Appleseed should be an example of the kind of change you intend to bring about elsewhere, it's worth considering. Perhaps we should all reflect on our discussions and decide later what might come of them." They agree.

The meeting with Ralph Nader was not at all unique. Within a year, there were hundreds of calls, many with similar requests. The diversity was astonishing—from the Conservation Law Foundation in New England, asking how chaordic concepts might be used for the restoration of the Northwest Atlantic marine system; from Peter Senge, founder of the Organizational

Learning Center at MIT, asking how the concepts might be used to reconceive that organization; from state directors of University Cooperative Extension; from U.S. Army generals. Later calls came from the Integrated Food and Farming Initiative; from health care, education, government, corporations; and from Bill Swing, Episcopal Bishop of California, founder of a global movement to unite people of every religious and ethical persuasion to seek an end to religious violence.

Within months it was apparent I would need a not-for-profit corporation to handle funds and employ a small staff. When I mentioned the need to Joel Getzendanner, he chuckled and said, "I though you might," then told me he anticipated the need and without saying anything to others, on his own time and from his own funds had incorporated such an organization and obtained tax clearance from the IRS. The corporation was inactive, waiting until I became aware of the need. I paid Joel his costs, the corporation was renamed the Chaordic Alliance and has become the primary organization for setting the four objectives in motion; and to which I now devote sixty or seventy hours a week without compensation.

I agreed to work with the group from Cooperative Extension. Immediately, two fine people, Larry Yee and Elwood Miller, each committed a year of sabbatical leave from their universities to work with me. I called Peter Senge to say I would be happy to work with the thirty members of his design team to reconceive the Organizational Learning Center at MIT. He told them of our need for financial support, and four corporations— Shell Oil, Harley Davidson, Phillips Components, and The Learning Circle—each volunteered gifts, from $15,000 to $30,000. I agreed to work with the Appleseed Foundation, and with a group of people from New England, now the Northwest Atlantic Marine Alliance.

The Cowell, Geraldine Dodge, Kellogg, Woodcock, Phalarope, and Jessie Smith Noyes foundations, as well as a number of corporations, other organizations, and individuals, have volunteered gifts ranging from a few dollars to $200,000. Greg Steltenpohl, founder of Odwalla Corporation, heard of the work. They contributed two years' use of a small building to house the fledgling effort. A young man, Geoffrey Strawbridge, appeared, explaining that the work was in harmony with what he felt called to do. He offered to work for nothing until the Chaordic Alliance could afford a modest salary.

The help that appeared did not begin to keep up with burgeoning interest and opportunities, but it was enough to keep the effort moving. More important, *we did not have to seek it out. It simply appeared, from people and places we could not have imagined.* Another simple tale shall stand as a symbol for hundreds such people.

At a critical point late in 1997, we received an anonymous message routed through a blind trust asking what we would do if we were to receive a major gift. I responded. Within weeks an extraordinary letter arrived:

> This is a letter to let you know that I would like to make a gift of one million dollars to the Chaordic Alliance. I would like to make this gift anonymously.
>
> Hope with a plan—that's what your work and ideas mean to me. Hope for the future of mankind, for our children, our grandchildren, and our great grandchildren, and ultimately, for our beautiful, miraculous, wounded earth. Hope that has a path; hope that feels linked to the reality of our wildly changing, technological world.
>
> I am impressed by your ideas that stress the importance of meeting core human needs in an organizational context.

Needs for dignity, for relationship, for shared meaning and purpose behind endeavor. Needs that are rarely addressed at the organizational base of our society, and needs, as you explain, that relate to the manageability, workability, and ultimate success of any organization.

I have faith in you and in your developing organization, and in the dream that we now share. My gift will come to you with a great deal of pleasure.

Sincerely,

Anonymous Donor

At about the same time, after a presentation to a large audience to which I explained that interest and projects had flooded the Alliance, forcing us to delay efforts to set in motion the third and fourth objectives, and our need for $3 million for that purpose, many people gathered around, excitedly asking questions. What were our plans? When did we expect to have the money? How could they help? What else did we need to get on with the work? One woman stood quietly in the background, thinking deeply, saying nothing. When the hubbub died down, she silently stepped forward, took my hand, and closed my fingers around some coins and bills. A tear glistened in the corner of her eye as she softly said, "It's all I have in my purse. Please, I want you to have it—for my grandchildren."

I stood silently, as the inevitable homily from my youth leaped into mind. "There's them as talks and them as does," I replied gently, "and you are clearly among the latter. Thank you." She vanished without giving her name. In my hand was four dollars and eighty-seven cents.

Let our two anonymous friends and donors be the symbol for people who daily confirm one of my deepest beliefs.

Life is a gift, which comes bearing a gift, which is the art of giving.

In this book it is impossible to give more than a hint of all that has emerged in the four years since realization that the first sixty-six years of my life were merely preparatory, and commitment to what that realization implied. What has emerged since and the societal change it promises is scarcely believable, and infinitely more important and exciting than VISA ever has been or ever could be. And it is emerging everywhere, not just at the Chaordic Alliance.

It is a story yet too green for adequate telling, which should ripen by the time this century comes to a close and the year 2001 begins. If The Essence That Is remains kind, and events allow, the second chapter of this odyssey will appear in another book. But, who knows, by then you may be a part of the odyssey and it will need no telling.

So this Epilogue ends with the same words as the Introduction. After all, I promised a chaordic book.

This is not a story of the past, although the past is in it. It is not my story, although I am in it. It is not your story, although you are in it. It is a story of the future—of a four-hundred-year-old age rattling in its deathbed and another struggling to be born.

All it asks is your commitment.

What Can You Do?

The most perplexing question throughout the writing of the book was, "What do you want the reader to do?" In time, the better question emerged. "Why do you think they will not know what to do much better than you?"

The Chaordic Alliance has only a quarter of the resources needed to set in motion the four objectives. We've done little to raise funds, preferring to concentrate effort and money on our objectives. You will understand why, as I wrote the book, Old Monkey Mind kept asking:

What if 200,000 people read the book and 1 in 10 cared enough to make a gift of $200?

What if 1 in 10 of the wealthiest 1 percent of the people who read the book cared enough to make a gift of 1 percent of their annual income?

What if 10 of the 500 largest corporations were to care enough to make a single gift of one-thousandth of their annual earnings?

What if 5 of the largest philanthropic foundations were to make a single gift of one-half of 1 percent of their annual giving?

What if only 1 of the 100 richest people made a single gift of a thousandth of their net worth.

If any one were to happen, within a year we could set in motion all four objectives with reasonable prospects of catalyzing the institutional change that a liveable future demands.

And what if every reader simply began the work, right now, right where they are—leading themselves, leading their superiors, leading their peers, freeing their subordinates to do the same—bringing into being chaordic organizations to permit it all to happen? And what if every reader shared this book with a half dozen friends?

And so the questions I can't answer go on and on. What is a grandchild worth? What are millions of grandchildren worth? What is the worth of all their children, and the children's children? And what is the worth of a beautiful, safe, productive earth on which they all can dwell?

You know what to do.

August 12, 1999

About the Chaordic Alliance

The Chaordic Alliance is a not-for-profit 501(c)(3) organization created to develop, disseminate, and implement new concepts of organization that more equitably distribute power and wealth, and are more compatible with the human spirit and the biosphere.

To achieve its purpose, the Chaordic Alliance has four primary objectives:

1. To assist in the evolution of new, successful chaordic organizations. Ideally, these organizations will span such diverse areas as education, government, social services, commerce, and the environment, to demonstrate that chaordic concepts have universal applicability. The Chaordic Alliance will develop methods and resources to help both existing and new institutions through the process of reconceiving themselves as chaordic institutions.

2. To create multidimensional models of chaordic organizations so that people have something to examine, experiment with, and compare to existing organizations. The models must contain the ethical and spiritual dimension generally lacking in current models. In addition, computer simulations will be created to allow people to quickly see how clarity of purpose and principles allow institutions to self-organize, evolve over decades, and link in new patterns for an enduring constructive society.

3. To further develop and disseminate an intellectual foundation for chaordic organizations. The intellectual foundation must integrate the economic, scientific, political, historical, technical, social, and philosophical rationale for such organizations and establish the common language and metaphors necessary for widespread understanding of chaordic concepts.
4. To assist in the creation of a global chaordic institution for the sole purpose of developing, disseminating, and implementing chaordic concepts of organization, linking individuals, institutions, and groups of all kinds committed to institutional and societal reconception in a vast web of shared learning. It must be organized on the principles it espouses and, itself, be a successful example of chaordic organization, enabling people to pursue chaordic concepts in unique ways, on any scale, at any time, for their own reasons.

The Chaordic Alliance is committed to creating the conditions for the formation of practical, innovative organizations that blend competition and cooperation to address critical societal and environmental issues. It grew out of the work of Dee W. Hock, Founder and CEO Emeritus, VISA International. VISA, which was based upon concepts of chaordic organizing, grew in two decades from a few hundred members to the largest enterprise in the world, fulfilling his vision of an enterprise that transcended nations, language, currency, custom, and culture, seamlessly blending competition and cooperation—chaos and order. In 1999, VISA linked 20,000 financial institutions, 14 million merchants, and 600 million consumers in 220 countries and territories, producing $1.25 trillion in volume. Mr. Hock is now Founder and Coordinating Director of the Chaordic Alliance:

The Chaordic Alliance
P.O. Box 907
Half Moon Bay, CA 94019-0907
Tel.: (650) 712-5830
Fax: (650) 712-5834
Website: www.chaordic.org
E-mail: chaordic@chaord.org

A Sample of Chaordic Alliance Participation in the Creation of New Chaordic Organizations

UNITED RELIGIONS INITIATIVE (URI)

URI is a global initiative to enable enduring daily cooperation among the people of the world's religious, spiritual, and ethical communities. Together, respecting each other's distinctiveness, the URI participants will seek to end violence between religions so they may work together for the good of all life. The modern idea for a forum of cooperation among the religions of the world had its beginnings in North America at the Parliament of World's Religions in Chicago, in 1893. Over a hundred years later, thousands of people from five continents are actively engaged in creating the United Religions, a global organization whose purpose is *to create a safe space for spiritual partnerships in which the people of the world pursue justice, healing, and peace, with reverence for all life.* The Chaordic Alliance began working with the URI's organization design team in early 1998 and has helped guide URI's development of its purpose, principles, concept, structure, and implementation.

The United Religions Initiative 1999 annual congress overwhelmingly approved the conceptual design and authorized the writing of a constitution and implementation of a plan to bring the new global organization into being in June 2000.

THE APPLESEED FOUNDATION

The Appleseed Foundation was founded by Ralph Nader and the Harvard Law School Class of 1958 to reclaim the law as a vehicle for achieving justice for all citizens. Appleseed's purpose is *to effect and enable constructive systemic change leading to a more just, equitable, and sustainable society.* To pursue this purpose, Appleseed is building a national network of locally self-organized and governed "Appleseed Centers for Law and Justice." These public interest law centers strive, in concert with the communities they serve, to identify and address systemic problems rather than to provide individual legal services. The Appleseed Foundation's chaordic structure coordinates the diverse actions of the local Appleseed Centers. The Chaordic Alliance assisted the Appleseed Foundation during its formation and continues to follow the growth of the various Appleseed Centers.

THE NORTHWEST ATLANTIC MARINE ALLIANCE (NAMA)

NAMA is a group of fishermen, community organizers, scientists, conservationists, educators, and others active in and knowledgeable about ocean fisheries management whose objective is to generate a new voice and institutional presence, open to all like-minded people, that will build on principles of ecological and economic sustainability, personal responsibility and accountability, resource protection, and distributed power and authority. NAMA's purpose is *to restore and enhance an enduring Northwest Atlantic marine system that supports a healthy and diverse abundance of marine life, and commercial, recreational, aesthetic, and other uses.* NAMA emphasizes the exchange of strategic information among participants and encourages equal opportunity among all parties to share in deliberations and decisions. Achieving its purpose will require fundamental restructuring of the participants' relationships to the marine environment and its resources, to the management structure that controlled those relationships, and to each other. If NAMA succeeds, it will provide a model for chaordic, self-organizing, community-based governance of any common, whether of land, forest, air, or ocean—a possible solution to the perplexing two-hundred-year-old problem of *ownership of the commons.*

Society for Organizational Learning (SOL)

SOL is an outgrowth of work begun at the MIT Center for Organizational Learning led by Peter Senge. In 1997, after working through the chaordic process with the Chaordic Alliance, SOL was created *to discover, integrate, and implement theories and practices for the interdependent development of people and their institutions.* SOL adopted a new constitution based on a chaordic model that integrates collaboration and governance among corporations, consultants, and university researchers. SOL is expanding internationally under a new constitution maximizing the potential for self-organized and governed national and local fractals.

The VValeo Initiative

The VValeo Initiative, the result of discussions among people from thirty leading health care organizations, is quickly expanding to include hundreds of participants, including the Department of Defense, the Veterans Health Care Service, and the Indian Health Care Service. VValeo's preliminary purpose is *to create a new concept of organization that will enable all individuals to have access to the information, assistance, and resources necessary for them to achieve their optimum health.* The Chaordic Alliance, in concert with the Sigma program at Case Western Reserve University, is working with the VValeo organizing group in planning a two-and-a-half-year effort to create a cooperatively owned health care organization open to all relevant and affected parties in the field of health, including patients, government, employers, insurers, health practitioners, and administrators. As this book went to press, a group of 200 people from every aspect of health was meeting to determine the future of the initiative.

THE GEODATA FORUM INITIATIVE

In June 1999, more than 350 representatives from federal, state, local, public, and private organizations involved in the immensely complicated field of geospacial data accumulation, processing, and mapping met in Washington, D.C. The field includes sixteen departments of the federal government and an estimated seventy to eighty thousand institutions from virtually every community in the country. The collection and use of such information materially affects the lives of every citizen in many ways. A substantial portion of the meeting was devoted to discussing four years of frustrating efforts to conceive of a governance structure that could effectively embrace such complexity and how chaordic concepts of organization might provide a solution.

A diverse group of dozens of industry leaders met for an entire day during the conference to investigate whether to undertake a two-year effort to create such a self-organizing and governing structure open to all relevant and affected parties for the evolution of the industry. There was unanimous agreement to explore in detail budgets and processes required and support for the conference planning committee to take steps to set the effort in motion. As this book went to press, a meeting of fifty people was being held to create a design team for the effort, affirm budgets, processes, and methods, and to commence the effort.

GENERAL

Inquiries have been received and preliminary conversations are under way with individuals and organizations from such diverse fields as education, community philanthropy, forestry, international private venture organizations, communications, and multinational corporations. The scant resources of the Chaordic Alliance, even though supplemented by many voluntary efforts from a considerable number of people, have been overwhelmed by interest in the concepts and opportunities to create more examples of chaordic organizations. Efforts to set in motion the third, fourth, and fifth objectives have been delayed due to lack of capacity and resources.

When the work to create more examples of chaordic organization began, it was expected that half or more of the efforts would fail to develop an acceptable concept of organization, and that others would fail to reach enough critical mass to bring such an organization into being, even if the concept and constitution were successfully completed. Although the difficulties of creating such organizations can hardly be overstated, only one attempt has failed completely, and that was the first that was attempted, Cooperative University Extension. All others are alive and moving forward, even though two, the Northwest Atlantic Marine Alliance and Community Alliances for Integrated Agriculture, are struggling to find sufficient resources to implement the conceptual structure and constitution they have created. The Society for Organizational Learning and the Appleseed Foundation are well under way and growing steadily.

However, it is a mistake to think of any of the efforts as a failure, for even if they fall short of the larger plan to create a national or global organization of the whole, many of the participants have used the concepts and ideas to improve smaller parts of the present structure and applied them successfully in other organizations of which they are part. I am constantly surprised and gratified at the number of people who return to relate the successes they have had and the degree to which the concepts and ideas have constructively affected their lives.